KANT

KANT

The Three Critiques

—— Andrew Ward ——

polity

First published in 2006 by Polity Press

Polity Press
65 Bridge Street
Cambridge CB2 1UR, UK

Polity Press
350 Main Street
Malden, MA 02148, USA

ISBN-10: 0-7456-2619-X
ISBN-13: 978-07456-2619-2619-2
ISBN-10: 0-7456-2620-3 (pb)
ISBN-13: 978-07456-2620-3 (pb)-26208

A catalogue record for this book is available from the British Library.

Typeset in 10.5 on 12 pt Berling
by Servis Filmsetting Ltd, Manchester
Printed and bound in Great Britain by
MPG Books Ltd, Bodmin, Cornwall

The publisher has used its best endeavours to ensure that the URLs for external websites referred to in this book are correct and active at the time of going to press. However, the publisher has no responsibility for the websites and can make no guarantee that a site will remain live or that the content is or will remain appropriate.

Every effort has been made to trace all copyright holders, but if any have been inadvertently overlooked the publishers will be pleased to include any necessary credits in any subsequent reprint or edition.

For further information on Polity, visit our website: www.polity.co.uk

Contents

CONTENTS

Preface

Over the last fifty years, there has been a widespread tendency among English-speaking philosophers to downplay Kant's idealism. This seems to me to have been a mistake – so far, at least, as gaining an understanding of Kant's own ideas is concerned. In this study, I offer an interpretation of the main themes in his three *Critiques* which places his mature thought squarely within the tradition of idealism: a tradition which includes the theories of Bishop Berkeley and of David Hume (however much Kant himself might have been surprised to learn that Hume falls into this tradition, and however much he would have disliked being compared with Berkeley).

Going along with the emphasis on idealism, I attempt to explain a number of Kant's central views – those concerning our knowledge of objects in space and time, the ground of our moral obligations and our judgments of beauty – as, in part, reactions to the scepticism and empiricism of Hume. The latter's views and, more to the point, the arguments that he provides for them are generally both clear and invigorating. While Kant's views are nearly always invigorating, his reasons for holding them are seldom clear, at least when considered out of context. By placing some of his key philosophical ideas alongside those of Hume, the aim is to elucidate Kant's arguments and, thereby, to offer an assessment of his conclusions.

A. W.

London, January 2006

Abbreviations and Conventions

CJ   *Critique of Judgment* (1790)
CPractR *Critique of Practical Reason* (1788)
CPR   *Critique of Pure Reason* (1st edition 1781, 2nd edition 1787)
Prol   *Prolegomena to Any Future Metaphysics* (1783)

Quotations from Kant's works are referred to by volume and page number in the German Akademie edition, *Kants gesammelte Schriften*, ed. Deutsche Akademie der Wissenschaften (Berlin: de Gruyter, 1900–), with the exception of quotations from the *Critique of Pure Reason*, which are referred to by the pagination from the 1st edition of 1781 (cited as A) and/or the 2nd edition of 1787 (cited as B).

Acknowledgments

I should like to express my thanks to Palgrave Macmillan for permission to quote from *Critique of Pure Reason* by Kant/Kemp-Smith (second edition) and to Cambridge University Press for permission to quote from *Immanuel Kant, Critique of Practical Reason* edited by Mary J. Gregor and with an introduction by Andrews Reath, 1997.

— Part I —

Critique of Pure Reason

1

A General Introduction to Kant's Copernican Revolution in Philosophy, and its Relation to Scientific Knowledge and Transcendent Metaphysics

I want to introduce Kant's philosophical approach in the *Critique of Pure Reason* – also known as the *First Critique* – by looking at what he took to be Hume's sceptical stance on causation, and how, in general terms, he sought to overcome it. When Kant himself set out the main threads of his argument in his own introductory essay on the *First Critique*, unappealingly entitled *Prolegomena to Any Future Metaphysics that will be able to Present itself as a Science*, it was his reaction to Hume's scepticism about causation that he particularly singled out. He did so not only because Hume's scepticism awoke him from his dogmatic slumbers, but, more crucially, because it gave him the hint of the *correct* approach to philosophical problems:

> Since Locke's and Leibniz's Essays, or rather since the beginning of Metaphysics as far as the history of it reaches, no event has occurred which could have been more decisive in respect of the fate of this science than the attack that David Hume made on it. He brought no light into this kind of knowledge, but he struck a spark at which a light could well have been kindled, if it had found a receptive tinder and if the glow had been carefully kept up and increased. (*Prol*, Preface; 4:257).

Hume's attack on causation was aimed at the principle that every event, or change of state, in nature must have a cause. He did not deny that we believed the principle to be true. What he denied was that we were justified in our belief. For the principle claims necessity as well as universality: it states that every event in nature must have a cause. How, asks Hume, could such a connection, a universal and necessary connection, possibly be proved? Not by experience; that is, not by perceiving how particular events in the spatio-temporal world behaved. For no amount of experience could prove that every *event* has a cause. The universal judgment is here taken to be entirely unrestricted, applying to all past, present and future events in nature, actual and possible. Evidently too, no experience could prove that it is *necessary* that any event has a cause. Experience can only tell us that such-and-such is or is not the case; it can never tells us that it must or must not be so.

But if experience will not do the trick, how could the causal principle be proved? The only alternative, Hume contended, is to show that it is true *in virtue of the meaning of the terms involved*. If the meaning of 'event' includes in it 'having a cause', then, indeed, we can justifiably assert that every event must have a cause. (Just as we can justifiably assert that every bachelor must be unmarried. In this latter case, the mere analysis of the subject term 'bachelor' and the predicate term 'unmarried' reveals that to deny the judgment would be self-contradictory.) But, as Hume argued, there simply is no such connection of meaning between the subject and the predicate terms in the principle 'Every event must have a cause.' To deny it is not self-contradictory. In Kantian terminology, the principle is not analytically true.

Since the principle is not analytically true, and, as Hume contended, this is the *only* acceptable way to prove that a judgment holds with strict universality and necessity, he concluded that our belief in the principle is unjustified.

Why, then, do we believe it? Here, Hume gives a psychological answer. It is the constant occurrence, throughout our past experience, of similar changes of state, under the same circumstances, that has led to our belief that the principle is justified. Far from the belief arising from, or being provable by, our rational faculties, it is merely the product of our enlivened imagination. In particular, the necessity that we ascribe to the principle is merely a 'subjective necessity' or *feeling* of inevitability (arising from our experience of past constant conjunctions), and not an objective necessity (not a requirement, discernible in the objects or in our judgment about the objects, that nature is uniform). Accordingly, so far as reason or understanding is concerned, our experience of nature could have been entirely chaotic. Moreover, there is absolutely no rational ground for supposing that our experience – even granting that it has, *in fact*, been as regular as clockwork up to now – might not turn random, acausal, at any moment in the future. The supposition that the future course of events will resemble the past cannot even be shown to be probable, let alone necessary.

It is important to grasp the extent to which Kant agreed with Hume's position. First, he accepted that the causal principle cannot be proved by experience (since it claims necessity and universality). Second, he accepted that the necessity and universality attaching to the principle do not derive merely from the meaning of the terms involved. That is, he agreed with Hume that the principle is not analytically true. Third, he accepted that there is no way in which we could determine with certainty the truth of any *specific* causal claim in nature. That any particular *kind* of event actually occurs (e.g. that water in the liquid state does, under certain circumstances, turn to ice), and *why* it occurs (what its cause is), have to be left to experience to discover. We cannot prove that particular kinds of changes of states must occur, or what specifically their causes in nature must be.

But he disagreed with Hume about the status of the general principle that every event, or change of state, in nature must have a cause. Although he thought that Hume was correct to maintain that this principle is not analytically true, he rejected what he took to be Hume's conclusion from this observation: namely, that the principle cannot be justified.

How, though, can the causal principle *legitimately* carry necessity and universality, if not in virtue of the meaning of the terms involved?

To understand Kant's answer to this question is to be well on the way to understanding many of the central ideas in the *Critique of Pure Reason*. He was not exaggerating when he claimed that Hume had struck a spark which, if carefully kindled, would produce a new light on metaphysics. For Kant thought that the *status* of the causal principle could be generalized to take in not only all the leading judgments in metaphysics, but also all the fundamental judgments in two areas of what he saw as unquestionably *genuine* repositories of knowledge of objects: namely, pure mathematics and pure natural science (pure natural science forms the non-empirical basis of Newtonian physics). And this thought, in turn, led him to conclude that there must be something wrong with Hume's scepticism. Since, as he affirmed, there certainly *are* two areas where we can find examples of judgments which, while not analytically true, hold with necessity and universality, viz. in pure mathematics and pure natural science, what is required is not a wholesale *dismissal* of all such knowledge claims, but an investigation of *how* such judgments can be true, in those two areas where they clearly exist.

In brief, Hume's scepticism alerted Kant to the fact, or to what he took to be the fact, that lying at the basis of three central areas of knowledge or alleged knowledge of objects – mathematics and natural science, on the one hand, and metaphysics, on the other – are a host of judgments or principles of exactly the same status as the causal principle. As he saw it, the fundamental judgments in all three areas claim to hold with necessity and universality, and yet none of them can be proved in virtue of the meaning of the terms involved. Accordingly, if the only way of seeking to establish such a judgment were through an analysis of the terms involved, it would follow that *none* of these areas could contain informative instances of knowledge that hold with necessity and universality. At least in the cases of mathematics and natural science, Kant regarded this conclusion as absurd. Accordingly, he maintained that Hume must have been mistaken in dismissing the causal principle merely on the ground that, though the principle claims necessity and universality, it cannot be established in virtue of the meaning of the terms involved. The correct conclusion, Kant held, is that there must be some *other* way to establish (at least some) judgments of this kind. The strategy of the *Critique of Pure Reason* may essentially be seen as proceeding in two stages: in the first stage, it investigates *how* it is possible to establish these judgments in mathematics and natural science (where, as Kant sees it, they quite evidently exist); and on the basis of this investigation, it proceeds, in the second stage, to enquire *whether* the leading judgments of metaphysics can also be established.

Kant's Copernican revolution

Kant's attempt to refute Hume's causal scepticism and so, too, his investigating how pure mathematics and pure natural science can exist are both intimately connected with his so-called Copernican revolution in philosophy. They are intimately connected, because he came to the conclusion that the only way to explain how mathematics and natural science can exist is by effecting a major *turnabout* in the way that we conceive the relationship between ourselves (the knowing mind) and the objects of our sense experience (the objects in space and time). His Copernican revolution equally has major repercussions for metaphysics and for morality. This second stage of his revolution will be touched on after I have said something about the first stage: his investigation of the possibility of mathematics and natural science.

The traditional way of conceiving the relationship between our-selves and the world that we are seeking to know by means of our senses – the world of objects existing in space and time – is to con-ceive of this world as existing entirely independently of the knowing mind. We, by means of our senses (in co-operation, perhaps, with our understanding), set out to discover how this mind-independent world is, both with respect to the rules governing the possible *structural* con-figurations of its objects and with respect to the laws governing their *behaviour*. As Kant sees it, mathematics as a science is the study of the former (the structure or form of objects), and natural science, that of the latter (the dynamical connections of objects). On the traditional way of taking the relationship between the mind and objects in space and time, it is up to our faculties of knowledge – our senses and under-standing – to attune themselves, if they can, to the objects of our attempted knowledge.

Unfortunately, if this traditional picture is accepted as the correct conception of the relationship between ourselves and the objects of our hoped-for mathematical and natural scientific knowledge, then, as Kant realized, there would be no possibility of our acquiring *any* infor-mative universal or necessary knowledge of these objects. *At best*, what we could hope to acquire would be empirical, hence only prob-able, knowledge. On the other hand, if we adopt the revolutionary point of view that the objects that we are seeking to learn about by means of our faculties of knowledge must themselves conform to those very faculties in order to *become* objects of the senses, then we might well be able to acquire some genuinely necessary and universal knowledge of objects *as possible objects of the senses*. For, independently of our acquiring any experience of these objects, we might be able to discover, by investigating our *own* faculties of knowledge, what condi-tions these faculties impose on the possibility of our experience and its objects.

In effect, the first major task that Kant sets himself, in the main body of the *First Critique*, is to show that his revolutionary way of con-ceiving the relationship between ourselves and the objects of our sen-sible knowledge – viz. that these objects must accord with our faculties of knowledge, rather than the traditional picture of trusting that our faculties of knowledge will be in accord with its sought-for objects – is, indeed, the correct one. This he seeks to accomplish by establishing two claims: first, that the dimensions in which the objects of our senses are located – namely, in space and in time – are depen-dent on us (are, in fact, properties of our mind); and second, that the fundamental laws governing the behaviour of the objects of our senses are dependent on concepts existing innately in us. If both of these conditions can be made out, it can be said that the whole *framework* by means of which objects of the senses can be known – the sensuous *forms* in which they are given (space and time) and the basic dynamical *laws* governing them – will be contributed by us. Clearly, such a picture of our relationship with the objects of our sought-after sensible knowledge is a far cry from the traditional one.

The revolutionary point of view according to which the objects of our senses should be taken to conform to our faculties for acquiring knowledge, Kant likens to Copernicus's revolutionary hypothesis concerning the spectator of the heavens and the heavenly bodies. On the traditional conception of the latter relationship, the spectator is at rest, and the observed behaviour of the heavenly bodies is dependent on their movement alone. On the Copernican hypothesis, the observed behaviour of the heavenly bodies depends, in part, upon the movement of the spectator. This hypothesis, Kant wishes to say, was firmly established on two grounds. First, it enabled Kepler to discover the three laws governing the motion of the planets. Second, it enabled a proof to be given of Newton's gravitational force of attraction (binding all objects together). Neither of these advances would have been possible on the pre-Copernican model.

How, though, does Kant propose to establish *his* Copernican revolution? It can be established, he thinks, in ways analogous to those that established Copernicus's own hypothesis. First, on Kant's revolutionary model of the relationship between our experience and its objects, he believes that we can explain how mathematics and natural science have provided us with universal and necessary knowledge of these objects. Second, he believes that it will enable us to provide proofs of the principles lying at the basis of natural science. Neither of these achievements is possible on the traditional model. Accordingly, just as Copernicus's own hypothesis was established because it, and it alone, enabled us to discover the laws of planetary motion and, at the same time, to provide a proof of Newton's force of attraction, so Kant's Copernican revolution is to be established because it, and it alone, can explain how we are in possession of universal and necessary objective principles in mathematics and natural science, and at the same time provide proofs of the first principles of natural science. The theory that Kant constructs, on the basis of his Copernican revolution, he calls 'transcendental idealism'.

In fact, as he sees it, there is a further ground for accepting his

Copernican revolution. He argues that, on the traditional conception of the relationship between the mind and its hoped-for objects, we are bound to involve ourselves in inextricable contradictions when we attempt to prove certain judgments which entirely transcend experience (for instance, a judgment concerning freedom of the will); whereas, on his opposing, Copernican-style conception, we can show that no such contradictions arise. Now a theory can only be justified if it does not lead to contradiction. Accordingly (on the assumption that there really are only these two theories), Kant regards the consistency of his own, revolutionary theory, compared with the unavoidable inconsistencies of the traditional theory, as a further proof of the correctness of his Copernican project, and hence of transcendental idealism. Moreover (as emerges in the later *Critique of Practical Reason* and *Critique of Judgment*), there are, on the alternative theory, *further* contradictions in our thought – our thought about morality and beauty – which, he will argue, can be resolved only by embracing his revolution.

Hume's scepticism about causation and Kant's Copernican revolution

In order to illustrate how the Kantian Copernican revolution bears on central issues in philosophy, let us return to Hume's scepticism about causation. Hume – at least as Kant reads him – sees nothing inconceivable in the behaviour of objects in the spatio-temporal world always having been, or suddenly becoming, totally chaotic. Since a state of lawlessness in nature implies no contradiction, it is by Hume's lights entirely conceivable. Moreover, although chaos in nature would obviously preclude us from connecting together objects, or their states, according to universal or necessary laws, Hume allows – again as Kant reads him – that we should still be able to *experience* objects and their changing states.

Now although this scepticism is diametrically opposed to the position that Kant adopts as a result of his Copernican revolution, there is a sense in which he accepts it. He accepts that if the *traditional* picture of the relationship between objects in the spatio-temporal world and ourselves is correct, then Hume's story of a nature in chaos cannot be dismissed. But now consider Kant's alternative, revolutionary picture. In particular, consider his claim that the laws by which the objects of nature can alone be experienced derive from certain fundamental concepts in us. If one of these fundamental concepts is the concept of *cause*, and the corresponding law is the causal principle (viz. every change of state must have a cause), then it would follow that we can only experience a change of state in so far as it is subject to causal law. Remarkable though such a conclusion would be if it could be shown, it can hardly be said fully to meet Hume's scepticism. Even granting that we cannot experience a nature which is non-causal in respect of any change of state, that would seem to put constraints only on our ability to perceive such a spatio-temporal world. But Hume's scepticism chiefly concerns the conceivability of a non-causal *nature*, not our capacity or incapacity to *experience* it. At this point, we need to bring in the other part of the Kantian Copernican revolution: that space and time are merely properties of our mind, and hence, that everything appearing therein must in reality be mind-dependent. If the objects of our senses (the objects in space and time) are, in reality, mind-dependent, then any condition on our being conscious of, and so of our experiencing, these objects must equally be a condition on the possible objects of our experience. For example, if we cannot think, and so experience, a change in the objects of our senses, except under the condition that the data apprehended by us be subject to the law of causality, then it follows – given the mind-dependency of this data – that there can be no acausal change in spatio-temporal objects. If everything that can appear in space and/or time is mind-dependent, then any restriction on our ability to *experience* spatio-temporal objects must equally be a restriction on the possible *objects* that can exist in space and time.

In sum, Kant accuses Hume of putting the cart before the horse. As Kant sees it, Hume assumes that spatio-temporal objects exist independently of our possible experience. On this traditional picture, it has to be admitted that we cannot see why these objects must conform to any of the concepts that may exist in us for connecting together the given sensuous data under laws. In particular, therefore, it is impossible to see why spatio-temporal objects must, in respect of their changes, be subject to the law of causality. On the other hand, if Kant's Copernican picture is correct, it would have the following consequences. First, we can have no experience of spatio-temporal objects changing their states except in so far as the apprehended manifold can be thought by us as subject to the law of causality. Second, all these changing objects are dependent for their existence on our capacity to think the given manifold by means of that law. Accordingly, not only must Hume have been wrong to suppose that we might be able to experience spatio-temporal objects changing randomly; more significantly, he must have been wrong to hold that there could exist any acausal changes in these objects.

Before turning to the second stage of Kant's Copernican project, I must stress that in this introduction I am aiming only to provide an overview of some of the main themes of the *First Critique*. In particular, what I have attempted in the last few paragraphs is nothing more than an outline of the *strategy* by which Kant hopes to answer Hume. Clearly, it is one thing to outline a strategy and another thing to show how it can be filled in to provide a convincing reply to scepticism. Most conspicuously, there are two issues that need to be addressed. First, we need to understand why space and time are held to have a mind-dependent status. Second, we need to understand why our capacity to have any experience of objects requires that the data apprehended through the senses must be subject to laws that derive from concepts existing in our mind. Without a proper appreciation of Kant's responses to these issues, there is simply insufficient detail to decide whether he has given a plausible, let alone a correct, response to Hume. In fact, both issues are discussed at length in the *First Critique*. Kant's treatment of them forms the backbone of his Copernican project.

Metaphysics

So far, we have concentrated on the first stage of Kant's Copernican revolution: the investigation of *how* the judgments in pure mathematics and natural science can exist (as they actually do). But we saw that he also maintains that metaphysics is essentially made up of judgments which have the same status as those in mathematics and natural science. With metaphysics, however, it is by no means clear that its central claims can be known to be true: the protracted and indecisive debates about every one of them strongly suggests that they cannot. In the section of the *First Critique* entitled 'Transcendental Dialectic', he turns to the second stage of his Copernican revolution: the investigation of *whether* the central claims of metaphysics can be substantiated. He concludes that our theoretical reason is unable to show any of them to be true *or* false.

His ground for reaching this conclusion is closely connected with the first stage of his Copernican project. For Kant's explanation of how judgments in pure mathematics and natural science can hold with necessity and universality, while yet not being analytically true, is that they make our experience, our empirical knowledge of spatio-temporal objects, possible. (I have tried to illustrate this with the particular case of the law of causality: this law is held to make possible our experience of *change of states* among spatio-temporal objects.) But the central (positive) claims of metaphysics – that the soul is immortal, that we possess free will, and that God exists – have *no* relationship to sense experience. They entirely *transcend* it: they can neither be shown to make sense experience possible nor, given their status, be confirmed or disconfirmed through sense experience. Since, as he argues, these are the only ways by which theoretical reason can establish any non-analytic judgment, he concludes that we cannot prove or disprove the central claims of metaphysics by theoretical means.

It is vital, however, to appreciate that Kant does not maintain that the impossibility of verification – either directly by sense experience or indirectly by showing that they make sense experience possible – renders the central claims of metaphysics to be effectively unthinkable. He allows that we can consistently *think* a judgment like the soul is immortal, even though we cannot confirm or disconfirm it by theoretical means. Certainly, a judgment can only be established – or even given any *determinate* meaning – by showing that it has a relation, direct or indirect, to experience. But Kant denies that it is necessary for thinking any of the propositions of metaphysics in an *indeterminate* way that we should be able to relate them to sense experience.

In actual fact (though here we need to go outside the *First Critique*), he holds that the central claims of metaphysics *can* be established. And he holds that they can be established by showing that they *make experience possible*. But, with the central claims of metaphysics, the experience is not sense experience, but *moral* experience, our recognition of duty and of the need to pursue the highest good. This recognition, however, is made known to us not by theoretical but by *practical* reason.

One way of understanding Kant's moral philosophy is to see it as attempting to prove the key judgments of metaphysics by showing that they make our moral experience possible. His idea is that we can only explain the existence of our moral experience – the demands of which we cannot doubt – by acknowledging the truth of the central claims of metaphysics (just as, in the *First Critique*, he argues that we can only explain the existence of mathematics and natural science – the reality of which we cannot doubt – by acknowledging that space and time are properties of our mind, and that the fundamental laws of nature derive from concepts in our understanding). We shall obviously need to consider Kant's proof of these metaphysical claims when we examine his Copernican revolution in relation to morality.

Returning to the Copernican revolution as this is exemplified in the *First Critique*, Kant's main negative point is that the *traditional* methods of the metaphysician must be given up. The central claims of metaphysics cannot be established by employing theoretical reason: they are not true solely in virtue of the meaning of the terms involved, and it is useless to seek to employ mathematics or any of the principles of natural science *outside* possible sense experience. Any attempt to establish the key judgments of metaphysics by employing mathematics or natural science is bound, Kant argues, to be dialectical (i.e. to be fallacious). Yet with respect to theoretical reason, it is only the employment of mathematics and natural science that can possibly yield informative judgments having the same status as the central claims of metaphysics. Accordingly, so far as our search for knowledge is concerned, the message of the *First Critique* is that this search is defensible where it is based on sense experience, or where it bears upon the possibility of our having sense experience, but indefensible with respect to the central claims of metaphysics. In their case, we should admit our necessary ignorance, and renounce our quest for theoretical enlightenment. We should concentrate solely on the quest for knowledge in those areas that are related to sense experience. Here, indeed, we can establish the existence of informative necessary and universal principles or axioms, in addition to an unlimited amount of empirical, and so probable, knowledge.

The Dialectic is frequently represented in a wholly negative way: as Kant's *criticism* of the use of theoretical reason outside the spheres of mathematics and natural science (as well as everyday sense experience). Certainly, the Dialectic does have this important negative side. But if we are to understand the place of the *First Critique* in Kant's overall critical system, it is imperative also to grasp a more positive side to his attack on metaphysics, as traditionally conceived.

We saw that, in the course of this attack, he maintains that it must be impossible theoretically to prove or disprove freedom of the will, the immortality of the soul, or the existence of God. But this impossibility, it transpires, is fortunate: fortunate for morality quite as much as for our positive beliefs in freedom, immortality and God.

Since, as he points out in the Preface to the second edition of the *First Critique*, if we do not embrace his Copernican revolution, we shall have to renounce these metaphysical beliefs; and this, in turn, will mean our acknowledging that the demands of morality are delusory (B xxvii–xxx).

But why does Kant suppose that his Copernican revolution is necessary for holding on to our central metaphysical beliefs? The answer is that he thinks that if we do not distinguish the world of our senses (the spatio-temporal world) from the world as it is in itself (the world that exists independently of our possible sense experience), then the deterministic laws that provably obtain in the sensible world must apply to us as moral agents. It would, in short, be impossible for us even to *assume* freedom of the will (see the Antithesis and Observation of the Third Antinomy). Equally, we should have to renounce our belief in a necessary Being who has created and sustains the universe; since, without the distinction, it is provably impossible that such a Being could exist (see the Antithesis and Observation of the Fourth Antinomy). Lastly, the belief that the soul is simple – and, therewith, the possibility of believing in the continuation of the soul after the death of the body – must be rejected, unless the world of the senses is distinguished from the world as it is in itself (see the Antithesis and Observation of the Second Antinomy).

Moreover, if it is impossible even to *assume* the existence of free will, God and the immortality of the soul, without embracing Kant's Copernican revolution, then since – as he himself argues – these are necessary presuppositions of morality, it follows that the demands of morality must themselves be delusory. That is why Kant asserts: 'I have therefore found it necessary to deny *knowledge* in order to make room for *faith*' (CPR, B xxx; italics original).

This famous assertion should not be taken merely as showing that, in order to save scientific knowledge, Kant accepted that we would have to deny ourselves any knowledge of the central claims of metaphysics (while leaving open the possibility of our believing in them). It implies something far stronger. It implies that if the traditional picture of our relationship with the world of the senses is correct, then we should actually be *precluded* from even believing in the existence of free will, God and immortality – since we would then be in possession of proofs of the impossibility of each of these beliefs. Only if we embrace Kant's Copernican picture can we deny the force of the proofs, and thereby make room for the beliefs that are necessary for morality. So the metaphysical discussions in the Dialectic secure our belief in God, freedom and immortality – and thereby in morality also – against inevitable *scepticism*.

The *First Critique*, then, not only seeks to explain how there can be universal and necessary knowledge of objects in mathematics and in natural science, it also seeks to leave a space open for morality. As Kant sees it, *neither* the theoretical *nor* the practical side to our lives can be sustained on the traditional picture. On his Copernican picture, on the other hand, we can – in fact do – have both. The positive contribution of the Dialectic is to show how it is possible for the moral life to exist – and therewith to lay the ground for the *practical* proofs of just those central metaphysical claims (concerning freedom of the will, the immortality of the soul, and the existence of God) that, as he had argued earlier, our *theoretical* reason is, in reality, powerless to prove or disprove.

2

The Division of Judgments, and the Status of Mathematics and Natural Science

Before embarking on a more detailed look at Kant's system, we need to do two things. First, we need to understand some of his terminology, especially with regard to his division of judgments into three types. Second, we need to understand more fully the status that he accords to judgments in mathematics and natural science.

The division of judgments

Kant identifies three possible types of judgment:

1 Analytic a priori judgments;
2 Synthetic a posteriori judgments;
3 Synthetic a priori judgments.

In order to explain this threefold division, he further distinguishes between analytic and synthetic judgments, on the one hand, and a priori and a posteriori judgments, on the other. These further distinctions can be explained as follows.

An *analytic* judgment is one in which the meaning of the predicate term is included in the meaning of the subject term. Example: 'All bachelors are unmarried (men).' Kant notes that the denial of an analytic judgment is self-contradictory (as in 'It is not the case that all bachelors are unmarried').

A *synthetic* judgment is one in which the meaning of the predicate term is *not* contained in the meaning of the subject term. Example: 'All men are mortal.' Accordingly, the denial of a synthetic judgment is not self-contradictory. (The judgment 'It is not the case that all men are mortal' is doubtless false; but it is not self-contradictory, given the meaning of 'men' and 'mortal', etc.)

An *a priori* judgment is a judgment that is thought of as holding independently of experience. Kant says that there are two 'sure criteria' of, two infallible ways of identifying, an a priori judgment. If a judgment claims to hold either with necessity or strict universality, then it must be an a priori judgment. For no judgment that depends on experience can be thought of as holding either necessarily or with strict universality. Experience can show that some judgment *is* or *is not* the case, but not that it *necessarily* is or is not the case (or *must* or *must not* be the case). Similarly, while experience can show that all instances *so far examined* of a particular unrestricted class are such-and-such, it cannot show that all past, present and future instances of that class are such-and-such. The most that our evidence to date can entitle us to claim, assuming it is wide-ranging and that no counter-examples have been encountered, is what Kant calls 'comparative universality'. That is, we may employ an inductive argument on the basis of our experiential evidence to date, and claim that all instances are *probably* such-and-such. But cases of comparative universality are not cases of strict universality (where 'no exception is allowed as possible' (B 4)). Throughout his critical works, whenever Kant discusses universality, he means strict, not comparative, universality unless he says otherwise.

It is worth noting that Kant does not *define* an a priori judgment as one that claims to hold with necessity and/or universality. For him, an a priori judgment is defined as one that is thought of as holding *independently of experience*. But if we can discover a judgment that does claim to hold with necessity and/or universality, then we can be sure that it is a priori. Necessity and universality are infallible means of *recognizing* an a priori judgment.

Given his definition of an a priori judgment, we can understand Kant's claim that besides a priori judgments (or principles) there may also be – indeed, are – a priori concepts. For example, he holds that the concept of *cause* is an a priori concept. By this he means that it is not derived, or formed, from any experience; it is, rather, a concept that we possess *independently of experience*. Such concepts may well be applied to what *can* be experienced, although this is not an essential feature of an a priori concept. What is essential is that an a priori concept is a concept that we possess independently of any experience.

An *a posteriori* (or *empirical*) judgment is a judgment that is thought of as holding on the basis of experience. It cannot, therefore, claim to hold with either necessity or (strict) universality. 'Copper dissolves in sulphuric acid' is an a posteriori judgment. We need to consult experience in order to confirm or disconfirm it. And the judgment that is, in fact, thereby confirmed carries only comparative universality, based on our past and present experience of the behaviour of copper in sulphuric acid.

Just as there can be a priori concepts, so there can be a posteriori ones. As one would expect, these are dependent (at least in part) upon experience. Our concept of *copper* is a posteriori, since it requires experience in order to be formed.

We can now examine Kant's division of judgments into three categories. In particular, we need to ask *how* each type of judgment can be established.

(1) *Analytic a priori judgments.* Since every analytic judgment depends, for Kant, only on the meaning of the terms involved, such a judgment can always be established by determining that the meaning of the predicate term is included in the subject term, i.e. by showing that the denial of the judgment is self-contradictory. All analytic judgments, therefore, must be a priori, since no recourse to experience is necessary to establish them. (The subject and the predicate terms *themselves* may require experience in order to be formed, as in the case of 'bachelor' and 'unmarried'. But the point is that once the meaning of the subject and the predicate terms is understood – whether they are themselves expressive of a priori or a posteriori concepts – there can be no need to consult experience in order to establish any analytic judgment. All that is required is an analysis of the meaning of the terms involved, together with the application of the principle of contradiction.)

(2) *Synthetic a posteriori judgments.* These judgments are not analytically true, and are established by recourse to experience. There is clearly no difficulty in grasping how there can actually be such judgments. When a judgment cannot be determined in virtue of the meaning of the terms involved (and so is synthetic), it is an entirely familiar, and frequently a successful, procedure to seek to establish it a posteriori, i.e. by consulting experience. The judgment 'All men are mortal' is synthetic. It is also a posteriori, since it is established on the basis of past experience and induction (the universality claimed is only comparative). Note that all empirical judgments – judgments that make recourse to experience – are synthetic a posteriori. For if a judgment requires experience to be established (and so is a posteriori), it cannot be true merely in virtue of the meaning of the terms involved. Hence, it must be synthetic as well as a posteriori.

(Granted what is said under (1) and (2), it is clear that there cannot possibly be any *analytic a posteriori* judgments. If such judgments existed, they would have to be true merely in virtue of the meaning of the terms involved yet require experience to be established. But since any judgment whose truth or falsity depends wholly on the meaning of its constitutive terms can always be established *without* consulting experience (a priori), it cannot require experience to be established.)

(3) *Synthetic a priori judgments.* These are not analytically true yet require to be established independently of experience. Undoubtedly, it is this class of judgments in which Kant is principally interested. Now although such judgments are not ruled out *ab initio* (as are analytic a posteriori judgments), it is not at all obvious *how* any claimed synthetic a priori judgment could ever be established. In order to establish it, we evidently cannot consult experience, otherwise the judgment would not be a priori but a posteriori. On the other hand, we plainly cannot seek to establish the judgment merely on the basis of the meaning of the terms involved. Only analytic judgments can be established in this manner; and *ex hypothesi* we are interested in establishing a synthetic, not an analytic, judgment. But if the judgment cannot be established either in virtue of the meaning of the terms involved or by consulting experience, how is a connection between the subject and the predicate of any supposed synthetic a priori judgment to be established?

Let us return to our earlier example. In the judgment 'Every change of state must have a cause', the concept *cause* is not included in the concept *change of state*. As Hume has shown, the denial of the judgment is not self-contradictory. So the judgment cannot be analytic. It is, therefore, a synthetic judgment. But the judgment also claims necessity ('*must* have a cause') as well as strict universality ('*Every* change of state'). So it is an a priori judgment: one that cannot be dependent on experience. But how can we hope to establish a genuine connection between the subject and the predicate in such a judgment?

It is, of course, just this question, when generalized to include all the axioms and principles of pure mathematics and natural science, as well as the significant judgments in metaphysics, that not only awoke Kant from his dogmatic slumbers but led him to propose his own revolutionary response (his Copernican revolution). Putting the point in his own terminology, Kant holds that *all* the fundamental judgments in these areas are synthetic a priori. Accordingly, the key question for him is to discover how such judgments can ever be established.

Let me reiterate the point that I made in my introduction, though without employing there the terminology of the *First Critique*. In raising the question, 'How is it possible to establish synthetic a priori judgments?', Kant is not questioning the legitimacy of such judgments in *two* areas: namely, pure mathematics and natural science. On the contrary, he believes that it is 'incontestable' that, in these two areas, we are already in possession of bodies of synthetic a priori knowledge of objects. Rather, his point is that until Hume's questioning of the synthetic a priori principle 'Every change of state must have a cause', it had not occurred to him (Kant) – or, he thinks, to anyone else – that this species of judgment forms the kernel not only of two bodies of undoubted scientific knowledge (mathematics and natural science), but of *metaphysics* as well (whose claim to be a science is by no means undoubted). Now that he has recognized the centrality of synthetic a priori judgments, he also realizes that the way to answer, if at all, the central questions of metaphysics is not essentially through any mere *analysis* of metaphysical assertions (the common pursuit of metaphysicians to date). How could it be, granted that these assertions are synthetic, not analytic? Instead, the central questions of metaphysics are to be answered, if they can be answered by theoretical reason at all, through first coming to understand *how* the fundamental synthetic a priori judgments are established in the two areas of science where it is incontestable that they do exist. Once this essential preliminary investigation has been achieved, Kant believes that we should be in a position to see *whether* the central questions of metaphysics can also be established.

The status of judgments in pure mathematics and in pure natural science

But now it may be objected that the claim that pure mathematics and natural science are bodies of synthetic a priori judgments is far from obvious. In his Introduction to the *First Critique*, Kant goes to considerable lengths to convince his readers that the axioms or principles of both disciplines are genuine instances of synthetic a priori judgments.

Mathematics

In the case of pure mathematics, he does not consider it incumbent upon him to prove that its judgments are a priori. He takes it as uncontroversial that the judgments of both geometry and arithmetic hold with necessity and universality. When it is said that the internal angles of a (Euclidean plain) triangle add up to 180 degrees, it is implied that this *must* be true of *all* triangles. The judgment, therefore, is a priori. And the a priori nature of this particular judgment, Kant plausibly holds, goes for all geometrical judgments. Similarly, in arithmetic, the judgment that 7 + 5 = 12 is a priori; since the judgment implies that *whenever* the numbers 7 and 5 are added, 12 *must* be the result. Again, this point can be generalized. The key issue for him is not whether mathematical judgments are a priori, but whether they are synthetic.

He thought that previous philosophers – including Leibniz and Hume – were guilty of a serious oversight in supposing that mathematical judgments are analytic (and hence that the denial of a true mathematical judgment is self-contradictory). This cannot be right, he argues, since we must have recourse to *construction* in order to determine the truth or falsity of any mathematical judgment. So, in the case of the geometrical question concerning the sum of the internal angles of a triangle, he holds that we need to *draw* a triangle, either in imagination or e.g. on paper, and proceed to prove the judgment by showing, *through the use of the diagram*, how the angles must add up to 180 degrees. The specific procedure is well discussed at A 713–24/ B 741–52, from which the following is an extract:

> [The geometrician] at once begins by constructing a triangle. Since he knows that the sum of two right angles is exactly equal to the sum of all the adjacent angles which can be constructed from a single point on a straight line, he prolongs one side of his triangle and obtains two adjacent angles, which together are equal to two right angles. He then divides the external angle by drawing a line parallel to the opposite side of the triangle, and observes that he has thus obtained an external adjacent angle which is equal to an internal angle – and so on. In this fashion, through a chain of inferences guided throughout by intuition, he arrives at a fully evident and universally valid solution of the problem. (A 716–17/B 744–5)

The essential ingredients in this example are, I think, these. First, the geometrical concepts involved (*line, triangle, angle,* etc.) are ones that we devise for ourselves, entirely a priori, 'without having borrowed the pattern from any experience' (A 713/B 741). Second, although the figure (the triangle) which we draw on paper is, of course, an empirical one, the way that we *use* the figure in the demonstration is entirely independent of any of the contingencies of this particular drawn figure (its size, the colour of the drawn lines and so on). As a result, the drawn figure can stand for *all* possible triangles. Third, the proof proceeds by means of the *construction* of the triangle, together with some further construction (extending the base line beyond one of the sides, etc.), in order to *demonstrate* – that is, to *show* – by means of the diagram that certain truths obtain for this particular figure and, therefore, for all possible figures that are constructed in accordance with these same a priori concepts.

In Kantian terminology, the method may be described as producing a proof on the basis of 'sensible intuition'. More will be said about intuition in the section on space and time. The point to note here about basing a proof on sensible intuition is that it involves recourse to the construction of figures, in a sensuous field, in accordance with our own a priori concepts. This construction can occur either by means of the imagination alone, in what Kant calls 'pure intuition', or by means of drawing a figure in reality, e.g. on paper, in what he calls 'empirical intuition'. But in either case, the construction must employ the a priori geometrical concepts, discounting any contingent features inherent in the drawn figure. And the demonstration itself – for Kant, a 'demonstration' can occur *only* in mathematics – consists in being able to *exhibit* (A 716/B 744) or *observe* (A 717/B 745) that certain relations obtain in intuition as a result of the construction. (A more general discussion, which was added in the second edition, is given at B 14–17.)

Without reference to intuition, Kant's claim is that there is no possibility of proving any of the axioms or first principles of geometry. Thus, the a priori concepts of *triangle, angle,* etc., however deeply they are analysed, will never entail that the denial of the judgment concerning the internal angles of a triangle is self-contradictory. Hence, the judgment cannot be an analytic a priori truth. I need to engage in a demonstration, a showing: I need, that is, to go *outside* the a priori concepts involved and *exhibit* in intuition, by means of the constructing of a diagram, that the corresponding judgment holds. That is why the a priori judgment is synthetic, and not analytic. Moreover, since geometrical demonstrations essentially involve proving synthetic yet necessary relationships about extension and figure (inherently spatial concepts), geometry is conceived as describing the structure of space. As Kant sees it, *geometry is a body of synthetic a priori judgments that determines the properties of space* (B 40).

A parallel approach is adopted with judgments of arithmetic. The judgment that 7 + 5 = 12 requires that the sum 7 and 5 must be constructed. For the concepts *7, 5* and *the sum of* – concepts which, as Kant sees it, are not derived from experience – never yield through analysis the concept *12*. They merely together tell us *how* the result is to be constructed, viz. by *counting* (whether by means of mental arithmetic or e.g. by using one's fingers). Only when the a priori concepts of 7 and 5 are realized in intuition, and then joined together, can the resulting number be brought into existence, i.e. *exhibited* by this constructive process of adding the two numbers. Since one must go outside any mere analysis of the concepts involved, and exhibit the result by construction in intuition, the judgment must be synthetic as well as a priori.

Although it is not difficult to see why, given Kant's claim about the manner of proving geometrical judgments, he should argue for a parallel process for arithmetic, it is not so easy to grasp why he thinks that arithmetic, together with pure mechanics, are possible only by means of our possession of an intuition of *time*. His argument seems to be that, in the case of arithmetic, the various concepts of number are all realized by *successive* addition or subtraction (*succession* being a temporal notion); and in the case of mechanics, its fundamental concepts are all concerned in some way with *motion* (which itself requires a recognition of how the same thing can be in distinct places, viz. through its existence in these distinct places, one *after* the other). At any event, in his discussion of the synthetic a priori judgments of arithmetic and pure mechanics, he links these judgments with the necessity of our having a sensible intuition of *time*.

Criticism of the thesis that mathematical judgments are synthetic a priori

By the end of the first quarter of the twentieth century, a consensus had grown up that Kant's view of the synthetic a priori nature of mathematics is untenable. The basis for the consensus can be illustrated most easily in the case of geometry. Euclidean geometry – the criticism runs – should be considered as *either* an a priori *or* an a posteriori discipline. Let us assume, first, that it is an a priori discipline. As such, the whole Euclidean system is a set of *uninterpreted formulae*, like a logical calculus. Proofs, on this account, are entirely formal, and there is no need to draw any diagrams, whether in reality or in the imagination, to establish any axiom or theorem. Thus Euclid's axiom 'A straight line is the shortest distance between two points' is taken as an uninterpreted definition of the term 'straight line'; and so on for all the other axioms of the system. The theorems of the system are established by means of rules of inference from these axioms. So understood, Euclidean judgments can have no application to the world, since the terms in the proofs are all uninterpreted, being either undefined terms or defined by means of the undefined terms. Admittedly, because the theorems result logically from the axioms, i.e. by means of the system's rules of inference, they do follow necessarily from the axioms. But since the basic terms are merely uninterpreted symbols, there can be no question here of any Euclidean judgment holding for the structure of *space*.

Second, let us assume that Euclid's system is a posteriori. As such, the Euclidean axioms can, in principle, be true judgments about the structure of space. Further, since they are based on experience, they must be synthetic (to deny any of them is not self-contradictory). But although the axioms may be true synthetic judgments, they are not, *pace* Kant, necessarily true. They will be merely true empirical generalizations about the structure of space. Thus the straight line axiom should here be taken as an empirical claim to the effect that since it has always been found *in fact* that the shortest distance between any two points in space is a straight line – where 'straight line' is given some suitable empirical definition, e.g. 'the path of a light wave in a vacuum' – it is held, on inductive grounds, that this is always the case. Consequently, the theorems of the system, since they follow logically, by rules of inference from these axioms, will equally express empirical generalizations about the structure of geometrical figures in space. They cannot, therefore, state anything with necessity or strict universality about the structure of space. On the contrary, all the theorems as well as all the axioms will have (at best) a posteriori validity because the content of the axioms – and so the theorems derived from them – are *dependent upon experience*. On this way of looking at Euclidean geometry, its theorems as well as its axioms will, if true, express synthetic a posteriori judgments about the structure of space.

But, the criticism concludes, you must choose one or other of these ways of viewing (Euclidean) geometry: either as a system that embodies purely a priori formulae or as a system that has axioms that are based upon a posteriori evidence about the structure of space. If you choose the first, the theorems of geometry do indeed follow necessarily from the axioms, but they have no reference to the structure of space. If you choose the second, the theorems do refer to the structure of space, but they carry neither necessity nor strict universality.

There is no *via media* between these two ways of viewing geometry. The main points of the objection were well summed up by Einstein: 'As far as the laws of mathematics refer to reality, they are not certain [necessary or strictly universal]; and so far as they are certain, they do not refer to reality.'

The force of this objection is not strengthened merely by the discovery or invention of alternative pure 'geometries'. Since these pure 'geometries' are uninterpreted marks on paper, they are not systems that make any claims about the structure of space, and it is doubtful whether Kant himself would even regard them as genuine geometries. (In themselves, they do not show that Euclidean geometry, when its basic terms are given a common-sense interpretation, cannot describe the structure of space.) What does appear to be a serious objection to the Kantian thesis about the status of Euclidean geometry is that some of these pure 'geometries', when given a physical interpretation, *fit* the spatial universe – the Einsteinian universe – despite contradicting Euclid's system. That non-Euclidean figures hold for certain regions of space has been thought to enforce the objection that, to the extent that one conceives of a pure 'geometry' as having application to the spatial world (when its basic terms are given a physical interpretation), it is a question of *fact*, an a posteriori matter, whether it will do so. In other words, if one considers geometry to be a body of *synthetic* judgments holding for the structure of space, as Kant does, then there can be no necessity or strict universality about its holding for space. No geometry, so considered, can be a body of synthetic *a priori* judgments.

In fact, the contemporary view is that Euclidean geometry does not fit *any* region of the spatial world; it is only a close approximation over short distances and under our local conditions. Consequently, the Kantian thesis that Euclidean geometry holds for the structure of space is not even accurate if its judgments are taken to express synthetic a posteriori, let alone synthetic a priori, truths.

I should add that, more recently, some philosophers have attempted a reinterpretation of the Kantian thesis about mathematics. This reinterpretation is known as 'the constructivist view'. It denies that the theorems in a system of geometry are already contained in the axioms independent of a certain type of *construction*. Rather, a proof has first to be given or constructed (in accordance with the axioms and rules of the system) *before* a theorem is true in that system, just as on the Kantian thesis it is the construction of a figure in intuition (in accordance with a priori geometrical concepts) that makes possible the holding of a geometrical judgment. Moreover, since, for the constructivists, it is this proof that alone determines the validity of the mathematical theorem, there is no question of its being falsified by recourse to experience, i.e. a posteriori.

Although the constructivist view of mathematics does, indeed, appear to give a sense to the thesis that the validity of mathematical judgments depends upon our carrying out a process of construction, it does not, so far as I can see, help Kant to prove or even to confirm the *mind-dependence* – the so-called *ideality* – of space and time (at least in the way in which he is seeking to prove it). Yet, as we shall find in the Transcendental Aesthetic, this is what he principally hopes to achieve with his thesis that the judgments of pure mathematics are synthetic a priori. So, even if it is accepted that a constructivist view does show that a Kantian-style thesis about mathematics is after all defensible – and the constructivist view itself remains a minority one compared with the position summed up by Einstein – it would not seem to be directly relevant to furthering Kant's own Copernican revolution.

Natural science

On the face of it, Kant does not provide any detailed reason for affirming that the first principles of physics are genuine instances of synthetic a priori judgments. (Physics is regarded as determining the behaviour, the dynamical relations, of matter in space.) Of course, there seems no great difficulty in comprehending why he should think that these principles *claim* this status. Thus the principle 'Action and reaction must be equal in all communication of motion' does claim necessity and universality, and it is also synthetic (B 17–18). The difficulty lies in understanding his grounds for affirming that the first principles of physics not only claim to hold but actually *do* hold as a body of synthetic a priori judgments.

In the Introduction to the *First Critique*, his assertion appears to rest solely on the near *unanimity* of opinion, among scientists, as to which group of synthetic a priori judgments forms the first principles of physics (or natural science). Undoubtedly, he does think of the first principles of physics as in a privileged position compared with those of transcendent metaphysics, where there is no unanimity about what judgments constitute its first principles. Undoubtedly, too, he is suspicious of the claims of transcendent metaphysics because of this lack of unanimity. But his ground for *accepting* a given group of synthetic a priori judgments as forming the genuine body of first principles of physics does not rest on the mere fact that this group commands unanimous assent among scientists. It is based primarily on the close parallel which he sees between the procedures in mathematics and physics.

This parallel is argued for in the second edition Preface (B x–xiv), just before he turns to consider whether a procedure similar to that employed in mathematics and physics might be attempted in metaphysics. With regard to mathematics and physics, his first point is that both are plainly in the canon of the sciences: they both possess a set of first principles, and they both yield, partly by means of their first principles, a vast body of results that are everywhere agreed to hold with a priori certainty. In fact, if we study the procedures of these two sciences, he believes that we shall find that their results are based either wholly (in the case of mathematics) or substantially (in the case of physics) on non-empirical foundations. A proof in mathematics, e.g. concerning some property of an isosceles triangle, depends on axioms or principles like 'A straight line is the shortest distance between two points' (together with certain non-empirical constructions and observations); and a proof in physics, e.g. concerning some property of moving balls on an inclined plane, depends on first principles like 'In all communication of motion, action and reaction must always be equal' (together with certain empirical constructions and observations). These axioms or principles are, in both cases, synthetic as well as a priori – even though the first principles of *physics*, as opposed to those of *pure* natural science upon which they depend, are not entirely free from the addition of some very general empirical input.

So Kant's claim that the first principles of physics are genuine instances of synthetic a priori judgments is by no means based solely on the unanimous assent concerning these fundamental judgments (as opposed to the palpable lack of such unanimity in transcendent metaphysics). Rather, it is based mainly on what he sees as a close parallel between the *procedures* in mathematics and physics, together with the extraordinary *success* of these procedures in yielding a huge number of results that are everywhere acknowledged to hold with necessity and universality. If the procedures in mathematics yield results, and a huge number of results, that have a priori certainty, and if closely analogous procedures in physics are similarly successful, then the first principles of physics (or natural science) *as well as* the axioms of mathematics must be genuine instances of synthetic a priori judgments. For the certainty of the results in physics, just as in mathematics, crucially depend upon their fundamental synthetic a priori judgments. There is no question, therefore, but that we are actually in possession of such judgments in natural science. What is needed is an *explanation* of how we can possess them.

The role of mathematics and natural science in Kant's overall strategy

Whatever reservations there may be concerning Kant's claims about the status of the fundamental judgments of mathematics and natural science, it is a central part of his strategy that these judgments – most importantly, those in mathematics – are acknowledged, at the beginning of his critical enquiries, as having genuine synthetic a priori validity. By the time he wrote the second edition of the *First Critique*, he had self-consciously adopted what he calls 'the regressive method' of substantiating his position. That is, he *begins* with what he regards as two sets of incontestably genuine synthetic a priori judgments – the judgments of pure mathematics and pure natural science – and proceeds to argue back from them to their necessary presuppositions. He had, in fact, given a key place to this regressive procedure, in the first edition, with regard to mathematics. For he makes it clear that what should *above all* convince his readers of the correctness of his views of space and time is that these views alone can explain our possession of the synthetic a priori judgments of mathematics (see A 46–9/B 63–6).

Of course, the regressive method does not *exclude* the use of a direct manner of proof, either of space and time or of the pure concepts of the understanding. And to the extent that the direct method is employed in the first edition, it is still to be found in the second. However, given Kant's own preference for the regressive method of proof for space and time even in the first edition, it would, I submit, be a mistake to deny its importance to his overall strategy. It is true that his famous transcendental deduction of the pure concepts of the understanding does not require the prior acceptance of the first principles of pure natural science: their certainty is employed only as a means of *rejecting* an empiricist derivation of the 'pure' concepts (B 128). But the transcendental deduction does require the prior acceptance of his views on space and time; and *these* views are, by Kant's own admission, made 'completely convincing' because they alone can explain the synthetic a priori nature of mathematics (A 46/B 63).

But how can the regressive method be of primary importance to Kant when, in the later *Critique of Practical Reason*, he claims that the

First Critique has been able to 'overthrow' scepticism with regard to natural science and mathematics (*CPractR*, 5:53)? There is, in reality, no inconsistency between this claim and the primacy of the regressive method. His point in the *Critique of Practical Reason* is that once it is recognized that the objects of the senses are mind-dependent (appearances), and not things in themselves, we can explain why scepticism concerning the objective validity of both natural science and mathematics can have no force. The sceptic alleges that no reply to his doubts can be offered; and he would be right, Kant agrees, if the objects of the senses were things in themselves. But, given that these objects are mind-dependent (appearances), we are enabled to overthrow scepticism by showing that both natural science and mathematics must apply to spatio-temporal objects. This attack on scepticism does not contradict Kant's employment of the regressive method in the *First Critique*. Far from it: the attack relies on our first accepting the existence of mathematics, as a body of synthetic a priori judgments holding for the structure of space and time, in order to render completely certain the *mind-dependence* (the *ideality*) of space and time. Once this has been achieved, Kant is in a position to explain (in the Principles of Pure Understanding) why pure mathematics and natural science must apply to the objects in space and time. It is the explanation of these two disciplines' *objective* validity – why they must apply to spatio-temporal *objects* – that Kant regards as overthrowing scepticism. The regressive method plays a vital initial role in this explanation because, as he sees it, that method can alone render fully convincing the ideal status of space and time.

3

The Transcendental Aesthetic: The Nature of Space and Time

In the Transcendental Aesthetic, Kant considers the relationship between space and time, on the one hand, and the modes or forms by which our senses are affected, on the other. These modes or forms he calls 'the forms of our sensible intuition'. He will argue that space and time must be identified with the forms of our sensible intuition. It is this identification that will enable an explanation to be given of *how* pure mathematics can be a body of synthetic a priori judgments. Remember that, for Kant, it is certain that pure mathematics is a genuine body of such judgments: the question at issue is to account for their certainty.

All very well, you may say, but what *are* the forms of our sensible intuition? In common with most philosophers of the seventeenth and eighteenth centuries (as well as many before and since), Kant takes it that our senses can only give us any awareness of an object that exists outside the mind by means of sensations that it causes – or otherwise occasions – within the mind. Our capacity to apprehend sensations, occasioned by this mind-independent object, he calls 'sensibility' or 'the faculty of representation'. The idea is that when this mind-independent object – to which he gives various names, including 'the transcendental object' and 'the thing in itself' – acts upon the mind's faculty of representation, or sensibility, it produces an empirical intuition. An empirical intuition is a sense field containing a manifold of sensations (or representations). This manifold is collectively termed 'an appearance'. An appearance always has two kinds of feature. First, there is the *matter* of the appearance: this corresponds to the content of the various sensations. In the case of an outer appearance – Kant's own example is the representation of a body – its matter corresponds to the appearance's particular colour, texture, hardness or softness, and so on (in other words, its secondary qualities). Second, there is the *form* of the appearance: in the case of an outer appearance, this corresponds to its particular extension and figure.

His claim is that although the matter of an appearance depends upon the way in which our faculty of representation happens to be affected by the transcendental object, the form or forms in which any possible appearance is located – the ways in which the sensations' contents can appear individually and be disposed collectively – must already exist in the mind. 'That in which alone the sensations can be posited and ordered in a certain form, cannot itself be sensation; and therefore, while the matter of all appearance is given to us a posteriori only, its form must lie a priori in the mind, and so must allow of being considered apart from all sensation' (A 20/B 34).

When it is said that the form of any appearance must already exist in the mind, Kant does not of course mean that the *particular* extension or shape of any actual outer appearance already exists in the mind. Its particular shape and extension will depend upon how, in a given case, the sensations are disposed. This, in turn, will depend upon the way in which we are affected by the transcendental object. But the possibility of our having sensations, and of our apprehending their contents in particular relationships, does require the mind to possess its own mode or modes of sensible receptivity. Without such a mode or modes of receptivity already existing in the mind, it would be impossible to be conscious of an appearance. For an appearance is constituted by an array of sensations, sensed in a particular relationship. In short, Kant's point is that if the mind did not possess a faculty for apprehending sensations and for sensing the relationships between them, there could be no consciousness of an appearance. Unless there exists in the mind a mode or modes of receptivity by which it *can* become conscious of sensations and their relationships, no consciousness of an appearance would be possible. So, while the matter of an appearance depends on the ways in which our mind happens to be affected by the transcendental object – and hence the specific contents of sensations can be determined only empirically or a posteriori – there must exist in the mind, independently of any action of the transcendental object upon it (and hence a priori), a mode or modes of sensible receptivity by which it is able to apprehend sensations, both singly and collectively. Such a mode of receptivity Kant calls *an a priori or pure form of sensible intuition.*

The point is illustrated, and further developed, by means of a thought-experiment with an outer appearance. If we subtract from the empirical intuition of a body the contribution made by sensations, viz. the body's colour, texture, etc.; and if we also subtract anything that the understanding may contribute, viz. features like force and permanence; we still possess the capacity to draw the *shape* or *outline* of that appearance – or indeed of any possible outer appearance – even though no *actual* appearance is now being apprehended. Our capacity to draw the form – the extension and shape – of any possible outer appearance, even when no appearance is actually present to the senses, shows that there must exist in the mind the capacity to form *pure* intuitions. This further supports Kant's claim that our sensibility must itself possess the form or forms necessary for apprehending and relating together the matter of any appearance. With respect to the form of an outer appearance, he says that 'extension and figure . . . belong to pure intuition, which even without any actual object of the senses or sensation, exists in the mind a priori as a mere form of sensibility' (A 21/B 35).

The mind, then, has a faculty of sensible receptivity (sensibility) through which it has the power to form pure intuitions. We have seen this power illustrated by the above thought-experiment; and Kant will later claim that it is crucially at work in the construction of geometrical figures and arithmetical products. He holds that the mind possesses *two* forms of sensible intuition: that by which extension and figure are represented is called 'outer intuition', and that by which succession and the simultaneous are represented is called 'inner intuition'. It is because the mind possesses these two a priori forms of sensible intuition that it can also become conscious of appearances – that is, of *empirical* intuitions. When the object which exists independently of the mind (the thing in itself, or transcendental object) affects our sensibility, we become conscious of appearance(s) in outer or inner intuition: in other words, we have an outer or inner empirical intuition.

Space and time

Now the key question is: When we perceive objects in space or time, what is the *relationship* between this space or time (and so spatial or temporal objects), on the one hand, and our forms of outer or inner intuition (and so appearances), on the other? Restricting the possibilities to space, does space exist *independently* of any property of our mind and, hence, of outer intuition? If so, space must either exist in itself or be a relation between things in themselves. In either case, our perceptual knowledge of spatial objects would have to be gained by means of an *inference* from what exists in the mind, i.e. by means of an inference from appearances in our outer intuition to spatial objects existing outside the mind. Or is space to be *identified* with a property of our mind – that is, with pure outer intuition? If so, our perceptual knowledge of spatial objects will be the same as, or at least a subset of, our knowledge of appearances in outer intuition. On this latter alternative, no inference to what exists outside the mind, viz. to things in themselves, would be required for gaining perceptual knowledge. Similar questions and replies go for time.

When Kant specifically turns to discuss space and time, rather than the forms of our intuition, he immediately signals that what concerns him is how space and time are related to our outer and inner intuitions: 'What then are space and time? Are they real existences? Are they only determinations or relations of things, yet such as would belong to things even if they were not intuited? Or are space and time such that they belong only to the form of intuition, and therefore to the subjective constitution of the mind, apart from which they could not be ascribed to anything whatsoever?' (A 23/B 37).

Three views of space and time are on offer here; and it seems clear that Kant regards them as exhaustive. According to the first, the Newtonian (or absolute) view, space and time exist not only independently of being perceived, but independently of any objects (understood as *things in themselves*) in space or time. This is the view being referred to when it is asked if space and time are real existences. According to the second, Leibnizian (or relational), view, space and time do exist independently of being perceived, but do not exist independently of things in themselves. Space and time are merely the relations holding between things in themselves, which we confusedly perceive by means of sensations in our minds. This is the view that is being referred to when it is asked if space and time are only relations or determinations of things (in themselves), yet such as would belong to things (in themselves) even if they were not intuited.

Kant rejects *both* these views in favour of a third: viz. that space and time are to be equated with our outer and inner a priori intuitions, respectively. This is the view that he is referring to when he asks if space and time 'belong . . . only to the subjective constitution of the mind, apart from which they could not be ascribed to anything'. He provides two types of argument for this third view and against the alternative, Newtonian and Leibnizian, views. The first type he calls the 'Metaphysical Exposition' of our concepts of space and time; and the second, he calls the 'Transcendental Exposition' of these concepts.

In dealing with both these expositions, I shall first discuss space and then deal, much more briefly, with time.

The Metaphysical and Transcendental Expositions of space

As regards the Metaphysical Exposition of space, its method is to begin with certain very general thoughts about space (e.g. that each subject thinks that there is only one, and not a multiplicity of, spaces in which he can place objects), and then to show that such thoughts can only be justified if space is a pure (or a priori) intuition. Kant presumably takes it that the proponents of the opposing views of space acknowledge that any acceptable view must accommodate these ideas. I shall follow the text of the B edition, which is divided into four arguments. (The A edition has five arguments; but the third is replaced in the B edition by the Transcendental Exposition.)

Metaphysical Exposition

The first two arguments of the Metaphysical Exposition are designed to show that we have an a priori, and not an empirical, conception of space.

Argument 1: In the opening argument, Kant considers whether our conception of space can have been arrived at from a number of outer *experiences*, viz. from an *empirical* consciousness of certain relations holding between the contents of sensations, relations like *alongside of*, *at a distance from*, and so on. However, if we had formed our concept of *space* from outer experiences, it must be possible to think of these experiences *independently* of thinking of the concept which has allegedly been acquired by means of them. For example, our empirical concept *table* can be formed by first having sensed instances of the concepts *leg*, *flat top*, etc., and acquiring the concept *table* therefrom. This is possible because the former concepts can be acquired from sensations *without* presupposing the latter concept. But, Kant contends, we cannot conceivably have built up our concept of *space* empirically by means of first observing certain relations between outer appearances. For, in order to be empirically conscious of outer appearances as e.g. *alongside of* or *at a distance from* each other, we must already have set the manifold of apprehended sensations (out of which the appearances are constituted) together in space.

It is worth remarking that, in the forthcoming Transcendental

Analytic, Kant does offer an *explanation* of why it is that we cannot be empirically conscious of the relations between outer appearances without presupposing the existence of space. This explanation hinges on the argument (which we will examine later) that, in order to be empirically conscious of *any* relations between appearances, certain synthetic a priori principles must first be applied to the manifold of apprehended sensations or representations. Some of these principles make possible the consciousness of the given manifold as collectively existing in one space, *thereby* allowing us to have empirical, relational knowledge of outer appearances. On this account, we cannot begin with an *empirical* consciousness of relations holding between outer appearances and *then* derive our concept of space therefrom. The very capacity to experience any relations between outer appearances already requires us to have set the manifold of representations constituting the given appearances in one space. It is instructive to compare Argument 1 regarding space with the parallel argument for time (A 30/B 46). In the latter, it is held that time cannot be derived from experiencing the relations of *coexistence* and *succession*, since these very experiences presuppose the conception of time as underlying them. This argument again relies on Kant's later contention that there can be no experience of coexistence or succession without certain synthetic a priori principles applying to the manifold of apprehended sensations or representations. These principles make possible the consciousness of the manifold as collectively existing in one temporal continuum, *thereby* allowing us to experience, to have *empirical* consciousness of, coexistence and succession. (I particularly mention the parallel argument for time, because Kant later examines how our consciousness of succession and coexistence arises, at much greater length than our consciousness of spatial relations. But see B 162–3, where both a spatial and a temporal relation are discussed.)

Argument 2: A further consideration is here employed to show that we have an a priori, and not an empirical, consciousness of space. Whenever we think of outer appearances, we are conscious of them as spatially located (even a single outer appearance has spatial relations). But we can think about space *without* being conscious of any outer appearances. For instance, whenever we imaginatively engage in geometrical constructions and demonstrations. Consequently, if we are capable of thinking of space as empty of outer appearances, while all outer appearances must be spatially located, it follows that our concept of space is a presupposition of our consciousness of the appearances of outer intuition. Our concept of space must therefore be a priori, since it makes possible our outer empirical consciousness, rather than being dependent upon it. (Again, see the corresponding argument in the Metaphysical Exposition of time.)

Note that Argument 2 does not depend, as some have claimed, on the doubtful psychological generalization that we can think of an entirely *void* space. When it is said that we can think of space as empty of objects, what is meant is that we can think of space without thinking of outer appearances, of the objects of an *empirical* intuition. As I have just indicated, Kant believes that this occurs when we imaginatively undertake geometrical constructions. It can also occur if we start with the consciousness of an empirical object, and then think away all features besides the *form* of the object. Kant gives us an example in his Introduction: 'Gradually remove from your experiential concept of a body everything that is empirical in it – the colour, the hardness or softness, the weight, even the impenetrability – there still remains the space that was occupied by the body (which has now entirely disappeared), and you cannot leave that out' (B 5–6; see also A 20–1/B 35).

The second set of arguments, numbered 3 and 4 in the B edition, are designed to show that space is an intuition, indeed an a priori intuition, and not a *general* concept.

Argument 3: According to the view that space is a general concept, we have built up this concept from observing the relationships between different sets of empirical objects, and then taken the general concept *space* to stand for any similar relationships between objects. But this view cannot be correct, claims Kant, because 'we can represent to ourselves only one space; and if we speak of diverse spaces, we mean thereby only parts of one and the same unique space' (A 25/B 39). In other words, if space were a general concept, we could sensibly talk of genuinely different spaces, each of which individually falls under this general concept. But the truth is that we think of space as essentially *one* continuum, and not as made up of a number of individual spaces, each instantiating the general concept *space*. Compare a familiar example of a general concept: namely, the concept *horse*. Here we can think, indeed must be able to think, of many possible individual horses – in Kantian phraseology, 'we can represent to ourselves many diverse horses' – and when we do talk about diverse horses, we plainly do not mean that these are, let alone must be, only parts of one and the same horse. In employing any general concept, we necessarily think of it as capable of having innumerable *instances*, each capable of existing in its own right, rather than as a mere part of *one* all-embracing instantiation of the concept in question. But we cannot think of space in this way: all the so-called individual spaces are thought of as essentially parts of *one* all-embracing space. Space, therefore, cannot be a general concept. We must, rather, acquire our idea of it through acquaintance, through intuition.

Moreover, because we think of space as essentially one, and not made up of separable spaces, the intuition of space must be a priori, and not empirical. Consider a single empirical intuition like the consciousness of a colour expanse. Here, we certainly can have the consciousness of distinct expanses of that colour; and although it is possible that all these diverse expanses may be discovered to be parts of *one* overall expanse (by finding empirically that there are further expanses of the colour joining all the original ones), there is clearly no requirement that this must be the case. We might, alternatively, be conscious of e.g. empty space between the various colour expanses. On the other hand, we must think of space as forming one continuum. We cannot *first* have the intuition of two spatial areas, and then *discover* empirically that there is intervening space joining them up (as can be done with the colour expanses). Our notion of the unity of space is not something that we have merely discovered empirically; it is, rather, something that we think of as *essential* to it. Our intuition of space is, therefore, an a priori and not an empirical one (since its unity is thought of as *necessary*).

The question of *why* we cannot conceive of genuinely distinct spaces will be taken up later by Kant (see *Two Problems about Kant's Account of Space and Time*). In the Metaphysical Exposition, he is taking it as given that each of us does think of space as essentially one.

Argument 4: An additional ground is provided, in Argument 4, for holding that space must be an intuition, rather than a general concept. We think of space as presented to us as *infinite* in extent. Now although a general concept can have an infinite number of instances falling *under* it, this must always be in virtue of a *limited* number of common characteristics between the instances. For no concept can be used if an infinite number of characteristics need to be instantiated before it can be applied. Space, however, is conceived as presented to us as infinite in extent, as having an unbounded number of parts. Although no general concept can be thought of as constituted by a boundless number of parts, an a priori intuition *can* be given to us as boundless in extent. Thus, whenever we draw a line, whether in fact or in the imagination, we can think of extending that line *without limit*; and it is by the thought of such a limitless progression or construction in a priori intuition that we are enabled to conceive of space as a presentation that is infinite in extent (cf. *Prol*, Sect. 12). Space must, then, be an intuition, indeed an a priori intuition (since the thought of its boundless nature is acquired through a process of geometrical construction), and not a general concept.

Transcendental Exposition

I turn now to the Transcendental Exposition of space (later referred to as a Deduction, see A 87/B 119). Not only is this the clearest and, given its premises, the most compelling of the two expositions, it also directly connects with Kant's attempt to explain the existence of synthetic a priori judgments in mathematics.

The term 'transcendental' surfaces many times in the *First Critique*, as well as in the other works of Kant's critical period, so it will be useful to quote his own definition of it in relation to knowledge: 'I entitle *transcendental* all knowledge which is occupied not so much with objects as with the mode of our knowledge of objects, insofar as this mode of knowledge is meant to be possible a priori' (A 11/B 25; italics original). So, for example, the transcendental exposition of space is called 'transcendental' because it is occupied with explaining how we can be in possession of a body of synthetic a priori knowledge (geometry) holding for the structure of space – and, in consequence (as will emerge later), for the empirical objects that can come in space.

The Transcendental, unlike the Metaphysical, Exposition does not begin with certain very general thoughts that we have about space, and then proceed to draw conclusions from them concerning our concept of space. Instead, it starts with an agreed body of synthetic a priori knowledge, and proceeds to argue that such knowledge is possible if and only if space is the form of our outer intuition.

Kant believes that he has already shown in the Introduction that geometry is a body of synthetic a priori judgments, and that these judgments hold for the structure of space. The point now is to explain *how* this can be. Since the judgments are synthetic, it cannot be that they are proved merely from analysis of the concepts involved. Such a procedure could only produce *analytic* a priori judgments. But neither can the judgments proceed by consulting experience. At best, this could only give us synthetic *a posteriori* truths about how the differing singular figures, presented in empirical intuition, have each, in fact, been discovered to be structured. Rather, the proofs will need to proceed on the basis of our own a priori *construction* of figures in intuition. That is, we shall need ourselves to produce the specific sense fields (by means of the construction of geometrical figures in accordance with our own a priori concepts), and to base the proofs on these constructions. Not only will this explain how we can be in possession of synthetic a priori judgments holding for the structure of outer intuition; it should also make it possible to understand how the necessity of these judgments applies equally to the structural relationships among the *appearances* presented in outer intuition.

By way of analogy, compare the case of a mathematician constructing geometrical figures on a television screen, and thereby (with a knowledge of the curvature of the screen) producing demonstrations – at least as Kant would have it – which hold for these figures. In theory, prior to any transmitted images appearing on the screen, the mathematician could determine the rules governing the possible structural relations of these images. The geometry of the screen would lay down, in advance of the appearance of any transmitted images, the rules concerning how they could be internally structured and related to one another. Of course, the images on the screen will be physical images; and as such, they will be taken, at the common-sense level, to exist whether or not we are, or could be, aware of them. Equally, at the common-sense level, the screen exists independently of our possible awareness of it. Such independence does *not* apply to what Kant understands by appearances and by a priori intuition. In particular, we do not first apprehend a unified intuition and then construct a geometrical figure upon it: rather, it is the construction of the figure, in accordance with our a priori geometrical concepts, that brings into existence a unified intuition. None the less, the analogy does bring out a crucial point in the transcendental exposition: namely, that it is because we possess the capacity to construct figures a priori in outer intuition, and thereby to demonstrate synthetic a priori judgments about these geometrical figures, that even prior to any experience, we can be in possession of synthetic, yet necessary, rules governing the structure of the appearances in outer intuition.

Still, it may be objected, all that the argument explains so far is how geometry, as a body of synthetic a priori judgments, can describe the structure of outer *intuition* (and thereby how we can grasp its application to what is given in outer intuition, viz. *appearances*). It has not explained how geometry is able to describe the structure of *space* (and the possible structural forms of *objects* in space). That, of course, is so *if* space is not identified with the form of our outer sense, i.e. with pure outer intuition. But unless we do identify the two, there can be no explanation of how geometry is a body of synthetic a priori truths holding for the structure of space. For if space referred not to our form of outer sense, but to what exists in itself (absolutely or relationally), then, since the mathematician produces his geometrical demonstrations by recourse to outer intuition, there can be no guarantee that what necessarily holds for any construction in intuition *must* hold for space (and, *a fortiori*, for empirical objects in space). In other words, if space is not a property of the mind but exists independently of it, any demonstration that rests on what *is* a property of the mind (outer intuition) cannot be acknowledged to hold with certainty for what exists *independently* of the mind. Since, however, geometrical demonstrations *are* acknowledged to hold with certainty for the structure of space, then space and the form of our outer sense, pure outer intuition, must be one and the same. Such an identification can alone account for the status of geometry.

There is a good summary of the upshot of the Transcendental Exposition at A 48–9/B 66:

> If, therefore, space (and the same is true for time) were not merely a form of your intuition, containing conditions a priori, under which alone things can be outer objects to you, and without which subjective condition outer objects are in themselves nothing, you could not in regard to outer objects determine anything whatsoever in an a priori and synthetic manner. It is, therefore, not merely possible or probable, but indubitably certain, that space and time, as the necessary conditions of all outer and inner experience, are merely subjective conditions of all our intuition, and that in relation to these conditions all objects are therefore mere appearances, and not given to us as things in themselves which exist in this manner.

Time is a pure (or a priori) intuition

As Kant's arguments for the nature of time run parallel to those for space, I shall not discuss them in detail, but merely summarize them. The importance of time to his Copernican revolution will emerge properly only later, when we examine the proofs for the fundamental laws of pure natural science and the conditions of our own continued self-consciousness.

In the Metaphysical Exposition of time, it is first argued that time is a priori, in that it is not dependent upon our experiences but is, rather, a precondition of our having any experience at all. Time contains only relations, three of them: 'succession, coexistence, and that which is coexistent with succession, the enduring' (B 67). What this comes to is that everything that appears to us, whether in space or as a mere modification of the subject's own thoughts, must do so under the aspect of time, and in accordance with one or more of these three time relations. For instance, when we experience spatial objects, and their states, we must always perceive them as coexisting or in succession (with their substance remaining – enduring – throughout any change). But our empirical consciousness of any instance of these relations itself presupposes our recognition of a single temporal continuum within which the apprehended sensations *can* be related. We cannot, therefore, derive our concept of time empirically, i.e. from the experience of coexistence or succession; rather, the experience of these relations always presupposes our recognition of time. Moreover, while we cannot be conscious of an appearance except under the aspect of time, we can think of time as empty of appearances – as in the imaginative construction of an arithmetical proof. Hence, time cannot be derived from our empirical intuitions, but must underlie them as an a priori condition.

It is argued, second, that time is an a priori intuition and not a general concept. For different times are necessarily all parts of one and the same temporal continuum, and time is also thought of as boundless or unlimited in extent. These are characteristics which, as Kant had maintained in his analogous discussion of space, can be given only through a priori intuition, and not by means of a general concept.

In the Transcendental Exposition of time, he again concludes, independently of the above considerations, that time must be an a priori intuition. For if, and only if, it is, can we explain our possession of certain synthetic a priori judgments which refer to temporal relations. Time makes possible the synthetic a priori body of propositions that is arithmetic: 'arithmetic creates its concept of number by successive addition of its units in time [i.e. one *after* the other]' (*Prol*, Sect. 10; 4:283). It also makes possible that a priori body of propositions dealing with pure mechanics, viz. by making possible the concept of *motion*: 'Only in time can two contradictory opposed predicates (being in two different places) meet in one and the same object, *namely one after the other*. Thus our concept of time explains that body of a priori synthetic knowledge which is exhibited in the doctrine of motion' (B 49; italics original). The point that Kant is making in these passages is this. If time were attached to things in themselves, absolutely or relationally, then the synthetic a priori judgments in arithmetic and mechanics could not be known to hold for relations in time (but only for relations in our inner intuition). For we prove them by *recourse* to the form of our inner intuition, as in the construction of an arithmetical sum. Whereas, if time is *equated* with the form of our inner intuition, we have no difficulty in understanding how such synthetic a priori judgments are possible. Now since it is certain that we are in possession of these judgments, and that they do hold for relations in time, it follows that time must be equated with the a priori form of our inner intuition.

The results of Kant's arguments can be summarized as follows. Time is the a priori form of our inner intuition (or inner sense). It is also the form of intuition in which every appearance without exception must be located, whether the appearance is additionally referred to outer sense (and so to space) or whether it is only located in inner sense (and so in time). Everything that appears to us is constituted of representations; and all representations are mental phenomena. But while some appearances are conceived merely as belonging to the subject's own inner states, the form of which is time, others are also referred to outer sense, the form of which is space. Yet, since all appearances are in time, as the form in which the subject apprehends *any* manifold of representations as an appearance, it follows that all appearances, whether referred to outer sense or to inner sense (as a modification of the subject's thoughts) must be in time:

> Time is the immediate condition of inner appearances (of our souls), and thereby the mediate condition of our outer appearances. Just as I can say a priori that all outer appearances are in space, and are determined a priori in conformity with the relations of space, I can also say from the principle of inner sense, that all appearances whatsoever, that is all objects of the senses, are in time, and necessarily stand in time-relations. (A 34/B 51)

Two Problems about Kant's Account of Space and Time

The first problem is this. Allowing that space and time are pure a priori intuitions, why should they not *also* attach, absolutely or relationally, to things in themselves? Admittedly, if they do, our mathematical judgments could not be known with a priori certainty to apply to them; but this is scarcely enough to show that a (possibly) differently structured absolute or relational space and time could not also exist. Yet Kant clearly holds that space and time belong *only* to the forms of intuition, and that they cannot be things in themselves or relations between things in themselves. (Indeed, if they were, this would have serious repercussions for his moral philosophy.) I believe that he would seek to justify his position along the following lines. Since it has been shown that space and time are pure intuitions, they are not the *type* of phenomena that can exist as things in themselves or as relations between such entities. A pure intuition is an intrinsic property or mode of the mind, and hence cannot exist in its own right (just as a pain cannot exist in its own right, but must exist as a mode *of* a substance). It makes no sense to suppose that what is an intrinsic property of the mind can exist on its own. A thing in itself, on the other hand, is essentially something that can exist in its own right. Equally, it makes no sense to hold that what is an intrinsic property of the mind can be a relation holding *between* things in themselves.

The second problem concerns Kant's claim that we can know with a priori certainty the structure of space and time (by means of mathematical demonstrations). Applying the point specifically to geometry, the objection is that even if we grant that geometrical demonstrations, presently carried out, can tell us *now* about how space must be structured, how do we know that these demonstrations will do so in the future? Perhaps the structure of space will change overnight, so that any knowledge that I now have about the structure of space will not be applicable to my experience tomorrow. His response to this does not emerge until the following chapter, the Transcendental Analytic, where the conditions necessary for the subject's consciousness of its own existence through time are discussed. Kant will argue that a subject can have this consciousness of himself only provided that he can be conscious of all the outer objects of his senses existing in *one* space. However, if the rules governing the structure of space, and so spatial objects, are capable of changing between times, this would be impossible. It would, Kant argues, be impossible for the same *I* to be conscious of the unity of space. Accordingly, I (the same subject) cannot be conscious of a space which, at different times, is governed by differing sets of synthetic a priori rules. (A modified version of this reply can be employed against the objection that even if I do have a priori knowledge of the structure of *this* part of space, why might it not have happened that if I (the same subject) had now been conscious of *another* part of space, I should have discovered a different set of rules applying to that region of space.)

It is, incidentally, the requirement that without the recognition of one space, there could be no consciousness of oneself as the same subject through time, that explains, for Kant, why we each think of space as *essentially* one (as he held in Argument 3 of the Metaphysical Exposition of space).

What has the Transcendental Aesthetic achieved?

Within the overall framework of the *First Critique*, the purpose of the Transcendental Aesthetic is to answer the question: How are synthetic a priori judgments possible in pure mathematics (where they are known to exist)? It has been answered by showing that space and time are not things in themselves or relations between things in themselves, but merely the forms of our sensibility. This answer equally shows that we cannot extend our mathematical knowledge to what exists outside our modes of intuition; in particular, it cannot be extended to things in themselves. While the synthetic a priori judgments of geometry and arithmetic are valid for space and time respectively – and thereby, as will be shown, for the empirical objects in space and time – they can have no validity beyond space and time (beyond, that is, outer and inner *intuition*) and the empirical objects that can exist in space and time (i.e. *appearances*). In short, their validity, as both synthetic *and* necessary, cannot be extended beyond the objects of our senses, beyond the objects of possible experience.

These last points are well summed up in the final passage of the Transcendental Aesthetic, which was added for the second edition:

> Here, then, in pure a priori intuitions, space and time, we have one of the factors required for the solution of the general problem of transcendental philosophy: *how are synthetic a priori judgments possible?* When in a priori judgment we seek to go out beyond the given concept, we come in the a priori intuitions upon that which cannot be discovered in the concept but which is certainly found in the intuition corresponding to the concept, and can be connected with it synthetically. Such judgments, however, thus based on intuition, can never extend beyond objects of the senses; they are valid only for objects of possible experience. (B 73; italics original).

Of course, the Aesthetic will only really have achieved these results if Kant is correct in his derivation of the concepts of space and time. We have seen that the Transcendental Exposition of space (and similarly of time) depends on a view of geometry (and arithmetic) which is no longer generally accepted. It might be replied that if we were to reject his view of mathematics, this would merely mean that he is not called upon to explain how there can be synthetic a priori judgments in mathematics, since there is nothing to explain. This, it is alleged, simply *lightens* his burden – he now need only explain how there can be genuine synthetic a priori judgments in natural science.

But that answer is unsatisfactory. The synthetic a priori nature of mathematics is required for what, as Kant himself acknowledges, are his strongest arguments for the *ideality* of space and time: namely, their Transcendental Expositions. His claim that space and time 'belong to the subjective constitution of the mind' plays a pivotal role in his defence of natural science against scepticism, and – at least as important to him – in his defence of freedom of the will. By his own lights, if the objects of our experience are *things in themselves* (which they will be if space and time are not ideal), there can be no possibility of proving the reality of either natural science or freedom of the will.

The result is that, if the Transcendental Expositions of space and time are rejected, the whole burden of proof falls on the Metaphysical expositions, since these expositions also seek to establish that space and time are merely forms of our intuition. Alternatively, one might try to show that, at least with respect to natural science, the kernel of Kant's arguments *does* go through even on a realist, rather than on an idealist, framework. Although a number of philosophers have made the attempt, I do not believe that this alternative strategy can be successful. When we consider Kant's proofs for the three principles given in the Analogies section – and it is these principles which constitute the basis of natural science as he conceives it – we shall find that their validity *depends* upon his idealism. Without it, as Kant himself realized, his mode of proof would lack cogency. In fact, his attempted proofs would be full of logical howlers.

4

The Transcendental Analytic: How Our Experience – Our Knowledge of Objects in Space and Time – is Made Possible

The Transcendental Analytic is the most complex part of any of the three Critiques. It is also among the most stimulating, requiring the reader to hold together a number of different theses and grasp how they interlock to form a single overall framework.

The structure of the Analytic is divided into two books: the Analytic of Concepts and the Analytic of Principles. In both, Kant is concerned with the contribution of *thought* or *understanding* to the experience of objects. But in the first, the Analytic of Concepts, he is mostly concerned with the contribution of thought to experience with reference to *any* form of sensible intuition. In the second, the Analytic of Principles, he is concerned with specifying more particularly how thought is related to *our* experience – that is, to the experience of objects in *our* forms of sensible intuition, space and time.

Analytic of Concepts

Its chief components are the Metaphysical Deduction and the Transcendental Deduction.

Metaphysical Deduction

The first major task in the Analytic of Concepts is the derivation of what Kant calls the Table of Categories (or Pure Concepts) of the Understanding from the Table of Judgments. The latter table, which – with a few minor emendations – is claimed to come from Aristotle, is supposed to provide an exhaustive list of all the possible ways in which the mind can *make judgments* or *think about* any kind of data whatsoever. Kant believed not only that Euclid had stitched up the fundamental axioms and principles of geometry and that Newton had identified the first principles of physics, he also believed that Aristotle had in essence codified all the conceivable ways in which the mind is able to make judgments, and so to have thoughts, about anything:

> That logic has already, from the earliest times, proceeded upon this sure path [of a science] is evidenced by the fact that since Aristotle it has not required to retrace a single step. . . . It is remarkable also that to the present day this logic has not been able to advance a single step, and is thus to all appearance a closed and completed body of doctrine. . . . The sphere of logic is quite precisely delineated; its sole concern is to give an exhaustive exposition and a strict proof of the formal rules of all thought, a priori or empirical. (B viii–ix)

Kant's belief that the Table of Judgments exhaustively enumerates all the differing ways of judging or expressing thoughts is not as ridiculous as it may initially seem. To begin with, he holds that the basic judgment forms must originate in ourselves: presumably on the not unreasonable principle that the mind needs to possess the fundamental ways of connecting data into a judgment in order to start thinking at all. Further, he argues that since they are not only to be found in ourselves, but must be employed in every area of our thinking, it is reasonable to believe that: (a) they are of limited extent; and (b) they are relatively easy to identify. Finally if, as he maintains, the Table of Judgments has had no major modifications in 2,000 years, it would seem very likely that we have by now exhaustively and systematically enumerated all our judgment forms.[1]

In fact, Kant makes the even broader claim that these judgment forms exhaustively enumerate the possible modes of thought of *any* finite mind, not merely the human mind. So far as I am aware, no explicit argument is offered for this claim. It may rest on the view that

---

[1] It has been argued by Arthur Lovejoy, and others, that in reality Kant took over the judgment forms from his immediate German predecessors, seriously distorting them in the process. This alleged distortion was undertaken, it is claimed, in order that these forms might then be seen to yield his categories (see following). If correct, Kant's claim to have discovered both the exhaustive list of categories and their a priori origin would obviously be greatly weakened. In particular, it would call into doubt his claim to have established that his list of categories, and so their corresponding principles, can *alone* make experience possible. It would not, however, overturn his key general argument that the possibility of experience does require the employment of *some* a priori concepts.

what is possible must be in principle conceivable by us, and that we can only conceive of an instance of thinking which we can identify as a thought. Given Kant's claim that the judgment forms enumerate all the ways that we can think (and so identify a thought), it would then follow that all possible modes of thought must accord with the judgment forms. Whatever his reason, the fact is that he does regard the Table of Judgments as providing an exhaustive list of ways in which any finite mind, not just any human mind, can have a thought about any material. (God, if there is one, is held not to be restricted by any judgment forms – and so by any categories – on the ground that these impose limitations, which cannot apply to a limitless being. *Thought* is not applicable to God; see B 71–2.)

Corresponding to the Table of Judgments, Kant contends that there must be a Table of Categories (see tables 4.1 and 4.2).

Each of the individual items in table 4.1 has its corresponding item in table 4.2. Thus, the hypothetical judgment form in the Table of Judgments corresponds to the category of *cause* in the Table of Categories. (I have followed the slightly simpler statement of the Table of Categories as set out in the *Prolegomena*.)

What does the Table of Categories enumerate? It is supposed to give an exhaustive inventory of the concepts by which the mind can grasp a rule-governed connection holding between any data – any manifold of representations – apprehended in any form of *sensible intuition*. Kant explicitly says that the categories can apply to any sen-

Table 4.1 Table of Judgments

	I *Quantity* Universal Particular Singular	
II *Quality* Affirmative Negative Infinite		III *Relation* Categorical Hypothetical Disjunctive
	IV *Modality* Problematic Assertoric Apodictic	

sible form of intuition; they are not confined to our particular sensible forms, viz. to space and time (see B 148).

If we consider one of our forms of sensible intuition, namely time, then Kant's general idea can perhaps be illustrated by an example which uses the temporal notion of *succession* or *change* and the category of *cause*. When we think of a change of state in an object as governed by a causal law, we think that if (or whenever) certain circumstances obtain, then that change of state must occur. Consequently, in thinking of an object's change of state as subject to causal law, we are thinking of a necessary connection between an object and its surrounding circumstances which, in respect of its structure, instantiates a rule expressed by the hypothetical judgment form: If (or whenever) X, then Y. In other words, to think of an object's change of state as governed by a causal law is to conceive of a rule-governed connection between a manifold of representations, given in the temporal form of intuition, which has a parallel structure to thinking of any type of data whatever as subject to a rule expressed by the hypothetical judgment form. (There is an attempt to explain the relationship between the hypothetical judgment form and the category of cause, as it applies to our (temporal) intuition, in *Prol*, Part II, especially Sects 20–2 and 29.)

Of course, even if the example of the relationship between the hypothetical judgment form and the category of *cause* is allowed to have some plausibility, it is far from clear how the correspondence is supposed to

Table 4.2 Table of Categories

	I *Quantity* Unity Plurality Totality	
II *Quality* Reality Negation Limitation		III *Relation* Substance Cause Community
	IV *Modality* Possibility Existence Necessity	

work for each of the other judgment forms and its corresponding category. This has encouraged commentators to affirm that the categories should be treated as independent concepts existing in the mind, rather than derivable from the judgment forms. It must be admitted that Kant does precious little to help us to see how exactly the correspondences are supposed to arise. None the less, I do not find his basic idea unpromising. Once it is granted that the mind has only a limited number of judgment forms by which it *can* connect any kind of data whatever in thought, then the concepts by which we can think a rule-governed connection in a sensible intuition must reflect the structure of this small, identifiable, class of judgment forms. After all, if we can know of any laws connecting together a manifold of sensible intuition, then these connecting laws – formulated, of course, as judgments – must express *thinkable* rule-governed connections. Hence, the expression of these connections must employ categories or pure concepts of the understanding. For the categories are the most basic concepts by which we have the capacity to think any rule-governed connections at all between representations given in a sensible form of intuition (as when a change of state is thought of as governed by a rule which employs the category of *cause*). They must, therefore, in respect of their structure or form, reflect the possible ways in which the mind can hold together, or grasp, any kind of data whatever in a (coherent) thought.

What is later termed the Metaphysical Deduction (B 159) is just the attempt to argue that, corresponding to the judgment forms, there must be a specific list of categories, or pure concepts, of the understanding, by which the mind has the capacity to think of the representations, given in any form of sensible intuition, as falling under rules. The list of categories must be an *exhaustive* list of connecting concepts, because the judgment forms from which the categories are purportedly derived are themselves an exhaustive inventory of the mind's ability to connect any kind of data whatever in thought. It is because Kant holds that the categories can be deduced from the judgment forms that he is able to claim that the categories are a *complete and systematic* list of the concepts by which the mind possesses the capacity to connect together, according to rules, any manifold of representations apprehended in a sensible form of intuition. There can be no further fundamental concepts of unity in a sensible intuition: apparent counter-examples will be merely one or more of these basic concepts as they are restricted to *specific* forms of sensible intuition, e.g. to space or time, perhaps with the addition of some *empirically* discoverable feature, e.g. that of *matter*.

Whatever we may think of the legitimacy of the Metaphysical Deduction, we do need to appreciate that the categories represent for Kant a complete list of the mind's fundamental concepts for unifying representations in any form of sensible intuition. To *unify* an intuited manifold of representations is to connect that manifold *according to a rule*; and the categories are the most basic concepts used in formulating these rules. (Rules, for Kant, always carry necessity and universality with them: they state how certain phenomena *must always* be connected.) Later, in the Principles of Pure Understanding, the particular rules, or principles, for applying the categories to *our*, spatio-temporal, intuitions will be discussed.

Before we leave the Metaphysical Deduction, the following point needs to be stressed. When Kant claims that the categories are an exhaustive list of the concepts by which the mind is able to unify representations given in any sensible form of intuition, he is not thereby claiming that we will ever *succeed* in this task of unification. For all that has been shown so far, the manifold of apprehended representations, out of which an appearance can be constituted, may not *accord with* any of the categories. In which case, the mind would simply be unable to bring the given manifold of representations under *any* rules whatever (since the categories are an exhaustive list of concepts through which unification can be thought). What the Table of Categories purports to exhibit is the list of all possible concepts by means of which the understanding, and so the mind, has the *capacity* to unify representations in a sensible intuition. But Kant does not suppose that, without further argument, his discovery of this complete list is sufficient for holding that any appearance *will* – let alone *must* – fall under any rules which employ the categories. For instance, the mere fact (if it is a fact) that our understanding has the innate capacity, in conjunction with a form of sensible intuition, to operate with the rule of cause and effect does not, by itself, prove that the appearances will be so ordered as to *allow* the mind to apply this rule to any of them. Yet, for all that has been shown so far, appearances would still be given to us in intuition as objects of the senses; it is merely that we would not be in a position to think of them as connected according to any *laws*. This very point is well made by Kant himself when he urges that, for all that has been shown so far, 'Appearances might very well be so constituted that the understanding should not find them to be in accordance with the conditions of its unity. Everything might be in such confusion that, for instance, in the series of appearances nothing presented itself which might yield a rule of synthesis and so answer to the concept of cause and effect. . . . But since intuition stands in no need whatsoever of the functions of thought, appearances would none the less present objects to our intuition' (A 90–1/B 122–3).

The Metaphysical Deduction has not demonstrated the necessary applicability of the categories to all objects of the senses. Admittedly, if successful, it *does* show that the mind has, independent of experience, all the fundamental concepts by which it is able to think of data, given in any form of sensible intuition, as unified – provided that the data have an order which allows these concepts to be applied. So, although the Metaphysical Deduction does not by itself prove that the categories must apply to the objects of experience (appearances), it can be said to have made a *start* in the Kantian attempt to answer the Humean sceptic. For, according to Hume, the concept of *cause* is one that we have entirely gathered *from* experience. It is not a concept that originates in us, but one that we come to form (illegitimately) as a result of the regularity that we happen to discover in nature. On Kant's account, we do have, really have, that concept (together with the other pure concepts or categories) in our understanding independent of any experience. But, to repeat, showing that the categories originate in us and are thus a priori, not a posteriori, concepts is only a start. The major task is now before him: viz. to show that the objects of the senses *must* accord with the categories. That task is first taken up, in a general way, in the Transcendental Deduction; and, illustrated and expanded with regard to our forms of intuition, space and time, in the ensuing Principles of Pure Understanding.

Transcendental Deduction

Introduction

The Transcendental Deduction seeks to prove that the categories make experience possible, *whatever* the subject's forms of sensible intuition. In order to help us to come to grips with the Deduction and the ensuing Principles sections, let us recap on three sets of claims that Kant believes either that he has himself already established or that he can reasonably take for granted:

1 If a subject is to have any knowledge by means of the senses, the transcendental object (a thing or things in themselves) must first

cause representations in the subject's a priori form(s) of sensible intuition. The objects of a sensible intuition are appearances (mind-dependent phenomena). Each appearance is constituted by a manifold of representations in a given sensible intuition.

2 Space and time are a priori sensible intuitions. Hence, the objects in space and/or time are merely appearances.

3 The understanding possesses, a priori, an exhaustive set of categories for unifying a manifold of representations given in any sensible form of intuition. In so far as the mind can unify a manifold of representations, that manifold must conform to rules that derive from these categories. Rules always hold with strict necessity and universality.

Claims (1) and (2) are dealt with in the Transcendental Aesthetic. Claim (3) is dealt with in the Metaphysical Deduction.

Exposition

Kant contends that knowledge of objects of the senses (appearances) is possible only in so far as the manifold of representations, given in any sensible form of intuition, can be connected together by categories of the understanding. Or, to put the claim the other way around: if the understanding is unable to combine a manifold of representations, given in a sensible form of intuition, in accordance with categories, then it would not be possible to have any experience on the basis of that manifold; that is, it would not be possible to have a perceptual consciousness of that manifold as an *objective* state of affairs. In fact, Kant wishes to make an even stronger claim than that. He wishes to claim not only that a manifold of representations could not be *perceived* as something objective, but that there could *exist* nothing objective in that manifold. No possible object of the senses can exist whose disposition is not in accord with categories. More particularly, his claim is that the apparently coherent notion that, within *our* forms of sensible intuition (space and time), there could exist either a change of state of a given object or a collection of coexisting objects, although this change or coexistence is not in conformity with any rules that derive from the categories, is, in reality, an incoherent one.

Interestingly, Hume appears to allow the very kind of thing that Kant is here opposing. That is, he appears to allow that nature (the world existing in space and/or time) might be in such disorder that no causal connections could be conceived to apply to any changing states of affairs:

> It seems evident that if all the scenes of nature were continually shifted in such a manner that no two events bore any resemblance to each other, but every object was entirely new, without any similitude to whatever had been seen before, we should never in that case have attained the least idea of connection among these objects. We might say, upon such a supposition, that one object or event has followed another, not that one was produced by the other. The relation of cause and effect must be utterly unknown to mankind. Inference and reasoning concerning the operations of nature would, from that moment, be at an end; and the memory and senses remain the only canals, by which the knowledge of any real existence could possibly have access to the mind. Our idea, therefore, of necessity and causation arises entirely from the uniformity observable in the operations of nature, where similar objects are constantly conjoined together, and the mind is determined by custom to infer the one from the appearance of the other. (*Enquiry concerning Human Understanding* (London, 1748), Sect. VIII, Part I)

This passage affirms that if nature were in such confusion that there was no regularity observable in the behaviour of objects or events, it would follow that we should never be able to connect together the parts of any event under the concept of *cause* (because, for Hume, our so connecting the parts together requires that they be experienced as constantly conjoined). Yet – it is urged – we should still be able to perceive that these chaotic changes were occurring. But, since we could not bring these objective changes under causal laws, we should have to be content with merely observing each singular change as it happened and of remembering the occurrence of previous ones. In other words, there could be no thought of any necessary connection binding the parts of any of these objective changes together, but only the perception of the present change, plus the memory of past lawless changes in nature. For Hume, it would seem that a spatio-temporal world in which the objects of our possible perception were in chaos is a coherent one.

Kant will maintain that such a picture is not coherent, once it is realized that the objects of perception are *appearances*, and never *things in themselves*.

There is, however, an important issue on which Kant agrees with Hume, and which plays a major role in the Transcendental Deduction. Employing Kantian terminology, it is this: Until the apprehended representations of a manifold have been related together in thought, there can be no single subject who is conscious of having apprehended *all* the representations of that manifold. Both Hume and Kant agree that each of us is not simply *given* the consciousness of ourselves as existing throughout a series of representations. Rather, this self-consciousness has to be constructed on the basis of the separately apprehended representations (the construction requires the understanding for Kant, but not for Hume). Prior to this constructive employment of the understanding, all that Kant contends can exist in any form of sensible intuition is a series of *separately* apprehended representations, each individually introduced in consciousness by the act of 'I think': as with 'I am aware of A', 'I am aware of B'. To have the thought 'I (one subject) am aware of *both* A *and* B' – in other words, for a *collective* consciousness of the sensible manifold to arise – the individual acts of consciousness need to be connected together by the understanding into a single act of consciousness. Only if this act of unification by the understanding occurs can there be the thought of one subject, one I, who is aware of all the manifold (both A and B).

Why is this important for the Transcendental Deduction? The reason is that since we are concerned with our knowledge of appearances, we need to ascertain the minimum conditions on there being a single subject who can be collectively conscious, through sensible intuition, of a manifold of representations. For, as Kant maintains, every appearance is constituted by a sensible manifold of representations. Consequently, since it is necessary for there to be a subject who has a *collective* consciousness of the representations of a manifold *before* knowledge of any appearance (constituted by that manifold) can arise for the subject, we shall need to investigate the conditions which permit the occurrence of such a collective consciousness. From the Aesthetic, we have learnt that a manifold of representations must first be given to us through sensibility, i.e. in a form (or forms) of sensible intuition, before we can have any knowledge of objects of the senses. It will now be argued that the understanding must *also* be brought into play for such knowledge to arise.

Kant's position is that unless the understanding can connect together all the separately apprehended representations of a manifold of sensible intuition by means of certain rules (deriving from the categories), it will be impossible for there to be *one* subject, *one* 'I think', that is aware of *all* the representations of that manifold. If this can be shown, it will follow that these rules must lay down the basic connecting laws governing a manifold of representations that can be thought by a subject to constitute an appearance. If a manifold of sensible intuition does not conform to any of these rules, there will be no single subject who is capable of being aware of all the apprehended representations of the manifold, and hence of an appearance constituted by that manifold. Accordingly, there can exist no such appearance, since an appearance exists only in so far as it is capable of being known.

Let us now look at the argument of the Transcendental Deduction in more detail. First, each appearance contains a manifold of representations; and since each representation occurs *separately* to consciousness, a combination of them is necessary, if there is to be a subject who is aware of the manifold as a whole (and hence of an appearance). 'Now since every appearance contains a manifold, and since different perceptions . . . occur in the mind separately and singly, a combination of them, such as they cannot have in sense itself is demanded [in order to be conscious of an appearance by means of that manifold]' (A 121).

Second, since every appearance is constituted out of a manifold of representations, it (the appearance) can only exist for a subject in so far as that subject can be aware of that whole manifold in *one* act of consciousness. For each representation is a mind-dependent item, and, consequently, can exist only as an actual or possible item of consciousness. Since each appearance is constituted by a manifold of representations, an appearance can itself only exist for a subject in so far as that subject can be conscious of the manifold collectively, i.e. in one act of consciousness. 'Save through its relation to a consciousness that is at least possible, appearance could never be for us an object of knowledge, and so would be nothing to us; and since it has itself no objective reality [i.e. it is not a thing in itself], but exists only in being known, it would be nothing at all' (A 121).

So, putting the first two points together, we have this. Each appearance is made up of a manifold of representations given in a form of sensible intuition. Representations are mind-dependent items, and each representation is originally apprehended (through sensibility) in a separate act of consciousness. Hence, if there is to be a subject who can be aware of an appearance by means of the apprehension of the representations of a manifold, it is not enough that the representations of a sensible manifold should exist in consciousness as they are first apprehended, i.e. in a series of *separate* acts of consciousness (as in 'I am aware of A', 'I am aware of B'); what is required is that they can be thought *together*, i.e. in *one* act of consciousness (as in 'I am aware of *both* A *and* B'). Unless there can be a subject who is conscious that *it* has perceived the *whole* manifold, there can be no subject who can be conscious of that manifold as an appearance. Moreover, if there can be no subject who can be *conscious* of an appearance, no appearance can thereby *exist*. For since every appearance is constituted by a manifold of mind-dependent items (representations), given in a form of sensible intuition, it follows that unless there is a subject who can be collectively conscious of the separately apprehended representations, no appearance constituted by that manifold can exist for a subject.

That is why Kant holds that the capacity to bring together the representations of a manifold of sensible intuition into one act of consciousness 'is not merely a condition that I myself require in knowing an object, but is a condition under which every intuition must stand in order *to become an object for me*' (B 138; italics original). The point he is here emphasizing is that the capacity to bring a sensible manifold into one act of consciousness is not simply a condition for a subject to *know* that there is an object of the senses; it is a requirement for there to *exist* a possible object of the senses, a possible object of sensible intuition, for a subject to know.

Third, how can the discretely apprehended members of a manifold of sensible intuition be thought together in one act of consciousness? Restricting the question to a manifold of intuition consisting of two representations: how can there be a subject who is conscious of having apprehended *both* representations? Kant's answer is that it is only by recognizing that the separately apprehended representations are *related* in the form of sensible intuition that there can be a subject who is conscious of both representations. He gives this answer because he holds that all representations are apprehended in a form (or forms) of sensible intuition. Our consciousness of the given (the serial representations) is always a consciousness of a sensible manifold, a manifold existing in a form of sensible intuition. Accordingly, it must be possible to be conscious of the separately given representations as related in that form of sensible intuition if there is to be a subject who is capable of a collective consciousness of that manifold.

For example (to take one of the forms of our intuition, space), it is by recognizing that B exists *at a distance from* A, or that B exists *alongside* A, that a subject can be conscious of having apprehended *both* A *and* B, i.e. in one spatial continuum. Or (to take the other form of our intuition, time), it is by recognizing that B *succeeds* A, or that B *coexists with* A, that a subject can be conscious that he has apprehended *both* A *and* B, i.e. in one temporal continuum. Since space and time are the only two forms of intuition in which I can apprehend *any* representations, it must be possible to recognize a manifold of representations as related spatially and/or temporally if there is to be a single subject, myself, who is collectively conscious of that manifold.

Suppose that the separately apprehended representations of sensibility could not be recognized as related in a form of intuition. In that case, there would be no subject who could be conscious of having apprehended *both* representations. For, without the possibility of recognizing any relation between the disparately apprehended representations A and B, there could be no *single* act of consciousness that encompasses A and B (merely the successive acts of consciousness: 'I am aware of A', 'I am aware of B'). Yet the only way in which it is possible to recognize a relation between apprehended representations is through the consciousness of their being *intuitively* related (as in the consciousness of the temporal relation: 'I am aware of A coexisting with B').

In short, unless the (separately) apprehended representations of a sensible manifold can be recognized as intuitively related, there could arise no consciousness that I (one subject) have apprehended all the representations of that manifold of intuition. Consequently, there could be no I, no subject, who is aware of an appearance constituted by that manifold.

Fourth, what makes it possible to think of the representations of a manifold as related in a form of sensible intuition? Kant's answer: What alone makes this possible is if the manifold conforms to the categories. In the Metaphysical Deduction, it has been shown that the categories are the mind's most basic concepts for *unifying* representations, for thinking of a manifold of intuited representations as falling under rules. Kant now maintains that only in so far as a manifold can be brought to what he calls 'synthetic unity' – that is, can be thought of as conforming to a rule or rules (derived from the categories) – is it possible to recognize a connection, a relationship, between the representations in any form of sensible intuition. For unless the apprehended representations of a manifold can be brought to synthetic unity, the subject cannot be conscious of those representations as existing together in a *single* intuition; that is, as existing together in e.g. *one* spatial and/or *one* temporal continuum. Admittedly, what particular *empirical* relation can be perceived in a single intuition will depend upon the content of the given apprehended representations; but unless these representations can be unified by means of some category or categories, they could not be thought as collectively existing in one intuition. Consequently, there could be no question of perceiving *any* empirical relationship by means of that manifold. Since the categories are an exhaustive inventory of the mind's ways of thinking a rule-governed connection between sensible representations, it follows that unless a subject can be conscious of a manifold as conforming to categories, it could not think of that manifold as related in an intuition. There would be no subject, therefore, who could be conscious of that manifold as an appearance.

How categories make possible the recognition of a relation between representations in a *temporal* intuition will be explored in our discussion of the Analogies section. But, to illustrate the line of argument in the last paragraph, consider the perception of a given empirical relationship, the freezing of water. Here there is the experience of a relationship between two states, fluidity and solidity, as existing together *in time* (and, hence, as existing in a single intuition). More especially, water in the fluid state is perceived as *succeeded by* its existence in the solid state. Kant's contention is that the possibility of recognizing such a temporal relation at all (succession) requires that the given manifold of representations can be brought to synthetic unity (by the application of the rule of cause and effect). Independent of the particular empirical, or *material*, content in the apprehended representations (fluidity and solidity), there is a requirement governing the *form* of the temporal experience – succession – namely, that the manifold of apprehended representations can be brought to synthetic unity (by means of the appropriate rule, that of cause and effect). Unless the manifold is capable of being brought to synthetic unity, there could be no possibility of recognizing the individually apprehended representations as existing together in a relation of time (more specifically, in the relation of succession). Hence, no *empirical* relation of succession – in this case, the *freezing* of water – could be perceived. (See B 162–3.)

So it must be possible for categories to be applicable to a manifold of sensible intuition if there is to be a single subject who can be conscious collectively of the representations composing that manifold (since without the recognition that the representations are related in the given form of intuition, no collective consciousness of them can occur). The thought, and so the existence, of any appearance requires that there be a single subject who can be conscious of the manifold of sensible intuition which composes that appearance. Since this requirement, in turn, entails that the manifold conforms to categories, it follows that every appearance must obey categories. These categories belong to the understanding. From the point of view of thought, therefore, it is that faculty which makes the existence, as well as the knowledge, of appearances possible.

A notion that has not been mentioned by name in the above exposition, but which explicitly looms large in the text, is what Kant calls the principle of the 'transcendental unity of apperception'. This is the principle – which I have in fact employed, although not under that name – that, in order for any knowledge of an appearance to arise, it must be possible for one subject to be conscious of having apprehended all the representations out of which the appearance is constituted. Although, according to Kant, an individual act of self-consciousness, or 'I think', has to accompany each apprehended representation of a manifold in turn, there is no immediate consciousness of one subject, one I, existing *throughout* that manifold. The consciousness that one subject, one I, has apprehended, in any form of sensible intuition, all the representations of a manifold – and so has existed throughout the manifold – can only come about if the separately apprehended representations can be conceived as related in that form of sensible intuition. Unless this unitary consciousness can arise, no subject can know of the existence of an appearance constituted by that manifold.

Now the categories are the mind's most fundamental concepts for unifying representations in any form of sensible intuition. They give rise to rules which, relative to a given form of sensible intuition, must be applicable to the manifold if any consciousness of a relation between the separably apprehended representations of that manifold is to be possible. Hence a manifold of representations given in a sensible form of intuition can only be perceived as an appearance, as an object of sensible intuition, in so far as that manifold conforms to categories. Since all appearances are mind-dependent, and each one is constituted by a manifold of representations, all appearances must conform to categories.

The requirement that a manifold, constituting an appearance, must conform to rules (derived from the categories) explains why our concept of an *object* of the senses – which is, of course, nothing other than the thought of an appearance – is always of something that *determines* the subject's apprehension in a specific way. For if, in order to be conceived as an appearance, the manifold must be thought of as governed by rules, it follows that the subject's *apprehension* of an appearance must itself always be *determined* in accordance with the rules governing the given appearance.

Summary

From the principle of the transcendental unity of apperception, Kant argues that the categories, the 'functions of unity' as he calls them, must be applicable to any sensible manifold of representations in so far as any objects of the senses are to be known by means of that manifold. The basic condition for any thought, and so for any knowledge, is that there should be one subject who is aware collectively of a manifold of representations. For all thought requires the consciousness of a number of representations. In the case of a manifold of representations given in a form of sensible intuition, if there is to exist a subject who is collectively aware of the manifold, it must be possible to recognize its discretely apprehended representations as related in that form of intuition. This itself is possible only in so far as the manifold can be brought to synthetic unity, i.e. can be thought as conforming to rule(s) (derived from the categories), since that alone permits the representations to be apprehended together in a single intuition. Accordingly, without the possible application of categories to a sensible manifold, its discretely apprehended representations cannot come collectively to the consciousness of any subject. No thought or knowledge, therefore, can arise from that whole manifold, since there is no subject collectively aware of it. Consequently, no consciousness of any appearance can thereby arise. On the other hand, if categories are applicable to a sensible manifold, there can be a subject who is conscious collectively of the representations making up that manifold, and thus of an appearance or appearances constituted by them. Hence, from the point of view of thought, it is the categories which make possible the knowledge, and so the very existence, of objects of the senses (appearances).

Analytic of Principles

Here the main conclusion of the Transcendental Deduction – that the categories must be applicable to the objects of experience whatever the form(s) of sensible intuition – is referred to our particular forms of sensible intuition, space and time.

To this end, Kant *schematizes* the categories. In effect, this means that the fundamental rules are given for *applying* the categories to the manifold of representations in so far as that manifold can yield objects existing in time. These fundamental rules are known as *the principles of pure understanding*. In specifying how the possible objects of perception can exist in time, the principles also specify the a priori conditions for the possible existence of objects in space. They do so because *all* the objects of our senses, all appearances, exist in the form of inner sense, i.e. in time, even those that also exist in the form of outer sense, i.e. in space: 'Just as I can say a priori that all outer appearances are in space, and are determined a priori in conformity with the relations of space, I can also say, from the principle of inner sense, that all appearances whatsoever, that is, all the objects of the senses, are in time, and necessarily stand in time relations' (A 34/B 51). The upshot is that the principles of pure understanding provide the exhaustive set of a priori rules for the possible existence of spatio-temporal objects.

In the Schematism chapter itself, we are not offered any detailed explanation of how Kant arrives at the particular content of the principles of pure understanding. We are simply presented with a list of principles which are said to arise when the categories are schematized for use with our temporal form of intuition. I do not believe that it can be claimed that the list self-evidently follows from a knowledge of the categories plus a recognition that all the objects of our experience exist in time. Still, this lack of self-evidence is not perhaps of any great significance, since Kant does later attempt to prove that these schematized categories, the principles of pure understanding, must be applicable to the objects of our possible experience. The ensuing and longest chapter in the Analytic of Principles is mainly taken up with this attempt.

Kant's reasoning may have been along the following lines: 'In the Analytic of Concepts, in particular in the Transcendental Deduction, I have shown that the categories must apply to the objects of an *intuition in general*, i.e. to the objects given in any sensible intuition whatever. This has the consequence that when the categories are applied to our particular forms of sensible intuition (by being schematized), they must be applicable to spatio-temporal objects – although the detailed proofs of their necessary application to these objects has still to be given'. On this view, the Schematism chapter provides an introduction to the Analytic of Principles, serving two chief purposes: on the one hand, of pointing out that the categories, in order to be applicable to the objects of our experience, will need to have added to them a temporal dimension; and, on the other hand, of listing what the resulting principles are. We are thus prepared for the proofs of these principles in the ensuing chapter.

But how has Kant determined what the content of the principles is? How, for example, does he know that the pure concept or category of *substance* – that is, of 'a something which can be thought only as a subject and never as a predicate of something else' – yields, when schematized, what he calls the *Principle of Permanence of Substance*, viz. 'In all change of appearances substance is permanent'? I suspect the answer is that, to some extent, he worked backwards. The principles of pure understanding – or, more strictly, those of the principles that are known as the Analogies of Experience – form the pure laws of natural science, the fundamental laws holding for appearances in both our inner and outer sense; and these laws must, with the addition of certain very general *empirical* features holding for the objects in space, yield the more specific first laws of physics. Since Kant has already affirmed, in his Introduction, that we are actually in possession of the first laws of physics, he may well have looked at these physical laws and asked himself what the *pure* laws of natural science would have to be like in order to yield, together with the general empirical considerations, the more specific and known first laws of physics. This is not, I take it, an objectionable procedure provided that (as Kant thinks): (a) it is certain that we are in possession of the first laws of physics; and (b) the categories form the basic concepts of these laws.

The Principles of Pure Understanding

The main headings under which all the principles of pure understanding collectively fall are given in the Table of Principles. This table (4.3) is supposed to correspond to the Table of Categories, since it results from the latter when the categories are schematized for use with our forms of sensible intuition.

Table 4.3 Table of Principles

	1. Axioms of Intuition	
2. Anticipations of Perception		3. Analogies of Experience
	4. Postulates of Empirical Thought	

Only under the Analogies of Experience and the Postulates of Empirical Thought are we also given the three subheadings (corresponding respectively to those under the headings of Relation and Modality in the Table of Categories).

I do not intend to go through all of Kant's arguments for the application of the principles to the objects of our experience. I shall look only at what seem to me to be the most important: namely, those that are given in the Axioms of Intuition and the Analogies of Experience. It is true that there is a most important argument, in the Postulates of Empirical Thought, concerned with our knowledge of the self. We shall examine the argument after discussing the Analogies.

The Axioms of Intuition

The main purpose of the Axioms of Intuition is to argue that mathematics must apply to the appearances. While Kant takes it as evident that mathematics is a body of synthetic a priori judgments holding for the structure of space and time (from which, in the Aesthetic, he went on to identify space and time with pure outer and inner intuition respectively), this does not strictly show that the appearances, the (empirical) objects in space and time, must be governed in their construction by these same judgments. Accordingly, it has not yet been shown conclusively that mathematics has *objective* validity.

However, since space and time are the sensible forms in which representations are intuited by us, and an appearance requires the synthesis of a given manifold of representations, it is, on the face of it, unsurprising that Kant should maintain that the very same rules that apply to the mathematician's construction of a geometrical figure in pure intuition (as in the imaginative drawing of a cube) must equally apply to our consciousness – and hence to the very existence – of any possible *appearance* (as in the perception of a house). Both mathematical figures and appearances in space or time are what he calls 'extensive magnitudes': that is, their existence is determined through a successive synthesis of their parts to produce a whole. And since appearances are merely *empirical* intuitions, it does seem evident that we must determine them – from the successively apprehended representations – in accordance with the same rules of synthesis that we apply to the determination of our *pure* intuitions, as in the construction by means of the imagination alone of a geometrical figure. 'As intuitions in space or time, they [appearances] must be represented through the same synthesis whereby space and time in general are determined' (A 162/B 203).

What is the significance of explaining why mathematics must have synthetic a priori validity with regard to the objects of our possible experience (appearances)? When Kant asks the question in the Introduction, 'How is pure mathematics possible?', he wants an explanation of how mathematics can be a body of synthetic a priori judgments that provides us with knowledge of the objects of our senses. Remember, he wants to understand how both mathematics and natural science can provide us with synthetic a priori knowledge of the objects of possible experience, in order to see whether metaphysics can also provide us with synthetic a priori knowledge of *its* objects.

So far as mathematics is concerned, we now have Kant's answer. Mathematics provides us with a priori knowledge of objects because, with respect to the *form* of appearances, it makes experience possible. We can have no sensible knowledge, no experience, except of objects in space and/or time. Since mathematical judgments determine the form of space and time, and hence (as has now been shown) the form of empirical objects, it follows that all our possible experience – since it has only to do with appearances – must accord with the synthetic a priori judgments of mathematics. Without the assurance of their necessary application to the objects of experience, mathematical judgments could not claim any objective validity: they would merely be playing with figments of our productive imagination. This point is often overlooked in discussion of Kant's view of mathematics. He is especially keen to stress it with regard to the synthetic a priori judgments of geometry:

> Although we know a priori in synthetic judgments a great deal regarding space in general and the figures which productive imagination describes in it, and can obtain such judgments without actually requiring any experience, yet even this knowledge would be nothing but a playing with a mere figment of the brain, were it not that space has to be regarded as a condition of the appearances which constitute the material for outer experience. These pure synthetic judgments therefore relate, though only mediately, to possible experience; and upon that alone is founded the objective validity of their synthesis. (A 157/B 196; see also A 223–4/B 271–2).

So the explanation of how mathematics can yield synthetic a priori knowledge of spatio-temporal objects is that these objects are appearances, and that, in respect of their form, mathematics determines our possible experience of the appearances. In effect, Kant had already implied as much right at the end of the Aesthetic (B 73), when he said that mathematical judgments can never extend beyond the objects of possible experience, i.e. to things in themselves. But he had not then strictly proved that the judgments of mathematics apply to the objects of possible experience (rather than solely to mathematical figures constructed in our pure intuitions of space or time). That task is formally accomplished in the Axioms of Intuition.

The Analogies of Experience

There are three Analogies: the First Analogy seeks to prove the principle of the permanence of substance, the Second Analogy the principle of succession, and the Third Analogy the principle of coexistence. These principles 'are properly the laws of nature' (*Prol*, Sect. 24; 4:302); and, if provable within the constraints of transcendental idealism, their proofs will provide very substantial backing to Kant's Copernican revolution as against the alternative realist position (since no proofs of these principles are available on the realist hypothesis). A grasp of their mode of proof is, therefore, essential for understanding Kant's attempt to explain how there can be synthetic a priori knowledge in natural science.

Before we look at their proofs, something does need to be noted from another section of the Principles: namely, from the Anticipations of Perception. In that section it is contended that both space and time are *continuous magnitudes*. This means that between any two points in space there is always a space, and between any two instants, or moments, in time there is always a time (see A 169/B 211). Accordingly, as Kant himself notes, there can be no space or time that is the smallest. (His basis for making these claims appears to be our knowledge that mathematics must apply to space and time as well as to their objects. Thus, a straight line in Euclidean geometry is made up of an infinite number of points, and yet can be constructed in space. Hence there can be no line or distance in space that is the shortest.) Although the contention that space and time are continuous magnitudes may seem unimportant, it will play a significant role in the attempt to establish the principle of the First Analogy – and, as a result, in making possible the attempted proofs of the principles of the Second and Third Analogies.

First Analogy

The three Analogies of Experience attempt to explain how we are able to experience objects as either *changing* their states or *coexisting* together. These are the two fundamental ways in which we can perceive dynamical relations among objects. Kant will argue that, in order to explain these possible experiences, the objects of our experience must themselves conform to the synthetic a priori rules (principles) given in the Analogies section. But if that is so, why is there any need for the First Analogy, given that the Second and Third deal, in turn, with conditions necessary for the perception of change of states and of the coexistence of objects?

The answer is: to explain a condition necessary for us to have the conception of *duration*, or a *length* of time, within which alone objects can be perceived as changing or coexisting. It is obvious enough that the perception of change presupposes the thought of a length of time, viz. the period during which the change occurs. But even the perception of coexisting objects requires the conception of temporal magnitude. Two things cannot be perceived as existing *simultaneously* unless we can think of a temporal period within which they both exist.

All the mind is initially presented with through sensibility is a series, a manifold, of representations, apprehended separately. Since representations are themselves mind-dependent, fleeting existences, there is nothing in this original apprehension to provide the subject with the conception of a length of time in which the manifold as a whole can be thought. Nor do we, the subjects of experiences, have any initial conception of our *own* continued existence. If we did, we could conceive of a manifold as existing *during* the period of our own apprehension of it. (We shall discuss the self's consciousness of its own existence in time after the Analogies.)

How, then, is the notion of a duration, a length of time, formed? Certainly our perception of *change* is, as Kant holds (in common with many philosophers), essential for generating that notion. But he adds to this the intriguing claim that if the perception of change is to provide us with the notion of duration, then this perception itself has to include the idea of the permanence of *what* changes. We must think that, in all cases of change, there is only a change of states of an underlying permanent substance. Without this thought of the permanence of substance, we could have no conception of duration; and, consequently, no experience of change or coexistence.

The clearest presentation of his argument for the permanence of substance is given almost at the end of the First Analogy (A 188/ B 231). There Kant assumes the opposite of his own position: that is, he assumes that there could be change in the appearances *without* permanence of substance. What would this be like? Consider one of his own examples: namely, the burning of a lump of wood. The result is ash and smoke. On the assumption that there is no need for permanence of substance in this change, we could experience the wood – understood as the parcel of substance constituting it – absolutely *ceasing to exist* followed by two new parcels of substance, constituting respectively the ash and the smoke, absolutely *coming into existence* (*ex nihilo*) in its place. Such a change is often referred to as a substance-change. On the alternative view, there is no substance-change, only a change of state of the original parcel of substance. Here we would think that the wood is, for example, made up of atoms, and that the action of burning causes these atoms to be redistributed into two parcels (ash and smoke). The substance originally constituting the wood has not absolutely ceased to exist; nor has the substance constituting the ash and smoke absolutely come into existence. There has merely been a *rearrangement* of the original amount of substance.

Kant wishes to argue that, in order to have the notion of a duration, within which we can alone experience the change from wood to ashes and smoke, we must plump for some version of the second view (*not* necessarily the atomic hypothesis). He denies that we can view the change as any kind of substance-change. This denial includes the possibility of our thinking of part, but only part, of the original parcel of substance absolutely ceasing to exist and/or part, but only part, of the subsequent parcel of substance absolutely coming to be. In no case of the experience of change can there be, on Kant's view, *any* degree of substance-change.

His argument hinges on the claim that in order to experience a substance-change, we should have to perceive what he calls an 'empty time', i.e. a period of time when nothing could be perceived as changing (why Kant thinks this will be explained shortly). Yet empty time is not a possible object of perception, given that time is merely a form by which we experience things. Certainly, if time existed independently of our possible consciousness, whether absolutely (*à la* Newton) or relationally (*à la* Leibniz), we could not rule out the existence of an empty time merely because of our inability to *perceive* it. But since time is only the form of our inner sense (which, like outer sense, is 'a property of our mind'), we cannot possibly accept a passage of time when nothing can be perceived as happening. We cannot, therefore, experience a substance-change.

But why should our experience of a substance-change *require* an empty time? If there is to be an experience of substance-change, the second parcel of substance must be perceived as absolutely coming into existence *after* the first parcel of substance has been perceived absolutely to cease to be. But at what point in the temporal continuum can the experience of this absolute coming to be take place? Since empty time is not a possible object of perception, there can be no perceived gap in the temporal continuum *between* the alleged experience of the absolute ceasing to be of the first parcel of substance and the alleged experience of the absolute coming to be of the second. But unless such a temporal gap is possible, what we are aware of cannot be experienced as a substance-change but as the *same* substance existing throughout, with only its *states* changing. To experience a change as a substance-change, and not as a mere change of states of one (continuously existing) parcel of substance, requires the possibility of perceiving a *break* in what exists. For the experience of a substance-change requires the perception of the first parcel of substance absolutely *ceasing* to exist followed by the perception of the second parcel absolutely *coming into* existence. But if empty time cannot be perceived, no such break in the perception of what exists can occur. Without the possibility of perceiving an empty time, the coming to be, far from being absolute, must be experienced as merely a new *state* of what was earlier being experienced, albeit in a different state. Neither the alleged absolute ceasing to be nor the alleged absolute coming to be can be perceived as forming part of a substance-change: both must be experienced as merely parts of a *change of states* of the same parcel of substance.

The argument is succinctly expressed in the following passage:

> If we assume that something absolutely begins to be, we must have a point of time in which it was not. But to what are we to attach this point, if not to that which already exists? For a preceding empty time is not an object of perception. But if we connect the coming to be with things that previously existed, and which persist in existence up to the moment of this coming to be, this latter must simply be a determination [a state] of what is permanent in that which precedes it. Similarly also with ceasing to be; it presupposes the empirical representation of a time in which an appearance no longer exists. (A 188/B 231)

As we noted from the Anticipations of Perception, Kant holds that both space and time are *continuous magnitudes*. Time is a continuum, so that between any two moments, there is a period of time. Consequently, there is no moment after the alleged experience of an absolute ceasing to be of the first parcel of substance which can be considered as the *first* or *next* moment following, i.e. such that there is no intervening temporal period. On the contrary, given that there is always a period of time between any two moments, whatever moment is selected for the alleged experience of the absolute coming to be of the second parcel of substance, after the alleged experience of the absolute ceasing to be of the first, there would have to be a period of empty time. But, as empty time is not a possible object of perception, there can be *no* moment at which either an absolute ceasing to be or an absolute coming to be can be experienced. Hence, whenever a change is perceived, it must be experienced as a continuous change of states of what is permanent (as with e.g. a change of position of atoms making up an empirical object). Since a substance-change is not a possible object of experience, it follows (on Kant's Copernican revolution) that the principle of the First Analogy has been proved: substance (in the field of appearances) must be permanent throughout all change.

Criticism of the First Analogy

It is a frequently heard criticism that Kant is guilty of an exaggeration in claiming that a single temporal continuum requires the *absolute* permanence of substance: the most that he can reasonably claim is that we require the *relative* permanence of any given parcel of substance.

There can be no objection – so the criticism runs – to any given parcel of substance absolutely ceasing to exist provided that, when this occurs, there has previously come into existence, *ex nihilo*, a compensating parcel of substance (which itself can later cease absolutely to exist provided that . . . etc.). In short, all that is required for the existence of a single temporal continuum is the existence of *overlapping* parcels of substance. Accordingly, no parcel of substance needs to persist *throughout* the temporal framework. (Kant allows that any given parcel of substance can *amalgamate* with another or itself *split* into smaller parcels of substance. What he denies is that any given parcel of substance can *absolutely* come into or go out of existence within a temporal continuum. It is the denial of absolute creation or annihilation that the criticism is challenging.)

Clearly, if there can be overlapping parcels of substance within the same temporal continuum then Kant's argument will have failed. The most he would have shown – as his critics urge – is that we need a certain *degree* of permanence amidst the changes in nature, if we are to form the conception of a single temporal framework. But, in fact, our previous considerations show that his argument has not failed on the grounds offered by these critics.

In order for there to be an *overlapping* existence of substances, there would first have to be an absolute coming to be of a parcel of substance within the existing temporal continuum, viz. the absolute coming to be of that parcel of substance which is to overlap with the (later) absolute ceasing to be of an original parcel of substance. But at what point in time could the new parcel of substance be experienced as absolutely coming to be? In order to experience something as occurring at some point within an existing temporal continuum, it must be thought of as coming to be *after* the previous changes of state in that continuum. However, since empty time cannot be perceived, the alleged absolute coming to be – if it is to be placed in that temporal continuum at all – would have to be experienced, not as a *genuinely* absolute one but as merely forming a further *part* of an existing changing state of one of the original parcels of substance. In other words, the alleged absolute coming to be would have to be experienced *not* as the creation *ex nihilo* of a parcel of substance, but as a *continuation* of some changing state of one of the original parcels of substance.

It is no good trying to circumvent this argument by holding that an absolute coming to be can be experienced as coming into existence *simultaneously* with some change of states in the already existing temporal continuum. If the alleged absolute coming to be can be experienced to occur at all in that temporal continuum, it must be possible to experience it as coming *after* the changes of states that have occurred prior to its coming to be. But, since empty time is not a possible object of perception, the alleged absolute coming to be must be perceived as a mere continuation of one of these changing states.

Within an existing temporal continuum, a genuine absolute coming to be cannot be experienced without the possibility of perceiving some period of time, however minute, between all earlier changes of state and its creation *ex nihilo*. Without the possibility of perceiving such a period, what we would be experiencing is the continuing alteration of an already existing parcel, and not the creation of a *further* parcel, of substance. In order to perceive a coming to be as the creation *ex nihilo* of a parcel of substance, that coming to be must obviously not be experienced as a continuation of a changing state of an already existing parcel of substance. It needs to be experienced, rather, as having an existence independently of any already existing substance (and hence, not as a mere state of that substance). But such an experience is possible only if we can perceive a temporal *gap* between all earlier changes of state and the present coming to be. Empty time, however, cannot be perceived. Hence we can never experience a coming to be as anything other than a subsequent part of some changing state of an already existing substance. Only in so far as a change or coming to be is thought as the *alteration of what is permanent* is it possible for us to conceive a duration in which the change or coming to be can be perceived. (Exactly parallel considerations go for any ceasing to be.) Consequently, the creation and annihilation of *overlapping* parcels of substance, within a single temporal continuum, cannot occur.

What the criticism has overlooked is the *idealism* in Kant's Copernican revolution. It is because he holds that time is only a form of our sensibility, and not something attaching to things in themselves, that he is able to argue as he does for the absolute (and not merely relative) permanence of substance. If he had maintained that the temporal continuum exists independently of our possible consciousness of it, his objection to the absolute coming to be or ceasing to be of substance, and thus to the possibility of overlapping parcels of substance, would be inadequate. For Kant's argument for the permanence of substance essentially hinges on the thought that since time cannot be perceived without the experience of change, it must follow that there can be no such thing as empty time. If the temporal continuum existed whether or not we could be conscious of it, Kant would have been unable to move from the mere fact that we cannot *perceive* a passage of time without the experience of change to the conclusion that there can be no such thing as empty time. But, given his idealism, the very *existence* of a single temporal framework depends on our capacity to perceive all change as happening to what is permanent. It is in the light of Kant's idealism about time, together with his claim that time is a continuous magnitude, that his proof of the permanence of substance must be seen.

(The Leibnizian, relational, view of time, would, I take it, also maintain that empty time is not a possible object of perception. For time, on that view, is considered to be nothing more than change or alteration among things in themselves. But the relationalist could not argue from a subject's mere incapacity to perceive empty time to its nonexistence: that move requires an idealist framework. Kant, of course, has rejected the relational as well as the absolute view of time in the Aesthetic.)

The Second and Third Analogies

The Second Analogy attempts to prove that the category of *cause* must be applied to the manifold in order to experience a *succession* or *change of states* in an object. The Third Analogy attempts to prove that the category of *community* must be applied to the manifold in order to experience the *coexistence* of objects. In developing his proofs, Kant is accepting that we do perceive that particular changes of state and particular coexistences among objects take place: the question at issue is to explain how these experiences can occur.

Let us concentrate, first, on the argument of the Second Analogy. Its principle is: 'All alterations [changes of state] take place in conformity with the law of the connection of cause and effect' (B 232). This principle – Kant sometimes refers to it as the Principle of Sufficient Reason – gives the rule for applying the category of *cause* to temporal intuition.

In opening up his argument, the initial point that Kant wishes to make is that the original apprehension of a manifold, i.e. as it is given through sensibility, is always successive, whether what is thereby experienced is an objective succession (e.g. a ship going downstream) or an objective coexistence (e.g. the coexisting parts of a house). Hence the original apprehension of the manifold cannot alone enable me to experience any succession in the object; that is, it cannot enable me to be perceptually conscious of the manifold *as* an objective succession. There is, however, an important difference between my experience of an objective succession and of an objective coexistence. When I experience an objective succession, the order of my apprehension must be thought of as *bound down* in its order by the actual order of succession in the apprehended manifold. For example, in the case of the ship going downstream, since the particular objective succession is a move *from* the ship upstream *to* the ship downstream, I need to recognize that my apprehension of the ship downstream *had* to succeed my apprehension of the ship upstream if, on that occasion, I am to perceive the successively apprehended representations as this particular objective succession. Compare the case of my experiencing coexisting parts of a house by first apprehending the roof and then apprehending the basement. Although my apprehension of the basement did *in fact* succeed my apprehension of the roof, there is clearly no requirement for me to recognize that the apprehensions *had* to occur in that order if, on that occasion, I am to perceive the successively apprehended representations as this particular objective coexistence. On the contrary, if the apprehensions had occurred in the *reverse* order, I should still have been experiencing, on that occasion, the same objective coexistence. In the case of coexisting objects, I am certainly not required to recognize that the order of my disparate apprehensions had to occur in the order in which they in fact occurred, if I am to perceive the successively apprehended representations of the manifold as a particular objective coexistence.

Returning to the experience of objective succession (the succession of states in an object), it is, Kant argues, the recognition that the order of my apprehension is bound down by the actual order in the given manifold that enables me to perceive the manifold of successive representations as an objective succession. But if the original apprehension does not enable me to perceive the manifold as a succession of states in an object, how does this experience arise? Since it is through sensibility that the manifold is *given* (and this by itself, as we have just seen, does not alone permit the experience to occur), and it is through the understanding that it is *thought*, it must be through the understanding that the experience becomes possible. For sensibility and understanding, taken jointly, are the only faculties through which our knowledge can arise (see A 15/B 29). The experience of objective succession becomes possible by the understanding introducing a suitable *rule* governing the apprehended manifold itself. This rule is the Principle of Sufficient Reason, according to which I think that there is something in the surrounding circumstances such that whenever, under these circumstances, the first state occurs (ship upstream), the second state (ship downstream) must succeed. If the content of the manifold is *itself* thought of as subject to this rule, it follows that I can recognize that my *apprehension* of this manifold must be suitably bound down in its order, i.e. that I must, under the circumstances, apprehend the ship downstream after apprehending the ship upstream. It is through the understanding submitting the given manifold to the Principle of Sufficient Reason that I am alone enabled to perceive the successively apprehended representations as an objective succession. (This principle is the only one, in the Table of Principles, that deals with succession.)

Let us now look at the other form of experience in time: namely, the perception of a manifold of representations as a particular *coexistence*. Say that, by first apprehending the roof of a house and then apprehending the basement of a house, I experience them as coexisting. To be conscious of these representations as coexisting is, of course, to be conscious of them as standing in a particular temporal relationship. What conditions allow me to think of the successively apprehended representations as standing in the relationship of coexistence (or simultaneity)? Kant's reply is that it is only in so far as I recognize that, on the occasion of apprehension, I could have apprehended the successive representations in the *reverse* order that the experience of their coexistence can arise. Although *in fact* the apprehension of a roof was succeeded by the apprehension of a basement, I need to recognize that these apprehensions were, on that occasion, reversible. In other words, I need to recognize that it *must* have been possible for me, on that occasion, to have apprehended the representations in the reverse order. The experience of an objective coexistence is made possible through the recognition of the *reversibility* of apprehension. (Compare, the experience of an objective succession from A to B: in that case, I come to the consciousness of that objective succession through the recognition that, on the occasion in question, the apprehension of B *must* have succeeded the apprehension of A and, hence, that it is *not* possible for the apprehensions to be reversed.)

Now the recognition of the reversibility of apprehension (in the case of coexistence) is possible only if I can think of the given representations themselves as subject to a suitable rule. For there is nothing in the original apprehension of the manifold, i.e. through sensibility, to show that the apprehension of representations is reversible. On the contrary, one of the representations is merely, as a matter of fact, apprehended after the other. It is only in so far as the understanding can supply a suitable rule to the content of the apprehended manifold that I can recognize that the apprehensions are reversible (and, hence, that I am experiencing a coexistence). Kant claims that this rule of the understanding is the *Law of Reciprocity or Community* (this gives the rule for applying the category of *community* to temporal intuition). By employing this rule, I am enabled, he holds, to think that there is a *mutual* causal influence between the content of the successive representations, and thereby to recognize the reversibility of the successive apprehensions.[2] So, in our particular example, it is my capacity to

[2] I shall not discuss whether, as Kant claims, it *is* the rule of reciprocity that makes the recognition of reversibility possible. The crucial points to appreciate are the parallel strategy of the Third to the Second Analogy, and the plausibility of Kant's contention that, in order to experience coexistence, I need *first* to recognize that my apprehension of the given manifold is reversible (and that this, in turn, requires the application of a suitable rule to the manifold). My experience of coexistence is made possible by means of the recognition of the reversibility of my apprehension, just as my experience of change of states is made possible by means of the recognition of the irreversibility of my apprehension.

think that there is something in the state of the roof of a house that is making possible something in the state of the basement of a house, *and vice versa*, that allows me to recognize that, on the occasion of my apprehension of the basement of a house succeeding my apprehension of the roof of a house, the order of those apprehensions could have been reversed. My experience of coexistence is only possible because my understanding brings the contents of the manifold of representations under a given rule (the Law of Reciprocity), thereby allowing me to recognize that the apprehensions are reversible.

In the course of the Second Analogy, Kant makes some illuminating comments about our concept of an *object* of the senses. These comments help to explain his strategy in the Transcendental Analytic as a whole. They are to be found around A 190–1/B 235–6.

He remarks that we think of an object of the senses as something that serves as a rule for our possible apprehension of a manifold of representations. More especially, it is the recognition of a specific rule governing our apprehension of a manifold that provides us with the conception of a particular type of object or objective occurrence. Thus, if I recognize that I must apprehend the representations of a given manifold in the way that I actually do apprehend them, then the content of my experience is conceived as a *change of state* in an object. On the other hand, if I recognize that it must have been possible to have apprehended the representations of that manifold in the reverse order, then the content of my experience is conceived as a *coexistence* of objects. If no rule can be thought of as governing the apprehension of a given manifold, then I cannot have any objective consciousness *at all* by means of that manifold.

The explanation of how we come to attribute objectivity to the representations of a manifold is summed up in the following quote: 'appearance, in contradistinction to the representations of apprehension, can be represented as an object distinct from them only if it [the apprehension] stands under a rule which distinguishes it from every other apprehension and necessitates some one particular mode of connection of the manifold. The object is *that* in the appearance which contains the condition of this necessary rule of apprehension' (A 191/B 236; italics original). We form our conception of an object of the senses, and indeed of a particular type of object of the senses (an objective succession or a coexistence among objects), through the thought of there being something in the manifold that *determines* apprehension in a given way (as irreversible or reversible). It is through the recognition that the apprehension of a manifold is thus determined or rule-governed that allows us to form the conception of something in the intuition that exists *distinct* from its mere apprehension. Moreover, we have seen that, in developing his argument in the Second and Third Analogies, Kant goes on to maintain that, for the recognition of my apprehension as determined or rule-governed, the manifold *itself* needs to be brought to synthetic unity in accordance with the Law of Causality (for the experience of succession) or the Law of Reciprocity (for the experience of coexistence). Only in so far as the apprehension of a manifold can be thought of as determined or bound down in its order (by the application of a suitable law to the manifold itself) can the conception of any *object* of the senses arise.

The way in which the application of categories makes possible temporal experience serves to elucidate a point in my exposition of the Transcendental Deduction. I said, under the fourth point of that exposition, that categories are required in order to be conscious of a relation holding between the representations that are given in a sensible form of intuition. While it may be conceded that such a relation must be perceived if the manifold is to be thought together in one act of consciousness, it may be objected that no ground has been offered for why the manifold should be subject to a *rule* or *rules* in order for any relation to be perceived. Why must a manifold be brought to synthetic unity – be understood as *falling under a rule* – if a relation is to be perceived among the representations in a given form of sensible intuition? With respect to temporal intuition, we can now see Kant's answer. It is only because the manifold is subject to the Law of Causality (for change of states) or the Law of Reciprocity (for coexistence) that it is possible to be conscious of the manifold as existing together in *time*, viz. through the consciousness that B comes *after* A or that B is *coexisting with* A. The application of a rule to a manifold, given in a temporal form of intuition, is alone what makes possible the perception of a relation in time between the representations of that manifold.

So, putting the point generally, without the application of a rule to a manifold of sensible intuition, it would be impossible to recognize that the order of apprehension of that manifold is *determinate*. It is the recognition of a determinate order governing apprehension that gives rise to the conception of a relation in the manifold of appearance. (Thus, it is the recognition that, under the circumstances, B *must* be apprehended after A that gives rise to the conception of a *succession* in the appearances; and it is the recognition that, under the circumstances, it must be possible to apprehend A and B in *reverse* order that gives rise to the conception of a *coexistence* in the appearances.) After all, there is nothing in the original apprehension of the manifold, i.e. through sensibility, that can of itself give rise to the recognition of any determinate order of apprehension (and thus to the consciousness of any relation holding between the representations in the given form of sensible intuition). Hence, it can only be by means of the understanding applying a rule or rules to the apprehended manifold that the conception of a relation between the representations can arise. Accordingly, the application of rules (derived from the categories) is necessary for a manifold of sensible intuition to be thought of, and hence to exist, as a possible object of the senses.

Criticism of the Second and Third Analogies

There is a notorious criticism of the Second Analogy – in fact, a parallel criticism goes for the Third Analogy – which has been made by two of the foremost commentators on Kant in the twentieth century: Arthur Lovejoy and P. F. Strawson. The easiest way to explain the criticism is by giving an example of how, as it is alleged, Kant argues invalidly.

Say that a spectator, on a certain occasion, perceives wax to melt. Kant correctly notes that, on this occasion, the spectator's apprehension is determined or necessitated in its order: since the perceived change is a change *from* solid *to* molten wax, the apprehension of wax in the molten state *must*, on that occasion, come after the apprehension of wax in the solid state. From this correct observation, it is alleged that he invalidly concludes that the change *itself* must be causally determined or necessitated (so that, on any similar occasion when wax is in the solid state, it must be perceived to change into the molten state).

The conclusion, it is said, is a flagrant *non sequitur*. It simply does not follow that because my apprehension is determined in its order, on any single occasion of the perception of a given change, that that change *itself* must be causally determined or necessitated. From the fact that wax melts, on one occasion (say, on an occasion when it is heated to 70°C), thereby determining the order of my apprehension, it simply does not follow that the change in the wax, from solid to molten state, must itself be subject to a rule governing its behaviour. More generally, it simply does not follow that any change we perceive, or could perceive, must be governed by the rule of cause and effect.

To suppose that it does is to confuse the correct claim that, on any occasion of our perception of change, the order of apprehension is determined or necessitated (by the order of the change of states), with the incorrect (or, at least, totally unsubstantiated) claim that the change of states itself must be causally determined or necessitated. Nothing that Kant has said in the Second Analogy or elsewhere has proved – as Kant undoubtedly thinks that he has proved – that Hume's scepticism about causation is untenable. For nothing in his argument shows the impossibility of a change occurring, and being perceived to occur, on one occasion, while yet that change should fail to occur, and be perceived to fail to occur, on any other similar occasion. For instance, nothing has been said to rule out the possibility of wax melting, and being perceived to melt, on one occasion (say, when heated to 70°C), while yet, on any exactly *similar* occasion, it should fail to melt and be perceived to fail to melt. The fallacy of which Kant's argument here stands accused was memorably summed up by Lovejoy as 'one of the most spectacular examples of the *non-sequitur* which are to be found in the history of philosophy'.

I do not think that this well-known criticism of the Second Analogy could be made by anyone who has grasped the centrality to Kant of his Copernican revolution, his transcendental idealism. For this criticism, in effect, assumes that the objects of our senses, the objects in space and time, are things in themselves, and not appearances. If that were the case, then Kant would *himself* agree that his argument could not succeed. (Precisely the same general comment goes for the arguments of the First and Third Analogies.) As he repeatedly stresses – including in the Second Analogy – how things may be in themselves, 'apart from the representations through which they affect us, is entirely outside our sphere of knowledge' (A 190/B 235; see also A 128–9).

Certainly, if the objects of the senses exist independently of their capacity to be known by us, we can have no right to conclude from the fact that, on a given occasion, the order of *apprehension* of a perceived succession is determined in its order (by the order in the succession) that the succession *itself* must be subject to a rule – and, in particular, to the Principle of Sufficient Reason. Since we are here supposedly concerned with objects whose existence does *not* depend on the possibility of our knowing them (things in themselves), there can be no reason, depending on the conditions of *our* knowledge, why an object that (we are assuming) has been perceived, on one occasion, to change its states – thereby determining our apprehension of the change on that occasion – should have to behave in the same way on *any* other similar occasion. There can, accordingly, be no ground for concluding, from the experience of change (however large), that *all* changes of state *must* be subject to the Principle of Sufficient Reason. Indeed, I take it that it was considerations of just this type that motivated Kant to re-examine the grounds for the traditional conception of the relationship between the knowing mind and the objects of knowledge – and which, therefore, partly led him to investigate the possibility of inaugurating his Copernican revolution, his transcendental idealism.

So, on the basis of his transcendental idealism, how would Kant have answered the *non sequitur* objection?

Granting that I can perceive a series of disparately apprehended representations as an objective change (from A to B) only in so far as I can recognize the order of my apprehension (of A succeeded by B) as determined or bound down to that order, the question arises as to how I can come to conceive 'this necessary rule of apprehension'. Since the original apprehension of the serial representations, i.e. through sensibility, cannot provide any grounds for holding that I *had* to be conscious of them in the order in which they were actually apprehended, the recognition that apprehension is bound down to its actual order must arise through the understanding submitting the manifold to a suitable rule: a rule, that is, which *does* thus determine the order of my apprehension. There is only one such rule in the Table of Principles, viz. the Law of Causality. If, through the understanding, the manifold can be brought to synthetic unity by means of this rule, it will follow that the manifold is subject to the law that there is something in the surrounding conditions, such that whenever A occurs (under those circumstances), B must follow. Once the apprehended succession is itself thought of as falling under this law, I can recognize that my apprehension of the succeeding representations is, on this occasion, *bound down* to that order. In short, I can only perceive an apprehended manifold of representations as an objective change, on any given occasion, through the understanding submitting that manifold to the Law of Causality; for it is the thought that the manifold is so governed that alone enables me to recognize my apprehension, on that given occasion, as suitably bound down in its order. This is why Kant holds that the very possibility of *experiencing* a manifold of representations as an objective change depends upon the understanding submitting that apprehended manifold to the Law of Causality. Now, given his transcendental idealism, Kant further holds that the very *existence* of any objective change depends upon the possibility of experiencing that objective change. All change in the objects of the senses, in nature, must therefore be subject to the Law of Causality.

I conclude that there are no grounds for holding that Kant's argument in the Second Analogy – and, by parity of reasoning, in the Third Analogy – commits the *non sequitur* of which he has so frequently been accused. To suppose that it does is to fail to see the argument within the context of transcendental idealism.

The criticisms that we have considered against the three Analogies all fail because they assume that the objects of the senses are things in themselves, rather than appearances. These criticisms would undoubtedly be devastating on that assumption. But, as I have tried to show, they fail when applied to appearances. This is in line with Kant's own case for his Copernican revolution. Far from these criticisms endangering that revolution, they actually serve to support it. They support it, because no valid proofs have been provided for any of the principles of the three Analogies on the assumption that the objects of our sensible knowledge are things in themselves. Indeed, if spatio-temporal objects were things in themselves, it is hard to see how we could ever *hope* to prove the truth of such synthetic a priori principles. As Kant pointedly observes:

> If the objects with which our knowledge has to deal were things in themselves, we could have no *a priori* concepts of them. For from what source would we obtain the concepts? If we derived them from the object (leaving aside the question how the object could become known to us), our concepts would be merely empirical, not a priori. And if we derived them from the self, that which is merely in us could not determine the character of an object distinct from our representations, that is, could not be a ground why a thing should exist characterized by that which we have in our thought, and why such a representation should not, rather, be altogether empty. (A 128–9)

On the other hand, given transcendental idealism – according to which space and time are forms of our sensible intuition (and, hence, spatio-temporal objects merely appearances) – the Analogies section has provided valid proofs for these principles. Since (as Kant holds) we are certain of the truth of these principles, his Copernican hypothesis is thereby strongly supported against the rival theory, according to which the objects of our senses are things in themselves.

The Self's Existence in Time and its Relation to our Knowledge of Objects in Space

In both editions of the *First Critique*, Kant argues against René Descartes's so-called problematic or empirical idealism, although his arguments in the two editions are somewhat different. I shall concentrate on the B edition version, known as the Refutation of Idealism. But before doing so, some general comments about his attitude to Descartes's problematic idealism are in order. (The views here ascribed to Descartes may not be his. They are intended to be the views that *Kant* ascribes to Descartes in both editions.)

According to Descartes, immediate experience does not prove the existence of objects in space outside us: only our *own* existence, understood as the existence of the self, and its states, in time (in inner sense), can be proved by recourse to immediate experience. Whereas the existence of our own self in time is proved on the immediate testimony of our own self-consciousness (and for just as long as we are thinking), the existence of objects in space outside us is doubtful on the evidence of our immediate experience. It is doubtful because, on the Cartesian view, in order to prove the existence of objects in space, we need to resort to an *inference* from what alone constitutes our immediate experience: namely inner, temporal experience (ourselves and our own states as existing in time). In other words, on Kant's reading of Descartes, the latter holds that objects in space, if they exist at all, exist as *things in themselves*, i.e. exist entirely independently of our capacity or incapacity to know of them by means of the senses. This account of the relationship between the mind and spatial objects, Kant calls 'transcendental realism'. It opposes Kant's own account, transcendental idealism, according to which the mind has *immediate* sense experience of spatial objects. The experience is immediate because, for the transcendental idealist, objects in space are mere appearances, and not things in themselves: they are, therefore, constituted by our own representations (synthesized, according to the categories, in our form of outer sensible intuition). For the transcendental realist, on the other hand, all experience of spatial objects, if it is to exist, must be *mediate* experiential knowledge. What we are immediately conscious of exists in inner sense alone, and hence can never by itself amount to knowledge of objects in space. Spatial objects, being for the transcendental realist things in themselves, must be wholly distinguished from the contents of sensibility, and indeed must be considered to exist entirely independently of the knowing mind.

Consequently, without a proof of the existence of a non-deceiving God, the transcendental realist's only method of gaining knowledge of objects in space would seem to be an inferential argument from what exists in us (representations in inner sense) to what exists entirely independently of us (things in themselves in space). The ground for making this inference would have to rest on the claim that the existence of objects in space outside us, hypothesized as the cause of our representations, best explains the existence and behaviour of these representations. But, as Kant points out, this inference is a very hazardous one, since, for all we can tell, our representations may have been caused by something entirely different from spatial objects, thus conceived: for instance, by some unknown cause within us. (Kant never questions the assumption that the representations *do* have a cause or causes.) Accordingly, if we can have only mediate experience, inferential experience, of objects in space outside us, the existence of such objects is uncertain. In effect, then, Kant agrees with Descartes to this extent: *if* spatial objects are conceived as things in themselves, then – without proving the existence of a non-deceiving Deity – their existence is doubtful. 'Problematic or empirical idealism' is the name he gives to the Cartesian claim that the existence of objects in space outside us is doubtful.

Kant argues against problematic idealism in the Refutation of [Problematic] Idealism (B 275–9; see also B xxxix–xli, B 291–4, and B 156). This B edition argument replaces the one he gave in the Fourth Paralogism of the A edition (A 366–80). In the earlier version of his anti-Cartesian argument, he had maintained that our knowledge of external objects (in space), like our knowledge of our own existence (in time), is immediate. Certainly, this earlier argument opposes problematic idealism. It opposes it, because Descartes held that the self is *more* easily known than objects in space (since the latter, he claimed, cannot be known through immediate experience alone, but require an inference from that experience). However, in the B edition, Kant holds, like Descartes, that there *is* an order of priority in our knowledge. As he now sees it, our experience of objects in space is immediate, while the experience of ourselves in time is mediate. The result is that in the B edition he can be seen as maintaining, *contra* Descartes, that the existence of objects in space is more easily known than the existence of the self in time.

Some commentators have suggested that, in the Refutation of [Problematic] Idealism, Kant abandons his transcendental idealism (and so, in effect, his Copernican revolution). Nothing seems to me to be further from the truth: the argument of the Refutation against problematic idealism requires that objects in space outside us are appearances, and not things in themselves. For only in so far as they are appearances can we have any *immediate* perception of them. The alternative interpretation, according to which Kant abandons his earlier idealist position, would also appear to be explicitly contradicted by comments at B 156, a passage which, like the Refutation itself, was added in the B edition.

Moreover, if Kant were now to maintain that we can have perceptual knowledge of things in themselves, this would, by his own acknowledgement, put paid to the central claims of his moral philosophy: an area of his thought as important to him as his theory of knowledge, and one which was especially exercising him by the time of the B edition of the *First Critique*. It is only if spatio-temporal objects are mere appearances – and hence have no existence independent of our actual or possible consciousness – that we can think of ourselves possessing the freedom required for moral responsibility.

Let us examine Kant's argument, in the B edition, for his claim that we can prove the existence of objects in space outside us.

His central idea is that each of us can have consciousness of ourselves as a subject existing in time (to which successive and simultaneous acts of awareness occur) only in so far as we have immediate and not inferential consciousness of objects existing in space. Since he agrees with Descartes that we *do* each have the consciousness of ourselves – the *I think* – as existing through time,[3] it follows that he disagrees with him that we can have this consciousness without having the immediate experience of objects in space.

Why does Kant suppose that, in order to have the consciousness of ourselves as possessing a temporal existence, we need immediate consciousness of spatial objects? A crucial part of his answer refers back to the claim in the First Analogy that our consciousness of *duration* requires the thought of the permanent throughout the experience of change. Yet, if we examine the contents of our own inner sense, we find that we can introspect nothing that we can think of as permanent: all we encounter is a series of momentary acts of awareness – thoughts, sensations and so on. (Kant's point here is clearly reminiscent of Hume's in his account of our belief in the self.) Even the expression

---

[3] In fact, this agreement is more apparent than real, since, for Descartes, the self that is allegedly known to continue to exist is a *thing in itself*, and not the phenomenal self to which Kant refers. The Cartesian view of the self will be discussed further when we come to the Paralogisms.

of the subject's own existence, given by means of the use of the 'I',
refers to no experience of duration given in inner sense. So far as the
use of 'I' is confined to the contents of inner sense alone, it is merely
a grammatical subject term affixed *in turn* to each of a series of
momentary states, as in 'I am aware of A', 'I am aware of B', and so on.
Consequently, if – as Descartes affirms – all we can be immediately
conscious of in perception is a series of disparately apprehended *representations* given in inner sense (from which we attempt to infer, from
effects to causes, the existence of spatial objects, conceived as things
in themselves), it would be impossible for each of us to have the consciousness of ourselves as persisting in time. It would be impossible
precisely because there would then be nothing in sensible intuition
upon which to base the thought of the permanent: there would only
be a series of fleeting existences (representations), each apprehended
in a separate act of self-consciousness. Yet, without the possibility of
basing the thought of the permanent on what exists in sensible intuition, there could be no consciousness of duration or of a length of
time. For sensible intuition is necessary for us to have *any* determinate
thought at all; and, more especially, there needs to be something in
sensible intuition on the basis of which the bare category of substance
can be used to think of the permanent.

But, *ex hypothesi*, we do have the consciousness of ourselves as
existing in time. Our experience of spatial objects must, accordingly,
be *immediate*. For, as Kant argues, it is only if we are able immediately
to experience objects existing in space that we can have any *intuition*
upon which to base the thought of the permanent. Immediate perceptual consciousness, therefore, cannot be held to provide us, as
Descartes maintained, with the mere awareness of *representations* or
images of spatial objects (the latter thought of as existing in themselves, and so ontologically distinct from what is given to us in inner
sense). If that were the case, we could at best have only mediate, or
inferential, consciousness of spatial objects, and this could not provide
us with any basis for thinking the permanent. It could not, because all
that we could then be immediately aware of would be fleeting existences (representations). Only the immediate experience of objects in
space outside us – that is, of appearances in *outer intuition* – can
provide us with the thought of the permanent, and hence with the
consciousness of duration.

More particularly, Kant claims, I can only come to the consciousness of my own temporal existence by means of an immediate perception of change in position of what is identified as permanent (matter)

in space. It is this experience of spatial change, of change in the position of spatial objects, that gives me the consciousness of *duration*, and thereby of my *own* temporal existence. For example, through the immediate perception of a change in the position of the sun relative to objects on earth, I come to the consciousness of a *length* of time in which this spatial change has occurred, and, in consequence, to the consciousness of myself as existing *during* or *throughout* that period of perceived change. By recognizing that I have experienced objects enduring in space (on the basis of the immediate perception of their change of position), I come to the consciousness of my own continued existence throughout the period of this experience.

We must, then, acknowledge the existence of objects in space to which our perceptions can give us immediate, not inferential, knowledge. Without the possibility of their immediate perception, we could have no intuition of anything as permanent. Since the awareness of duration requires such an intuition, it follows that our consciousness of ourselves as existing through time proves that, in perception, we are immediately conscious, not of *mere* representations (in inner sense), but of objects in space outside us (in outer sense).

Two further remarks. First, in contrasting immediate with inferential knowledge of objects in space outside us, Kant is not going back on his claim that a manifold of representations will need to be synthesized, in accordance with the categories, if the consciousness of objects is to be possible. This act of synthetic unity is no inference *from* what is given in apprehension *to* what can only be mediately experienced in space. The action of the understanding in synthesizing data is an action on apprehended representations to produce a unity of consciousness of those very representations (thereby giving rise to an immediate perceptual consciousness of objects in space). The Cartesian inference from what is in us, in time, to what is outside us, in space, is a move from attributes of the perceiving mind (representations) to what is ontologically distinct from those representations (viz., things in themselves). Second, Kant is not committed by his Refutation of Idealism argument to the implausible view that I can only have a temporal consciousness of myself to the extent that I am actually having, over any given period, an experience of objects in space. *Once* a subject has generated the conception of its own existence over time – by means of an immediate spatial experience of an object's change of position – it is of course possible for that subject to know that it has suffered from e.g. hallucination during a period of its own existence. On the Kantian account, however, this knowledge is possible only because of the subject's realization that, over the period in question, the subject *could* have had a spatial experience that not only itself conformed to the categories but was capable of being connected up with the earlier and later law-abiding spatial experiences.

Nature, Scepticism and the Possibility of Experience

This is an appropriate place to dispel a confusion that readers of the Principles of Pure Understanding and, indeed, of the whole Transcendental Analytic can fall into. Kant has argued that the objects in nature must obey the synthetic a priori principles derived from the categories of the understanding. This central thesis of the *Critique of Pure Reason* is expressed in a number of arresting phrases. In the *Prolegomena*, it is said that '*the understanding does not draw its laws (a priori) from nature, but prescribes them to nature*' (Sect. 36, 4:320; italics original). Two examples, giving expression to the same theme in the *First Critique*, are: 'That nature should direct itself according to our subjective ground of apperception, and should indeed depend upon it in respect of its conformity to law, sounds very strange and absurd' (A 114); and 'Thus the order and regularity in the appearances, which we entitle *nature*, we ourselves introduce' (A 125; italics original).

These, and similar passages, have sometimes encouraged the following interpretation of Kant's conception of the role of the understanding with respect to the possibility of experience: 'What we are initially presented with, i.e. through sensibility, is a *chaotic* series or manifold of representations; and it is the role of our understanding, by employment of its categories, to *sort out* the members of this unseemly medley of representations into rule-abiding bundles. Our consciousness of objects in space and time (or whatever be the form(s) of sensible intuition) takes place after the originally apprehended, and chaotic, manifold has been *reprocessed*, in accordance with the categories.'

This is a confused interpretation. It is no part of Kant's contention that the manifold of representations, from which we are enabled to have the consciousness of appearances, is originally apprehended in a chaotic way. The mind and, in particular, the understanding do not, as it were, look along the manifold of the subject's representations and, then, *reshuffle the pack* in accordance with rules employing the categories. Sometimes the following analogy has been offered by advocates of this mistaken interpretation: it is as though the mind is first presented with a random collection of letters of an alphabet, and then rearranges them into strings of coherent words and sentences in accordance with a rule-book for this purpose.

The picture of the mind's operations on this interpretation, requiring as it does a possibly miraculous feat of 'transcendental psychology', is not what Kant is driving at when he says that the understanding 'prescribes' its laws to nature, and that we ourselves 'introduce' the order and regularity into nature. Admittedly, once the manifold has been apprehended through sensibility, it is we ourselves, by employing the understanding, who can be said to make possible the fundamental laws of nature. But this is not because the understanding rearranges a chaotically apprehended manifold. Indeed, if the given manifold *were* chaotic, there could be no experience of nature. Rather, to say that the understanding makes the experience of nature possible – and hence, in respect of its fundamental laws, makes nature itself possible – is to say that unless the understanding has submitted the manifold of representations to its fundamental a priori principles (which itself requires that the apprehended manifold has an initial order that permits subsumption under these principles), we could not think of the apprehended manifold as disclosing any objects of the senses. Hence, if we *are* experiencing objects by means of that manifold, we can say that this has been made possible by the understanding submitting the apprehended manifold to its own rules. But to say this should not be taken to imply that the apprehended manifold is initially given to us in a chaotic fashion which, by means of the categories (schematized in accordance with our forms of intuition), the understanding rearranges into a fully ordered set of relationships. To repeat: if the apprehended manifold were chaotically given, the understanding would be unable to think of any categories applying to the manifold. Experience would, therefore, be impossible.

So the regularity that Hume (of *The First Enquiry*) holds, or seems to hold, to be only a contingent feature of nature, and which Kant maintains is necessary, is not made possible, on the latter's view, by some mysterious acts of transcendental psychology – whereby what is originally apprehended as a random manifold is rearranged by the understanding in accordance with its own synthetic a priori principles. We must presuppose an orderliness in the originally apprehended manifold of representations; for, without it, no principles of the understanding could be applied to that manifold. But the order and regularity that Kant is claiming we are responsible for refers to the fundamental laws of *nature*, not to the order that needs to exist in the originally apprehended manifold of representations. Nature must, in all its relations, obey laws, because our possible experience of nature requires that the understanding is first able to think of the given manifold of representations as conforming to necessary and universal laws. The manifold, as it is originally apprehended through sensibility, is orderly (if it is) because of the action of the transcendental object upon the faculty of sensibility; and unless this apprehended manifold is orderly, no experience can occur on the basis of its apprehension (since the understanding would not be able to apply the categories to it). None the less, the experience of *nature* cannot be given to us merely through the original apprehension of an orderly manifold. The representations of the manifold must first be thought of as *necessarily* connected (unified), i.e. by means of rules deriving from the categories. This is an affair of the understanding. The consciousness of necessity cannot be given through sensibility, however orderly the apprehended manifold may be: it requires the application of the principles of the understanding.

But the principles which the understanding thereby introduces are concerned only with the *form* of experience, not with its *content* (its *matter*). Consider the Principle of Sufficient Reason, the Law of Causality. When Kant claims that all succession of states among appearances must be subject to this rule, he is not claiming that we can tell, independent of experience (a priori), what *particular* changes of state will occur or what the *particular* cause of any such change will be. Both of these matters must be discovered empirically (a posteriori). What he is maintaining is that if, on one occasion, a certain change of states occurs among appearances – e.g. the melting of wax – then we can know a priori that there is something in the circumstances of the solid wax, on that occasion, such that were those same circumstances to occur, on any other occasion, a similarly solid piece of wax *must* melt. He is not asserting that we can tell a priori that wax will ever melt or that, if it does, we can tell a priori what the cause is. Put generally, all we are entitled to claim a priori is that any change of state or coexistence that can be experienced must be subject to the Law of Causality (for change of states) or the Law of Reciprocity (for coexistence). But we cannot know a priori either *what* changes or coexistences will occur in nature or *what* their causes are (see A 766/B 794).

So far as the form of experience is concerned, it is not only impossible for us to experience a spatio-temporal world in which changes of state or the coexistence of objects *have* been lawless, it is also impossible for us to experience a world which either suddenly or gradually *becomes* lawless. Were the apprehended manifold of representations impossible to bring under any of the pure laws of nature, that manifold could not be recognized as disclosing anything objective. *Objects*, therefore, could not have been experienced to behave lawlessly; nor could they be experienced to do so in the future (nor could there be any change in the laws governing their behaviour, because this would mean that the 'rules' governing them were *not* strictly necessary and universal). Although the specific *content* of the empirical laws holding of spatio-temporal objects must be discovered by experience, the *form* of these laws must be those given in the principles of pure understanding. These principles are the most basic rules by means of which we are enabled to think of any apprehended manifold, given in our forms of sensible intuition, as *determining* apprehension – and hence as disclosing anything objective.[4]

---

[4] I suggest that we can now see how to defend Kant against the perennial criticism that he misreads Berkeley in accusing him, 'the good Berkeley', of 'degrading bodies to mere illusion' (B 71). Berkeley, it is countered, has a perfectly respectable distinction between objects that really do exist in space and mere illusory perceptions. His distinction hinges on differentiating between those series of representations that are found, on apprehension, to exhibit order and regularity (veridical perceptions of bodies) and those that are not (illusory perceptions). But Kant is no doubt aware that Berkeley *supposes* that he can distinguish veridical from illusory perceptions by means of observing the degree of regularity in the apprehended series of representations; his point is that no genuine distinction can be made on these grounds alone. As he has argued in the Transcendental Analytic, the possibility of even thinking of spatio-temporal objects requires that the serial representations are not merely found to have a certain orderliness in their apprehension, but are subject to certain a priori *rules* of our understanding. Without the application of these rules – which no mere *apprehension* of regularities could vouchsafe – it would be impossible to locate any series of representations in space or time. Space and time are a priori intuitions which are necessarily thought of as unified – all outer objects must be placed in one space and one temporal continuum – and this would be impossible without the application of rules stemming, not from the serial representations, but from the understanding. Accordingly, if you reject (as Berkeley rightly rejects) the existence of space and time as absolute existences, while failing to appreciate (as Berkeley fails to appreciate) that space and time are each singular intuitions whose very existence requires the application of a priori rules of the understanding to the apprehended manifold, then you will have no genuine method of distinguishing veridical from illusory perception. Everything which you claim is a veridical perception – on the sole ground of observed order and regularity in the apprehended series of representations – will have the same status as those apprehended series of representations that are found to be disorderly: they will be degraded to mere illusions.

Has Kant answered Hume?

We are now in a position to consider one of the most disputed questions in the history of philosophy: Has Kant answered Hume's scepticism about causation?

A major difficulty in reaching a balanced verdict on the question is this. When Kant casts a critical eye over Hume's causal scepticism, he bases his criticism on Hume's account as this is given in the *Enquiry concerning Human Understanding*. In that work, Hume assumes that the objects of the senses, the objects in space and time, are things in themselves, which we come to know via their 'appearances' or 'images' (both terms are used by Hume himself in the *Enquiry*) which they cause in us. And, as I have tried to make clear, Kant's position is that *if* the objects in space and time were things in themselves, then Hume would be correct: we would have no right to claim that every change in nature must have a cause. It is only because – as Kant argues – the objects of the senses are appearances that Hume can be answered.

So it might seem that the essential issue between Hume and Kant is not, after all, whether the argument of the Second Analogy is valid, but whether spatio-temporal objects are appearances or things in themselves (since the argument of the Second Analogy, like that of the other Analogies, presumes, and requires, that appearances are the objects of experience). However, this diagnosis of the issue between the two philosophers cannot be regarded as final. The reason is that Hume himself did not, in reality, hold that the objects of the senses are things in themselves. He merely assumed that they are, at least for the major part of the *Enquiry concerning Human Understanding*, because this would have been the accepted theory among his readers. In the concluding section of that work – and after discussing the idea of causation – he makes clear that he does not think that this theory of perception can be justified.

When we turn to his more full-blooded account of our perception of the external world, given in his earlier *A Treatise of Human Nature* (Book I, Part IV, Sect. II), it emerges that (i) he agrees with Kant that the objects of our senses are appearances, not things in themselves; (ii) he holds that the data, out of which our perceptual beliefs arise, must possess certain kinds of *orderliness* in their apprehension. When these two points are put together, it turns out that, on Hume's full-blown account of our perception of the external world, it is *not* possible for the objects of nature to be in chaos. On the contrary, he argues that it is only in so far as the series of our impressions of the senses regularly present themselves either with a certain kind of *constancy* (thereby giving rise to the idea of *coexistence*) or with a certain type of *coherence* (thereby giving rise to the idea of *change of state*) that we can come to form the belief in external objects. And since for Hume, as for Kant, these objects exist only as possible objects of our consciousness, it follows that the objects of the senses, the objects of nature, must behave in regular ways.

No doubt, it would be a mistake to overdo the analogy between these two philosophers' accounts. There are some notable differences of emphasis regarding the respective roles of the imagination and the understanding in making possible our consciousness of spatial objects. Yet, even here, both philosophers stress – in contrast to Berkeley – that the mere *apprehension* of regularity in the manifold is insufficient to produce the idea or belief in external objects. For Hume, as for Kant, there has, in addition, to be a complicated interaction between the apprehended manifold and the mind before any consciousness of external objects can arise. But whereas Kant emphasizes the role of the *understanding* in this additional process, Hume emphasizes – in fact, relies entirely upon – the role of the *imagination*.

None the less, I hope that enough has been said to show that the differences between Hume and Kant, in regard to the consciousness and existence of external objects, is not as great as is often made out. Employing Kantian terminology, the important similarities include the following. First, both hold that the objects of nature are appearances, and hence exist only in so far as they are capable of being experienced. Second, both hold that the mind must itself play a constructive role in making possible the consciousness of these objects. Third, both hold that nature cannot be in chaos; its objects, rather, must have a high degree of regularity in their behaviour. (Kant, of course, requires, *thoroughgoing* determinism in nature. It is possible that Hume might be slightly less rigorous in his demands. But even this is not obviously so.)

Is there, then, no significant divide between them with regard to our consciousness of a spatio-temporal world? It might plausibly be said that there is; but that it is one concerning the consciousness of *ourselves* rather than of spatial objects. Although Hume, like Kant, does not allow that we can be perceptually conscious of objects in chaos, he does appear to allow that if the manifold of representations were in disorder (so that no consciousness of external objects could arise), each of us could still form the belief in ourselves as continuously existing subjects. At least, that is what he seems ready to allow in the main body of the *Treatise*, since he there explicitly allows that we could each have the consciousness of ourselves, throughout a series of impressions and ideas, without believing that the impressions of the senses manifest external objects (see Book I, Part IV, Sect. VII). But he soon came to the conclusion that his account of the generation of our belief in an enduring self was unsatisfactory, and he wrote a section in his Appendix to the *Treatise* admitting as much. Unfortunately, he does not make it clear what exactly he is dissatisfied with in his earlier account of our belief in the self.

Still, in the light of Kant's argument in the Refutation of Idealism, we can see why Hume should at least have had cause for unease. On the Humean account, the belief in an enduring self is supposed to arise from the mind feeling a connection between the train of recollected impressions and ideas, thereby making 'the whole seem like the continuance of one [subject]' (Book I, Part IV, Sect. II). There is no requirement that some of these impressions must first be thought of as manifesting *objects in space*. Yet, as Kant argues in the Refutation of Idealism, the idea of duration must originally arise from the perception of change in the spatial position of objects. There is nothing in inner sense alone, i.e. without recourse to objects in space, that can give rise both to the thought of the permanent and to the requisite conception of change. Consequently, the idea of duration and, thereby, the belief in a subject existing through time cannot arise in the manner originally suggested by Hume. Even if it were plausible to hold that the whole train of impressions and ideas *do* feel so connected or glued together that they all seem like the parts of one subject, this feeling could not, by itself, generate the consciousness of a subject existing *through time*. Temporal consciousness of the self additionally requires the experience of motion (or change in position) of what is thought of as permanent. Accordingly, reference to objects *in space* – to their changing position – is essential.

I am not suggesting that this was Hume's own reason for dissatisfaction with his account of the self. It seems more likely that this arose from his original psychological explanation of how we come to feel a connection between the impressions and ideas in the memory. But whether one accepts a Kantian or a Humean ground for dissatisfaction with the latter's account of our belief in a continuously existing self, its failure does have repercussions for a sceptical response to Kant's – and, in fact, to Hume's – claim that objects in space cannot behave in a chaotic fashion. The sceptic might reply that there is nothing in this claim to rule out our experience being or suddenly becoming wholly *phantasmagoric*. Admittedly, in such an eventuality, we would no longer have any consciousness of objects in space; but this, far from countering scepticism, is merely a yet more forceful statement of it. Instead of supposing that we could experience objects behaving in a random or acausal fashion, we now have the nightmare thought that our experience could be entirely phantasmagoric.

But this sceptical counter-attack is unconvincing. In order to have the thought 'I am having a phantasmagoric experience', it is necessary to have the consciousness of oneself as a temporally extended subject, i.e. throughout the period of one's kaleidoscopic experience. Yet, given the acknowledged failure of Hume's own account of the self, the sceptic is in no position to suppose that he could have such a consciousness of himself *without* recourse to the immediate perception of objects in space. (This, of course, is no more than to repeat the point that Kant makes against Descartes's problematic idealism.)

In conclusion, I should say that, from Hume's point of view, there would seem to be a definite attraction in adopting the Kantian alternative to his own acknowledged failed account of the self. A crucial point to bear in mind about Kant's account is that, like Hume's, it is seeking to explain only our *consciousness* of the I or self existing over time. It is not attempting to prove, as Kant rightly thinks of Descartes's account as attempting to prove, anything determinate about the self as a subject existing in itself. From Kant's own position in the Refutation of Idealism, it follows that we can tell nothing (nor it is intended that we should) about the nature of the self as it is in itself – just as from his account of the existence of objects in space, we can tell nothing (nor is it intended that we should) about the transcendental object. Like Hume's, his account of the self denies that we can know, either by introspection or by theoretical reason, anything positive with regard to how the self may be in itself.

We have already seen that it would be inappropriate to claim that Kant has or has not answered Hume with regard to causation. Both are much more nearly in agreement when their respective positions are properly laid out. It would equally be inappropriate to claim that Kant has or has not answered Hume with regard to our knowledge of the self's temporal existence. Here, too, both philosophers are seeking to do similar things: viz. to give an account, and only an account, of the *consciousness* or *belief* in our continued existence. It may well be that Kant's explanation of how this consciousness is made possible is more persuasive than Hume's. That looks to me to be the case. But if it is, this is an improvement on the Humean position; it is not something that, in spirit, opposes it.

With regard to the spatio-temporal world, the phenomenal world, the systems of Hume and Kant can more profitably be compared than contrasted.

Synthetic a Priori Judgments and the Possibility of Experience

In the Introduction, Kant set down two questions (B 20):

1 How is pure mathematics possible?
2 How is pure science of nature possible?

We can now summarize his answers. In both cases, the explanation of their possibility – that is, of how the two disciplines can provide us with synthetic a priori knowledge of objects – is that their judgments *make our experience possible*. Without this 'third something' (A 155/B 194), viz. the possibility of experience, there would be no bridge connecting the subject and the predicate in the synthetic a priori judgments of mathematics and pure natural science by means of which their objective validity could be established.

In the particular case of pure mathematics, we have already seen that its existence is explained, because mathematical judgments not only describe the necessary structure of space (geometry) and time (arithmetic and pure mechanics), but describe the possible structural relationships of any object that can be experienced in space and/or time. This is finally established in the Axioms of Intuition. It is the bearing of mathematical judgments upon what can be experienced in space and time that gives these judgments objective validity (or what Kant also calls 'real possibility' (B xxvi)).

In the particular case of pure natural science, its existence is explained because the synthetic a priori principles of nature, as proved in the Analogies section, describe the fundamental laws governing our possible experience of any temporal connections between objects or their states.

So, with respect to the fundamental judgments of both mathematics and natural science, it is their laying down the formal conditions whereby any possible experience of objects can occur that explains their holding for all the possible objects of our experience. For, given that space and time are pure intuitions and their objects merely appearances, it follows that the formal conditions that make our *experience* of objects possible must, at the same time, hold for all the possible *objects* of our experience. On the other hand, if space and time were attached to things in themselves, it would be impossible to explain the existence of mathematics and natural science as bodies of synthetic a priori judgments holding for the objects (now: things in themselves) in space and time. Kant's Copernican revolution, therefore, is justified, since it alone can (a) *explain* the objective validity of the synthetic a priori judgments which are everywhere acknowledged to lie at the basis of the sciences of mathematics and physics; and (b) *prove* the fundamental dynamical laws lying at the basis of physics (proved in the Analogies).

What, now, of the possibility of *metaphysics* yielding us any knowledge of objects? By proving that the categories lie at the basis of the fundamental judgments of mathematics and natural science, metaphysics has *to a limited extent* been established. For these a priori concepts certainly belong to metaphysics, and they have been shown to yield synthetic a priori knowledge of the objects of experience, i.e. in mathematics and natural science. Accordingly, where a priori concepts of metaphysics can be shown to have a necessary application to or use in experience, metaphysics can provide us with knowledge. Kant is *not* denying outright the possibility of metaphysics as a science. To the contrary, he believes himself to have justified one of its parts as a science, viz. 'the part that is occupied with those concepts a priori [the categories] to which the corresponding objects, commensurate with them, can be given in experience' (B xviii).

The question for the Dialectic is whether those judgments of metaphysics which entirely *transcend* experience – especially judgments concerning the immortality of the soul, the freedom of the will, and the existence of God – can be shown to be possible, i.e. *really* possible, now that we understand how synthetic a priori judgments are possible in the only two areas where it is certain that they exist: namely, pure mathematics and natural science. Kant will argue that the transcendent judgments of metaphysics – judgments concerned with the *supersensible* – are not provable by theoretical reason, precisely because they do transcend the limits of possible experience. They cannot be proved *in* experience (clearly not, since they are, in intention, a priori as well as synthetic); nor can they be shown to *make experience possible*. They therefore lack the necessary credentials to be established by theoretical reason.

The Distinction between Phenomena and Noumena

In the final chapter of the Analytic of Principles, entitled 'The ground of the distinction of all objects in general into phenomena and noumena' (A 235–60/B 294–315), Kant has two connected aims. First, he wishes to remind us of what is a suitable object for the categories of the understanding (answer: whatever can be sensed). Second, he wishes to explain, in a summary way, why it is that the categories, though essential for knowledge of sensible objects, can be of no help in providing us with knowledge of what lies outside experience, viz. the supersensible. Whatever can have no reference to our senses is not a suitable object of our theoretical knowledge.

This latter topic, what is *not* a suitable object of our knowledge, will be extensively discussed in the Dialectic, where Kant will seek to show in detail why the attempts by the rationalist to gain knowledge of the supersensible must fail. Equally, his arguments are designed to nullify attempts to disprove the existence of these same supersensible entities or capacities, especially God, the soul and freedom – all of which have clearly been central to debates in metaphysics. (Here, it is worth re-emphasizing that, throughout the *First Critique*, Kant is above all concerned with what can or cannot be a suitable object of *theoretical* reason, thereby leaving it open that some, at least, of what cannot be known from a theoretical point of view can be known from a *practical* point of view.)

The distinction between phenomena and noumena, as it is drawn in the final chapter of the Analytic, has occasioned a substantial amount of secondary literature. It would be foolish to deny that some puzzling remarks are made, particularly in one of the passages that was removed for the B edition (A 248–53). But, generally speaking, I believe that there has been too much concentration on Kant's comments on the distinction in this chapter at the expense of what is often more fully discussed, and clarified, in other parts of the *First Critique* (or in the *Second* and *Third Critiques*). For my part, I would urge any reader of the *First Critique* to bear in mind the explicitly *summary* nature of this concluding chapter of the Analytic, and, where puzzles arise, to see whether the points of puzzlement are more expansively discussed in other parts of the work, as well as in the later *Critiques*.

Kant's major concern in the phenomena/noumena chapter – a concern that runs through the whole of the ensuing Dialectic – is to stress that, in our laudable attempt to extend our knowledge, we are perpetually in danger of overstepping the legitimate limits on the use of certain of our concepts. Although these legitimate limits in fact apply to any of our concepts, it is only with respect to the a priori concepts of the understanding, the categories, that he thinks there is a serious likelihood of our attempting to employ them beyond their proper domain. Accordingly, it is the categories that are singled out for discussion in this chapter. To this end, Kant distinguishes between the empirical and transcendental employment of a category. The empirical employment of a category is 'its application merely to appearances, that is, to objects of possible experience'. The transcendental employment, on the other hand, is its attempted application 'to things in general and in themselves'. It is only the former use of a category, its empirical use, that is held to be legitimate. Why? Essentially his answer is quite simple. The Table of Categories is, as we know, supposed to provide an exhaustive list of the pure concepts of the understanding, i.e. those a priori concepts which can be employed for unifying data in a '[sensible] intuition in general'. But these concepts, so considered, are *unschematized*. That is, they make no reference to what *kind* of sensible intuition the categories are applying. Yet it is only when the categories are restricted to some specific form(s) of sensible intuition that they are able to unify a manifold, since it is the given form(s) of sensible intuition which determine *how* these concepts can actually be applied. Thus, in the case of our own form of inner intuition, the categories make possible the experience of objects in time; this they do through principles which specify how the varieties of temporal experience are possible.

But if the categories remain *un*schematized, we can draw no conclusions whatever as to how objective data can exist in an experience. Without application to a specific form of sensible intuition, the bare categories are, as Kant puts it, 'without sense', and so they lack 'determinate meaning'. They lack determinate meaning precisely because, until the form of sensible intuition is known, there can be no indication as to how the categories are to be used in order to determine the experience of objects. How, for instance, can the pure concept of *cause* be employed to make possible an experience until it is known what form or forms of intuition our senses range over?

Consequently, we cannot know how things in themselves may exist by means of the categories. For things in themselves are necessarily the objects of a *non*-sensible intuition – that is, an *intellectual* intuition – while the categories can have a use only in conjunction with some form(s) of *sensible* intuition, and hence, only *vis-à-vis* appearances. By themselves, the categories are insufficiently determinate to characterize anything: when unschematized, they are empty forms of thought.

So we have a legitimate and an illegitimate use of the categories. A legitimate use requires that they are schematized; that is, that they are employed *in conjunction with* sensible intuition. As such, they lead to principles of the understanding; these are rules which, relative to a specific form of sensible intuition, determine the manner in which objects of experience (appearances) can alone exist. The categories, then, are *empty* forms of thought until they are used together with a given sensible intuition; when so used, the principles which contain them do *determinately* provide the form, the structural connections, which must hold for the appearances of that sensible intuition. An illegitimate use of the categories is their attempted employment, whether unschematized or schematized (viz. as principles of the understanding), *outside* sensible intuition. When the categories transcend their use as principles for determining the form of a possible experience, when we attempt to apply them to what cannot be encountered in any sensible intuition, they can tell us nothing about the character of what exists:

> Accordingly the Transcendental Analytic leads to this important conclusion, that the most that the understanding can achieve a priori is to anticipate the form of a possible experience in general. And since that which is not appearance cannot be an object of experience, the understanding can never transcend those limits of sensibility within which objects of experience can alone be given to us. Its principles are merely rules for the exposition of appearances. (A 246–7/B 303)

It is at this point that we are explicitly introduced to the distinction between phenomena (appearances, conceived as the objects of experience) and noumena (things in themselves). Kant maintains that despite the foregoing strictures on the use of the categories, we are easily subject to the illusion that they can be legitimately employed *outside* experience. When this illusion takes hold of us, we suppose that the categories can be used to *characterize* or *determine* what transcends experience, viz. noumena or things in themselves.

The illusion comes about, he thinks, in the following way. Although the unschematized categories are, in reality, mere empty forms of thought for unifying a given sensible manifold, their origin is in the understanding, independent of our, or indeed any, sensible intuitions. At the same time, it is acknowledged that what we sense are the appearances, and not the things as they are in themselves. Things in themselves can only be thought (not sensed) as the ground or cause of what does appear to us. They must, therefore, be conceived by us as wholly intelligible entities; that is, we must represent them to ourselves by means of *thought* or *understanding* alone. So the question naturally arises as to whether these things in themselves, these noumena, can be determined by means of those features of our thought which we alone possess for determining objects, viz. the categories. Now, since the categories are independent of sensibility, and yet can be used to determine certain objects (the objects of the senses), we are easily misled into supposing that by employing the categories, we must be able to determine, to know about, the purely intelligible entities, the noumena, as well as the sensible entities, the phenomena.

Indeed, it is just a train of thought along these lines that, Kant holds, misled Leibniz into supposing that we can come to have determinate knowledge of things in themselves by means of our understanding alone. Whereas (as Kant sees it) the most that we are entitled to claim is that since we admit that the objects of our senses are mere appearances, there must be something, unknown for what it is like in itself, that is the cause or ground of these appearances. When the thing in itself is thought of in this merely *relative* way ('that which is the cause or ground of appearances'), Kant calls it 'the transcendental object'. What we cannot legitimately do is think of the thing in itself independently of the appearances which it grounds, i.e. think of it in a non-relative way, and thereby *positively* characterize it. Our understanding, by means of its forms of thought (the categories), requires *sensible intuition* in order to think about any object in a non-relative way. But, of course, the object then thought about will be an appearance and not a thing in itself. Accordingly, we can know nothing determinate about the thing in itself by the use of our understanding. We must merely think of it under the *in*determinate concept of *the transcendental object*.

A criticism which is often heard is that Kant has no right to claim, as he does, that the transcendental object is the *cause* of appearances (see e.g. A 288/B 344 and A 494/B 522). He has no right, it is said, because the concept of *cause* only applies, by his own lights, *within* experience. But this criticism is at best misleading. It is true that the *schematized* concept of *cause* can be used only within sensible intuition. (Thus, the bare category of *cause*, when schematized within our temporal form of intuition, yields the Principle of Sufficient Reason, which must apply, but can apply *only* to the experience of succession.) However, Kant never affirms that a judgment containing an *unsche-*

matized category cannot be made about what exists, or may exist, outside possible experience, provided that we do not suppose that we have thereby said anything determinate, i.e. can really understand in what way, if at all, the given category can then operate. As he says, in reference to judgments containing unschematized categories, 'I can *think* whatever I please, provided only that I do not contradict myself' (B xxvi; italics original).

But how can Kant be in a position to claim that the objects of the senses have a cause (or ground) *at all*, even one whose operation we cannot understand? I think that the truth is that he does not have any profound answer to this question. Rather, as the opening paragraphs of the Aesthetic make clear (A 19–20/B 33–4), he always assumes that sensations (which provide the material for our consciousness of appearances) *are* the 'effect' of a thing or things in themselves. Indeed, he admits in the *Prolegomena* (Sect. 13, n. III; 4:293) that 'it has never entered my mind' to doubt the existence of things in themselves as the cause of representations. The only question for him is whether, when we do have experience of spatio-temporal objects, these objects should be regarded as things in themselves or as mere appearances (sets of representations) caused in us by a thing or things in themselves. As we have seen, he has argued for the latter alternative: given the status of space and time, we must think of the objects of experience as mere appearances. Accordingly, their cause – a thing or things in themselves – cannot be determinately known, since none of the categories can be employed outside sensibility to characterize objects. It must merely be *thought* as an unknown something which is their cause (the transcendental object). Later, in the Concluding Note on the Antinomies (A 565–7/B 593–5), he also calls this type of cause an 'intelligible cause' to signal that it is a mere thought-entity for which we can have no perceptual evidence. None the less, he there argues, our reason requires us to assume such a cause of the appearances in order to satisfy its demand for something that is sensibly *uncondi-tioned*, and which can therefore be thought of as grounding the contingency of appearances. So Kant maintains that the assumption of an intelligible cause of the appearances is, first, one that cannot be shown to be self-contradictory and, second, one that our reason naturally requires us to make in order to ground the admitted contingency of appearances – even though we must equally accept that we can have no experiential justification for assuming it.

The general distinction between an indeterminate and so, for us, an acceptable concept of a noumenon and a determinate and so, for us, an unacceptable concept of a noumenon is identified in the B edition by referring to the former as the negative concept and the latter as the positive concept of the noumenon. To have a concept of a noumenon in the *negative* sense is to have the concept of something which is *not* an object of a sensible intuition (and hence something that cannot be determinately known, i.e. characterized, by means of any of the categories). For us to have such a concept is not only legitimate; it is necessary. It emphasizes that the appearances are not the only objects that the understanding either can or must think, at least indeterminately. The transcendental object answers to this concept of a noumenon in the negative sense.[5] But it does not do so exclusively, since, as Kant recognizes, we need to acknowledge the logical possibility of there existing *other* non-sensible objects, i.e. ones that are not thought of as grounding the appearances (see B 309). Strictly, therefore, a noumenon or thing in itself, taken in the negative sense, should not be equated with the transcendental object: only when it is thought as grounding the appearances is it being identified as the transcendental object.

To have a concept of a noumenon in the *positive* sense, on the other hand, is to have the concept of an object of a *non*-sensible intuition. We cannot form the remotest notion of what it would be like to possess an understanding that can characterize an object by means of a non-sensible intuition; that is, by means of an intellectual intuition. Our understanding, after all, can characterize only objects of a sensible intuition (appearances). Indeed, Kant maintains that if there does exist an understanding which is capable of an intellectual intuition, it would be radically different from ours; it would not employ categories *at all*. It is, therefore, wholly illegitimate for us to seek to characterize a noumenon or thing in itself, and so to form a concept of it in a positive sense. This is not, of course, because such entities can definitely be asserted to be non-existent, but because even

---

[5] In a passage in the A edn, omitted in the B edn, Kant says that the transcendental object 'cannot be entitled the noumenon' (A 249–53). But what he means by this is that the transcendental object cannot be entitled the noumenon *in the positive sense*, as this italicized expression is explained in the B edn. (The terminological distinction between positive and negative senses of a noumenon is introduced only in the B edn.) He is not denying, in the A edn, that our thought of the transcendental object = X is the thought of a something in general that is the ground of the appearances; on the contrary, this is just what he is there saying (see also A 494/B 522). What he is denying is the possibility of our ascribing to the transcendental object any determinate, non-relational *properties*: it can only be thought as an unknown something. It thus answers to his concept of a noumenon *in the negative sense*.

forming any determinate idea of such entities is entirely beyond our capacities.

None the less, metaphysicians have repeatedly attempted to prove non-trivial propositions about supersensible entities. Despite having just shown why, in general, such attempts must fail, Kant turns in the Dialectic to a consideration of particular areas where positive claims are made about the noumenal world.

5

The Transcendental Dialectic: Why No Theoretical Knowledge in Transcendent Metaphysics is Possible

In the Dialectic, Kant is concerned to unmask the fallacious arguments by which certain philosophers have attempted to reach substantial, a priori conclusions about three actual or supposed existents. These existents are (a) the thinking subject; (b) the spatio-temporal world (the cosmos); and (c) the ground of all that exists or could exist (God). In each case, the philosophers concerned have assumed that they are referring to something that exists *as a thing in itself.*

Theoretical reason is first and foremost identified as the faculty which makes deductive inferences. But Kant claims that it also has the power to produce transcendental ideas – non-empirical concepts – specifically relating to the thinking subject, the spatio-temporal world, and the ground of everything that could exist. He holds that we are easily led by our reason into supposing not merely that we can form such ideas, but that we can give deductive proofs for the existence or (in some cases) the non-existence of the *objects* of these ideas. In fact, as he will argue, the most that reason can achieve is to allow us to *think* of these ideas without self-contradiction.

With regard to the thinking subject, our reason fashions the psychological idea. This idea contains defining attributes of the thinking subject: attributes which no sensible intuition could divulge to us, e.g. that this subject is a *simple substance* and is *permanent.* The fallacious arguments by which our reason seems to prove the reality of these a priori attributes, Kant calls 'paralogisms' (fallacious syllogistic inferences); and the corresponding chapter in the Dialectic is entitled 'The Paralogisms of Pure Reason'.

With regard to the spatio-temporal world, our reason fashions the cosmological ideas. There are four of them. These ideas – or, more accurately, the principles which our reason allegedly proves by employing them – seem to provide the answers to our questions concerning the spatio-temporal world when considered *in its totality*. For instance, our reason fashions the idea of a *free acting cause*. By means of this idea, we are easily persuaded by our reason that we can answer the question of whether causality in accordance with the laws of nature is sufficient, on its own, to provide a full explanation for the existence of change among the objects of the senses. But, unlike the use of reason with regard to the psychological idea, Kant contends that here its use comes into conflict, or is in danger of coming into conflict, with itself. In order to give a full explanation of the action of spatio-temporal objects, we seem forced to conclude both that there must be a free acting cause, and that there cannot be a free acting cause. Moreover, for each of the four cosmological ideas, he maintains that there is a corresponding antinomy or conflict of reason. The chapter dealing with these conflicts is referred to as 'The Antinomy of Pure Reason'.

With regard to the ground of all that exists or could exist, our reason fashions the theological idea. This is the idea of a being, God, who contains *all perfections* (the *ens realissimum*) and who is, at the same time, understood as providing the ultimate explanation for the existence of everything else. The speculative arguments by which our reason appears to demonstrate the reality of this ideal being are criticized in the chapter of the Dialectic entitled 'The Ideal of Pure Reason'.

The Paralogisms of Pure Reason

In this section, Kant criticizes the attempt by the rationalist – here called 'the rational psychologist' – to reach four positive conclusions about the existence of the self, or soul. It is important to remember that the self that is under discussion is the subject as it is in itself (the transcendental subject). The first of these positive rationalist conclusions is that the self must be a *substance* or *self-subsisting being*: something that is not *dependent on* anything else for its existence. The second is that the self must be a *simple* substance. The third is that it must be a *permanent* substance (even beyond this life). And the fourth is that the self can exist *distinct from* anything material.

The rationalist arguments are all based on the mere thought of oneself as the subject of experiences. Any attempt to reach conclusions about the self that are based on the actual contents of one's inner experiences, although, perhaps, of interest to the *empirical* psychologist, would be worthless for giving us any knowledge of the self that exists outside experience, viz. the transcendental subject. What the rational psychologist is after, however, are truths about the self that no experience could determine: most crucially that it is capable of enduring *beyond* its present connection with the body. It is the French philosopher René Descartes who is most famously associated with the attempt to reach a priori conclusions about the nature of the transcendental subject; and there can be little doubt that it is Descartes's arguments and, more importantly, his conclusions that Kant is principally attacking.

In the first of the Paralogisms, the rationalist claims that since the pronoun 'I' can never be employed except as the *subject* of predicates, it follows that its use must refer to a substance and not to a mere attribute or determination of something else. A substance, after all, is precisely that which is always a subject, and never an attribute of anything else.

Against this Paralogism, Kant counters that from the correct observation that the term 'I' can be employed only as the *grammatical* subject and never as the predicate of a judgment – and, in this sense, it is analytically true that our use of the 'I' necessarily refers only to the subject of my judgments – nothing can be inferred as to the mode of existence of the subject, considered as a thing in itself. In order to determine this subject's mode of existence, we would need to have intuition of what our use of the term 'I' is referring to. But this, in the nature of the case, is debarred to us, since all our intuition is *sensible* intuition. We cannot learn anything about the nature of that which is the *ground* of all our sensible intuition (the transcendental subject) through such intuition. In short, no conclusion can be drawn concerning the nature of the transcendental subject – whether e.g. it is or is not a self-subsisting being – from the analytic proposition that the pronoun 'I' can be used only as the grammatical subject, never as the predicate, of any of my judgments.

Equally, the claim of the Second Paralogism, that the subject must be a *simple* substance, cannot be established – as the rational psychologist holds – from the mere fact that, in order to have any thought, the constituents of that thought must be ascribed to a *single* subject: namely, to myself. For all that this shows is that whenever I do have a thought, I must be aware of the whole thought: there cannot be a plurality of *I*'s, each aware of only a part of the thought, since that could not produce the unity of consciousness required for entertaining the whole thought. But although all the constituents of a thought must be ascribed to a single subject, to one *I*, it does not follow that this subject exists as a simple *substance* rather than as a mere *determination* of something else (as a determination of something else, it could not have a separate existence). It is an analytic proposition that whenever a thought is entertained, there must be one subject, one *I*, entertaining it. But it is a synthetic proposition that this subject is, in its mode of existence, a simple substance, and not a mere determination of something else. We have no intuition available for proving this synthetic proposition. How could we, since this subject is never given as an *object* of sensible intuition? It is, rather, thought only as that which grounds our inner sensible intuitions. Accordingly, no conclusion can be drawn concerning the self's separate or independent existence from the acknowledged necessary unity of consciousness in the entertaining of any thought. Yet, the *raison d'être* of seeking to prove the simplicity of the soul or subject is to show that, since it is simple, it must *continue* to exist even when the body decomposes.

Admittedly, what is simple cannot cease to exist through decomposition. On the other hand, as the body dies (decomposes), the soul can cease to exist by its states and powers simply *fading away to nothing* (like a sound gradually fading away to nothing) (see B 414). Therefore, even by acknowledging that the subject is, in some sense, simple, we would still be unable to conclude that it must persist *after* the decomposition of the body. Only if the subject can be shown to be permanent, can its continuance beyond this life be assured. The question of its permanence is considered in the Third Paralogism.

In the Third Paralogism, Kant accuses the rational psychologist of fallaciously arguing from the analytic proposition that all my temporally distinct thoughts must be ascribed to the same grammatical subject (identified by use of the 'I') to the synthetic conclusion that there must be one and the same thinking substance existing *throughout* all these diachronic mental states.

In the A edition, Kant illustrates the synthetic nature of this conclusion by an example that owes a great deal to the English philosopher, John Locke.[1] Following Locke, Kant points out that even if the thinker of any *particular* thought is a substance in its own right, it does not follow that the *same* thinking subject or substance must be sustaining *all* one's diachronic thoughts. Perhaps one's previous thoughts (now memories), together with everything else that can come to one's

---

[1] See 'Of Identity and Diversity', in Locke's *Essay concerning Human Understanding*, 2nd edn (1694).

consciousness, are passed on from one substance to another which, in turn, passes these on, together with its own new thoughts, to a third substance. This third substance could then be conscious of all the previous thoughts (as memories) as 'mine', even though there would not have been the same thinking subject existing throughout. It would seem, then, that there could be (diachronic) unity of consciousness of a series of experiences – the consciousness that *I* have been collectively aware of *all* the serial experiences – *without* there existing one thinking subject (one substance) sustaining all these acts of consciousness.

There is, however, a significant difference between Locke and Kant. Whereas Locke argues that the identity of a person (or self) would be unaffected by such replacement of thinking substances, Kant claims that, although there would be unity of consciousness throughout, there would *not* be the same person (or self) existing throughout. As he says in relation to the Lockean-style replacement of thinking substances: 'The last substance would then be conscious of all the states of the previously changed substances, as being its own states, because they would have been transferred to it together with the consciousness of them. And yet it would not have been one and the same person in all these states' (A 363–4, note). In other words, whereas Locke does not tie the identity of a person to the identity of a thinking substance, Kant does so *despite* agreeing with Locke that the subject, identified by the use of the 'I', would have no consciousness of any change of thinking substance during the series of mental states.

I suggest that the reason for this difference stems from their contrasting views of reward and punishment. Both Locke and Kant conceive of the person as the proper subject of praise and blame. But they do not agree about the conditions that need to be fulfilled in order for praise and blame, and so reward and punishment, to be appropriate. For Kant, but not for Locke, it is the person, *conceived as the thinking substance*, who is praised and blamed (as capable of pure practical reason). Hence, if there should be a Lockean-style replacement of thinking substance, during the life of a human being, we do not have, for Kant, the same person existing throughout, despite the preservation of unity of consciousness.

Interestingly, we find that in the B edition Kant accepts that during the life of any human being – and so of an *embodied* mind – there can be only one thinking substance. In fact, this position is essential for the everyday application of his theory of reward and punishment. What he now says is that we cannot tell whether this subject will continue to exist *after* the death of the body.

But why does he suppose in the B edition that we can, after all, be assured that there is no change of thinking substance during this life? The answer is that each thinking substance is manifested to the outer senses, whether to one's own or to those of others, as an *embodied* consciousness (what Kant calls a 'man' and what I have called a 'human being'). Accordingly, if there were a change of thinking substance, there could not be one *continued* life of a given human being through that change. Instead, from the point of view of *outer sense* (a property of the mind), there would be an absolute existence change of material substance: one human body would be absolutely replaced by another. Since, as the First Analogy has shown, spatial substance must be permanent, it follows that there can be no change of thinking substance during the life of a human being, i.e. during *embodied* existence. As Kant puts it: 'Thus the permanence of the soul, regarded merely as an object of inner sense, remains undemonstrated, and indeed undemonstrable. Its permanence during life is, of course, evident per se, since the thinking being (as man) is itself likewise an object of the outer senses. But this is very far from satisfying the rational psychologist who undertakes to prove from mere concepts its absolute permanence beyond this life' (B 415).

So, with respect to the attempt to prove the permanence of the thinking subject beyond this life, Kant contends that the rational psychologist has confused the analytic judgment that each of us is conscious of our own identity, in the sense of being capable of having the thought 'I have been conscious of all my changing thoughts', with the synthetic judgment that each of us is conscious of our own identity as a thinking subject throughout any changes that may occur (*including* the death of the body). We have no intuition available to prove or disprove this synthetic, and substantial, judgment. For the judgment clearly goes beyond anything that we can establish in experience, and it contributes nothing to the possibility of experience.

The final Paralogism is an attempt by the rationalist to argue directly for our capacity to exist independently of anything outside of us, including our own body. As given in the B edition, the rational psychologist argues that since I can distinguish my existence as a thinking being from anything outside me (including my own body), it follows that I must be able to exist distinct from my body. Kant claims that this argument – like those of all the former Paralogisms – confuses an analytic judgment with a synthetic (and substantial) one. In this case, the analytic judgment is that, in identifying myself through representations of inner sense alone, I must be identifying myself apart from all *other* things, including my body. But it does not follow from this that I can exist independently of anything outside me, including 'things outside me through which representations are given to me' (B 409). It does not follow because, for all I know, I myself may cease to exist as a thinking being when representations, and hence representations of my body, are no longer given to me. In the nature of the case, I can have no knowledge of what the transcendental subject, the subject as it is in itself, is like. For all I can tell, it may be one and the same as the ground of the representations of my body (a transcendental object). And if it is, it will follow that when the transcendental object ceases to exist, my existence as a thinking being must also cease. (Remember that, for the rational psychologist, my body is a thing in itself, and that for Kant I can know nothing theoretically about the true nature of any such entity.)

In brief, the mere possibility of thinking of myself on the basis of inner representations alone fails to show that I should be able to *exist* as a merely thinking being, and so be capable of existing distinct from anything outside my thoughts – including my own body.

The criticisms of the four Paralogisms have shown that, by the use of theoretical reason, we simply cannot know whether we exist as self-subsisting beings or as mere determinations of something else, or whether we shall continue to exist beyond this life, i.e. beyond our lives as embodied beings. In order to establish anything synthetically about these matters, we need to have recourse to intuition. Our intuition is sensible only. The rational psychologist, on the other hand, needs to demonstrate synthetic judgments that entirely *transcend* anything that sensible intuition can confirm or disconfirm. From the point of view of theoretical reason, therefore, we must remain in ignorance concerning any claims both about our status as substances and about a future life. Our theoretical reason can no more gain any knowledge, can no more characterize, the transcendental subject than it can the transcendental object (even assuming that they are different).

The Antinomy of Pure Reason

An Antinomy of Pure Reason is a pair of arguments – a Thesis and an Antithesis – whose conclusions contradict, or appear to contradict, each other. There are four Antinomies. Each is concerned with an issue involving the spatio-temporal world, or cosmos. The Thesis of each Antinomy is supposed to represent the position of the rationalist or, as he is here called, 'the dogmatist': someone who has recourse to non-empirical explanations within the spatio-temporal world. The Antithesis of each Antinomy is supposed to represent the position of the empiricist: someone who insists on empirical explanations exclusively.

Kant holds that when the spatio-temporal world is taken to exist in itself, as both the dogmatist and the empiricist maintain, the Thesis and Antithesis of each Antinomy are valid. Consequently, if the world does exist in itself (and hence transcendental realism is true), all four Antinomies do indeed present pairs of arguments whose conclusions are mutually contradictory. But he also claims that if the spatio-temporal world exists as an appearance only, then no contradictions obtain. This he sees as further proof of the correctness of transcendental idealism. Given, as he assumes, that transcendental realism is the only alternative to transcendental idealism, a proof that transcendental realism leads to contradiction (and in four cases), while transcendental idealism does not, is an indirect proof of the correctness of the latter theory.

The first two Antinomies are entitled Mathematical Antinomies (they deal with questions of addition or division), and the second two are entitled Dynamical Antinomies (they deal with questions of causation). In the case of the Mathematical Antinomies, Kant's contention is that, granted transcendental idealism, both the Thesis and Antithesis of the two Antinomies are *false*. In the case of the Dynamical Antinomies, he contends – again, granted transcendental idealism – that both the Thesis and the Antithesis of the two Antinomies *may be true*.

The Mathematical Antinomies

The (dogmatist) Thesis of the First Antinomy is that the world is infinitely extended in space and in time.

The (empiricist) Antithesis of the First Antinomy is that the world is finitely extended in space and in time.

The (dogmatist) Thesis of the Second Antinomy is that every composite object in the world is made up of simples.

The (empiricist) Antithesis of the Second Antinomy is that no composite object in the world is made up of simples, and that there nowhere exists in the world anything simple.

Whether, with regard to the Mathematical Antinomies, the arguments of the Theses and Antitheses really do entail their respective conclusions has been much debated. Plainly, if they do not (or if only one of the pairs of arguments in each Antinomy is valid), there can be no genuine contradictions of the sort that Kant alleges. Consequently, there will not exist *these* grounds – contradictions generated by the First and Second Antinomies – for abandoning transcendental realism.

I shall, however, pass over the question of the validity of the dogmatist and empiricist arguments. Instead, I want to focus on the question: How does Kant propose to show that, on the assumption of transcendental idealism, the presumed contradictions vanish? Appreciating the key role that transcendental idealism plays in his attempt to defuse the Mathematical Antinomies should help both to refine our grasp of Kant's idealism and to reinforce its centrality to his Copernican revolution.

The First Antinomy

Let us concentrate on the First Antinomy. The key feature of Kant's account is that he rejects *both* the Thesis *and* the Antithesis conclusion: the world, he holds, should be considered as neither infinite nor finite in (spatial or temporal) extent. On the face of it, this is a highly paradoxical position. Surely the world must be either infinite or finite in extent, *even if* no valid argument has been produced to show which it is.

But we need to distinguish two claims: first, the claim that the world is either infinite or not infinite in extent; second, the claim that the world is either infinite or finite in extent. The first claim *is* analytically true; but in denying that the world is infinite in extent, I am not thereby asserting that it is finite in extent. The first claim, therefore, does not presuppose that the world is given as either infinite or finite in extent. In the case of the second claim, on the other hand, the denial of the infinite extension of the world *also* asserts its finite extension. And, Kant maintains, both disjunctions – that the world's extension is infinite and that it is finite – can legitimately be rejected because the extent of the world is given as neither infinite nor finite.

Admittedly, if the world existed in itself, i.e. independently of our capacity to know it, then we could rightly say – indeed, we must say – that it is either infinitely or finitely extended. But where the extent of the world *depends* on our carrying out an empirical synthesis of our representations (which have no existence independent of consciousness), the world is not given as either infinite or finite in extent. For, even when we do carry out such a synthesis, the world is never experienced as given to us *as a whole*; all that is experienced is a successive series of conditions, which can never be given as complete, whether as a determinately finite or determinately infinite series of conditions. No perception can show that, in the series of conditions, there are no conditions for the presently outermost experienced condition (and hence that the series is finite): the most that can be claimed is that no condition has so far been discovered for that experienced condition. Equally, no perception can show that the series of conditions is infinite: the most that can be claimed is that for every condition so far experienced, we have found on investigation that it is itself conditioned. In short, since the size and age of the world – that is, the *phenomenal* world – depend on the empirical synthesis of successive conditions, which can never be perceived as complete, it follows that the world's extent cannot exist as an unconditioned whole, whether as finite or as infinite.

These considerations are well made at A 504–5/B 532–3:

> If we regard the two propositions, that the world is infinite in magnitude and that it is finite in magnitude, as contradictory opposites, we are assuming that the world, the complete series of appearances, is a thing in itself that remains even if I suspend the infinite or finite regress in the series of its appearances. If, however, I reject this assumption . . . and deny that the world is a thing in itself, the contradictory opposition of the two assertions is converted into a merely dialectical opposition [only an apparently contradictory opposition]. Since the world does not exist in itself, independently of the regressive series of my representations, it exists *in itself* neither as an *infinite* whole nor as a *finite* whole. It exists only in the empirical regress of the series of appearances, and is not to be met with in itself. If, then, this series is always conditioned, and can never be given as complete, the world is not an unconditioned whole, and does not exist as such a whole, either of infinite or of finite magnitude. (Italics original)

Certainly, we should never give up the *search* for conditions (and we can say that, so far, we have never failed to find conditions for any experienced condition). But since the extent of the world, being the mere sum of appearances, depends upon carrying out an empirical synthesis, and this synthesis can never be determined as complete, it follows that the world is not given as either finite or infinite. Accordingly, both the Thesis and the Antithesis of the First Antinomy must be rejected as resting on a false presupposition: namely, that the world exists as a thing in itself (and so as an unconditioned whole). From the perspective of the transcendental idealist, the seemingly unexceptional claim that the world must exist as either infinite or as finite in extent is demonstrably false.

The Second Antinomy

Turning to the Second Antinomy, Kant denies the analogous transcendental realist claim that either every composite thing is made up of simples (and so must have a finite number of parts) or no composite is made up of simples (and so must have an infinite number of parts). Since composite objects exist not as things in themselves, but as mere appearances, it follows that no composite object, no appearance, is given as made up of *either* a finite *or* an infinite number of parts. The number of parts of any appearance (since the parts are themselves mere appearances) can be given only in so far as the empirical subdivision of the original appearance takes place. Agreed, if appearances were things in themselves, the number of their parts must exist independently of carrying out the division; and in that case, it could rightly be said of appearances that they must be made up of an infinite or finite number of parts. But since appearances are mere representations, the number of parts of any object is first given *through* the empirical series of divisions. Although, as Kant concedes, we can know that the division of a composite object is capable of proceeding to infinity (since the appearance is given as a spatial whole and, like space itself, can be divided *ad infinitum*), it does not follow that the appearance can itself be affirmed to be *made up of*, or *constituted from*, an infinite number of parts. The number of its parts is given only through carrying out an empirical process of decomposition which, since the appearance is infinitely divisible, can never be experienced as complete: 'Body is therefore infinitely divisible, without consisting, however, of infinitely many parts' (A 525/B 553).

So, as with the First Antinomy, the alleged contradiction between the Thesis and the Antithesis of the Second Antinomy is seen not to be genuine. The opposition is only an apparent opposition, resting on the false presupposition that what is given to us as an object of experience is a thing in itself. Once this presupposition is dropped, it can be seen that we cannot claim of any composite object that it must be made up of either an infinite number of parts or a finite number of parts. If a composite object is a mere appearance, the number of its parts is dependent on the successive empirical process of decomposition. This process can never be experienced as complete. While an appearance is infinitely divisible, we can be given the number of its parts only through carrying out a successive, though incomplete, empirical process of division (see A 526/B 555).

Concluding comments on the Mathematical Antinomies

We can now see that although idealism plays a major role in Kant's treatment of both the First and Second Antinomies, it does not play an identical role. With the First Antinomy, his argument hinges on the claim that since we cannot determine, for any given condition of an empirical series, whether there is a still remoter condition, or whether the given condition is itself unconditioned, it follows that the world (being a mere phenomenon) is not given to us as either a finite or an infinite whole. With the Second Antinomy, his argument relies on the claim that although a phenomenal substance must be infinitely divisible (since here we are presented with a whole *intuition*, and we can know, therefore, that the regress, i.e. the division, is capable of proceeding to infinity), the number of its parts can be given only through the empirical process of decomposition, which can never be taken as complete. Consequently, we cannot assert that the object has a finite number of parts (only that the incomplete process of subdivision has so far determined it to have a particular finite number); and we cannot assert that the object must have an infinite number of parts (since no successive process of subdivision can be perceived as giving us an infinite division).

Kant's method of attempting to resolve the Mathematical Antinomies has invited the following instructive criticism: 'His solution depends on taking the implausible line that spatio-temporal objects can exist only if it is *possible* for us to perceive them. This is implausible, because it rules out the existence of imperceptibly small objects or objects that are too distant for us to be capable of seeing.' This criticism depends on too narrow a sense of what can count, for Kant, as a possible object of perception. He is not requiring that, from our present vantage-point or with the senses as we now employ them, we must be able to perceive certain distant or microscopic objects. He would regard our present vantage-point or our current employment of the senses as merely *empirical* or *contingent* restrictions on what can be experienced. Conditions can be conceived whereby a perception would determine the existence or non-existence of the object in question, e.g. if we travelled closer to an alleged star, or if our sense organs were provided with higher powers of resolution (see A 226/B 273). True, if the synthetic a priori laws of nature *preclude* the possibility of our perceiving a putative object, then it would count for Kant as 'imperceptible', or as 'incapable of being seen', in the relevant sense: no such object could exist in the spatio-temporal world. For nothing can count as a possible object of our experience unless it conforms to the categories as these apply to our forms of sensible intuition (space and time). But such conformity obtains in the examples just considered: in these cases, it is conceivable that, were the contingent conditions altered, we would have a perception of the existence or non-existence of the object in question. On the other hand, no possible perception could determine the finite or infinite extent of the world, or the finite or infinite number of parts of a composite object, because no experience could in principle settle the issue one way or the other.

Transcendental idealism, then, defuses the Mathematical Antinomies by showing that, in both cases, the Thesis and Antithesis rest on a mistaken presupposition concerning the existence of the world, or cosmos. If the world existed in itself (and hence independently of our experiencing it, just as the transcendental realist would have it), there could be no escape from these Antinomies along the lines that Kant suggests. But the Antinomies cannot be generated if the world exists in appearance only.

The Dynamical Antinomies

The Third Antinomy

Thesis: The (dogmatist) Thesis is that causality in accordance with the laws of nature is not the only causality. Fully to explain what happens in the spatio-temporal world it is necessary to affirm not only a causality of nature but a 'causality of freedom'.

The causality of nature is not enough, because if everything were to take place merely through this causality, the series of conditioned causes would never have a first cause. It would not, because, according to the laws of nature, a cause which produces an effect must *itself* have a prior cause, otherwise the action of the cause would never have come into existence to produce its effect. However, this regressive series of causes must have a beginning, or first cause, because otherwise the series would never be completed; and that would contradict the law of causality itself, which states that everything that happens must have a *sufficiently* determining cause. As the Thesis puts it: 'The proposition that no causality is possible save in accordance with laws of nature, when taken in unlimited universality, is therefore self-contradictory; and this cannot therefore be regarded as the sole kind of causality' (A 446/B 474).

The Thesis conclusion is that another form of causality – a causality of freedom – must additionally be assumed: one in which a cause must exist which is *not* itself subject to a prior determining cause, but is, rather, that through which a series of natural events is set in motion. Such a cause would possess what Kant calls an 'absolute spontaneity': it must begin *of itself*, or be *self-caused*. This cause, since it cannot be preceded by an earlier cause by which its causality operates, while it makes possible the experience of change in the spatio-temporal world, possesses *transcendental freedom*.

The dogmatist immediately infers from the Thesis conclusion that once we have shown the necessity of spontaneous causation in order to explain the *beginning* of the events in the spatio-temporal world, it is permissible to allow *within* the series of events subsidiary causes which are also capable of beginning spontaneously a series of events in the world. It is permissible, in other words, to ascribe transcendental freedom to certain substances within the world, even though, in the case of these substances, their causality must be preceded by earlier events in the temporal series. The possible existence of such subsidiary spontaneous causes is clearly required if there are to be beings, like ourselves, acting within the world, yet capable of being regarded as transcendentally free.

Kant sums up the dogmatist's case for the possibility of transcendentally free subsidiary causes (given the alleged Thesis proof of transcendentally free causation of the world as a whole) in the following passage:

> Since the power of spontaneously beginning a series in time is thereby proved (though not understood), it is now also permissible for us to admit within the course of the world different series as capable in their causality of beginning of themselves, and so to attribute to their substances a power of acting from [transcendental] freedom. And we must not allow ourselves to be prevented from drawing this conclusion by a misapprehension, namely that . . . no absolute first beginning of a series is possible during the course of the world. For the absolutely first beginning of which we are here speaking is not a beginning in time but in causality. (A 450/B 478)

Antithesis: The (empiricist) Antithesis is that we must assume that everything that happens in the spatio-temporal world takes place in accordance with laws of nature. Transcendental freedom cannot be thought to exist in the world of our experience.

If causality through freedom were allowed, this would mean that a series of events could start up that was not subject to the causality of nature. But the law of natural causality has universal scope: everything that can be experienced as happening in the spatio-temporal world must be subject to it. Should transcendental freedom occur, the unity of experience would be broken, since that unity requires that every experienced event, actual and possible, must be ascribed to some previous cause. Hence, a spatio-temporal world that is not entirely subject to the causality of nature cannot be so much as thought by us as an object of possible experience. Otherwise put, without thorough-going natural determinism between events within the world of our experience, the criterion for distinguishing veridical perception from dreams and hallucinations would be severed. (It might be objected that the Antithesis argument presupposes transcendental idealism rather than transcendental realism. But that is not so. The argument is only that we could have no unified experience, or distinguish possible experience from illusion, if transcendental freedom is permitted; it is not claiming that the spatio-temporal world could only *exist* in so far as it accords with natural laws.)

The empiricist – the advocate of the Antithesis argument – is especially keen to insist on the universal applicability of the law of nature *within* the world of our experience. Even if spontaneous causation with respect to *starting up* the events of the world is admitted to be possible, no substances within the world of our experience can be credited with transcendental freedom. The distinction between veridical perception and illusion could no longer be made with any certainty if subsidiary substances manifested transcendental freedom (A 451/B 479).

As I mentioned earlier, Kant takes the line with the Third (as well as with the Fourth) Antinomy that whereas Thesis and Antithesis do contradict one another, when the objects of the senses are equated with things in themselves, there is no contradiction between them if the objects of the senses are equated with appearances, with representations in us (and so distinguished from things in themselves). He takes the line, in other words, that if transcendental realism is accepted, the arguments of the Third (and Fourth) Antinomy lead inevitably to contradiction; whereas, if transcendental idealism is accepted, there is no contradiction between the Thesis and the Antithesis – even though it is not possible to *prove*, by theoretical reason, that both are true.

In fact, the defence of the claim that, granted transcendental idealism, we may postulate transcendentally free causation to explain the beginning of events in the world *as a whole* is hardly discussed. After setting out the Thesis and Antithesis, together with some additional observations by the dogmatist and the empiricist, nearly all of the ensuing discussion is directed to showing that it is not self-contradictory for the transcendental idealist to think that there exist, *within* the spatio-temporal world, beings who realize transcendental freedom. Presumably, Kant takes it – I think rightly – that if he can defend transcendental freedom within the spatio-temporal world, a modified version of that defence can be applied to the beginning of the whole world. And indeed there are difficulties for the defence of transcendental freedom within the world that do not apply to its defence with respect to the beginning of the whole world. It is only Kant's defence of freedom within the world that will be examined.

Yet, since the transcendental idealist is himself committed to the view that everything that happens in the spatio-temporal world must have a cause, and a cause that can be located within the world, it is not prima facie evident how accepting transcendental idealism *is* going to permit us to think of the existence of beings in the world who are capable of exercising transcendental freedom. How can there be room for such beings if all spatio-temporal events, including human actions, must have a cause within the world?

In the attempt to answer this question, Kant considers a rational agent – a being who thinks of himself as capable of acting on reason alone – from two different standpoints. First, this agent may be considered as an appearance, as a phenomenal subject. Considered from this point of view, every one of the agent's acts of will must, of course, fall under the law of natural causality. Second, this agent may be considered as a thing in itself, as a noumenal or (as Kant frequently calls a purely rational being) an intelligible subject. From this latter standpoint, the agent is not in space or in time; and his acts of will do not fall under any of the laws of nature.

In broad outline, Kant's defence may now be put as follows. In so far as a rational agent is considered as a phenomenal subject, every one of his actions must fall under the law of natural causality; and, in particular, it must be possible to think of his acts of will as resulting from his personality traits, his empirical character, in conjunction with his beliefs about the surrounding circumstances. But, equally, every one of the agent's actions can be seen as expressing the free choice of the intelligible subject. For this subject, being outside the temporal series, does not fall under the law of natural causality. So although it must be possible to regard his acts of will, from the point of view of the world of appearances, as arising from the agent's empirical character, this requirement cannot interfere with the freedom of the agent, considered as an intelligible subject. It cannot, because, whereas the phenomenal cause forms part of the temporal series, the intelligible subject is an atemporal entity, and thus can be conceived as giving rise to action *spontaneously*, i.e. uncaused by any antecedently existing factors. Consequently, when a rational agent is considered from both the phenomenal and the noumenal standpoints – which is perfectly permissible, granted transcendental idealism – it can be seen that there is no contradiction. On the one hand – that is, from the phenomenal standpoint – we must think of the agent's actions as entirely subject to natural causation; on the other – that is, from the noumenal standpoint – we can think of these same actions as manifesting the transcendental freedom of the agent.

Criticism of the Third Antinomy

Numerous criticisms have been thrown at Kant's attempt to allow human beings the logical possibility of acting in the world through transcendental freedom. I shall concentrate on one particular criticism because it seems to me to bring with it all the major difficulties besetting the defence.

But before involving ourselves in the details of the criticism, there is one feature of Kant's defence that needs to be clarified. It has been alleged that his defence of transcendental freedom within the world must be flawed, because it leads to the following absurd consequence. Since it depends on the phenomenon/noumenon distinction, it must surely extend to everything that exists in the spatio-temporal world: not only to other animals, but e.g. to sticks and stones (after all – it may be presumed – these appearances too will have their noumenal counterparts). But this attempt to reduce the defence to absurdity is based on a misunderstanding. Kant explicitly limits it to beings within the world who are capable of activating themselves by reason alone. He does so because, he holds, we cannot conceivably ascribe the operation of reason to phenomenal factors: the faculty of reason, in so far as we acknowledge it to be genuine, must be conceived as operating free from such factors (A 546–8/B 574–6). It must, therefore, be conceived as belonging to a rational being's existence, not as a phenomenon, but as a noumenon. Furthermore, except in the case of human beings, he holds that we have no evidence for supposing that anything in nature possesses the power of acting on reason alone: even other animals seem capable of being motivated only by sensuous impulses. So far as we can tell, then, human beings are the sole candidates in the world even for being *considered* as genuinely transcendentally free agents, i.e. as creatures who really are capable of activating themselves by reason alone.

The criticism that I wish to examine begins by correctly pointing out that Kant is concerned to defend transcendental freedom because, on his account of morality, it must be possible to ascribe this kind of freedom to any rational agent to whom the concept of duty applies. As he himself insists, it must be possible to say of such an agent, who has not done what he morally ought to have done, that he could *spontaneously* have acted otherwise, i.e. he could have done his duty by exercising his power of transcendental freedom. But – the criticism maintains – it is absolutely impossible to say this, since, according to transcendental idealism, we must be able to think of every one of the agent's actions as causally determined by *antecedently* existing factors: more specifically, by the agent's empirical character in conjunction with his beliefs about the surrounding circumstances. The noumenal or intelligible subject, therefore, is morally superfluous. Although this subject may itself be free from the causality of nature, it cannot *affect* what happens in the phenomenal world because every one of the agent's actions is *already* determined by phenomenal factors (by the empirical character and so on). Any break now in that phenomenal series – running from the agent's beliefs about his surrounding circumstances through its co-operation with his empirical character to the production of the immoral action – would negate the Principle of Universal Natural Causality. Hence, by his own lights, Kant's conception of transcendental freedom can never be exercised in the phenomenal world.

To tackle the objection, we need to investigate Kant's conception of *an empirical character*. He thinks of each phenomenal object as possessing a set of causal behavioural powers: it is this set of causal powers which is collectively identified as the object's empirical character. We discover what a given object's empirical character is like by noting how the object behaves in the various types of circumstance in which it exists. Thus, part of the empirical character of a tennis-ball is its elasticity: its disposition to bounce under given circumstances (this we discover from observation of its behaviour). Analogously, Kant thinks of each human being as having an empirical character, or set of dispositions to behave, which we come to know by observing its behaviour in the various types of circumstance in which it lives: 'Man is one of the appearances of the sensible world. . . . Like all other things in nature, he must have an empirical character. This we come to know through the powers and faculties that he reveals in his actions' (A 546/B 574).

In constructing his defence of freedom around the notion of an empirical character, Kant should be seen as responding to the type of account of freedom offered by Hume. Like Kant, Hume maintains that the actions of human beings are as much subject to natural causal law as the behaviour of everything else in nature. And it was Hume who originally pointed out that it is because of the observed regularity of a human being's behaviour, under similar circumstances, that we are enabled to ascribe a *character* to that human being, and thereby to predict his future actions.[2] But Hume held that, given the regularity in nature – including the behaviour of human beings – all we can understand by free action is action that springs unconstrained from certain of our sensuous desires or inclinations. These impulses are themselves the expression of the corresponding sensuous dispositions with which a given human being has been born or has otherwise naturally acquired. On this picture, an action can arise *only* from a pre-existing sensuous disposition lying in the agent: none of his actions can be regarded as capable of arising *spontaneously* (through reason). It is this feature of Hume's account to which Kant took sharp exception. If every act of will must be regarded – that is, from every standpoint – as caused to occur by what exists *in antecedent time*, then, as Kant sees it, a human being would be unable to regard any such act as

---

[2] 'By means of this guide [experience], we mount up to a knowledge of men's inclinations and motives, from their actions, expressions, and even gestures; and, again descend to an interpretation of their actions from our knowledge of their motives and inclinations. The general observations, treasured up by a course of experience, give us the clue of human nature, and teach us to unravel all its intricacies. . . . Even the characters, which are peculiar to each individual, have a uniformity in their influence; otherwise our acquaintance with the persons and our observation of their conduct, could never teach us their dispositions, or serve to direct our behaviour with regard to them' (*An Enquiry concerning Human Understanding*, Sect. VIII, Part I).

within his power; it would, rather, have to be regarded as predetermined in nature: '[F]reedom consists not in the contingency of the act (that it is determined by no grounds whatever), i.e. not in indeterminism . . . but in absolute spontaneity. Such spontaneity is endangered only by predeterminism, where the determining ground of the act is in *antecedent time*, with the result that the act being no longer in *my* power but in the hands of nature, I am irresistibly determined' (*Religion within the Limits of Reason Alone*, Bk I, General Observation, note 3; 6:50; italics original). At the same time, Kant acknowledges that *if* transcendental realism is assumed, Hume is correct to this extent: that all of an agent's acts of will can only be taken as arising from factors which pre-exist those acts of will and which, given his beliefs about the surrounding circumstances, render them causally necessary. Therefore, on Kant's concept of *freedom*, Hume's account, far from being consistent with freedom of the will, must inevitably lead to its denial, and therewith to the impossibility of morality.

If, however, we embrace transcendental idealism, it is at least not self-contradictory to regard a human being's conduct as capable of arising spontaneously. For it then becomes logically possible to regard every manifestation of a rational agent's empirical character as expressing the free choice of that agent, considered as an intelligible subject. The idea is that although the agent, *qua* phenomenal being, is born with, and perhaps further naturally develops, a set of sensuous dispositions, it is the intelligible subject which chooses whether, on the one hand, to allow an action to occur by means of whichever of these sensuous dispositions is, under the given circumstances, naturally manifested (as a sensuous impulse) or, on the other, to begin a series of phenomenal events on the basis of reason alone. Whichever of the two possible causal grounds actually prevails (sensuous impulse or reason alone), the ensuing conduct must fall under a universal rule. For suppose that, on a certain occasion, the agent's action comes about by means of a particular sensuous impulse. Granted the thoroughgoing determinism in nature, this means that, under exactly the same circumstances, the same sensuous impulse will occur and, as a result, the same action will follow. But suppose that, on the occasion in question, the agent's action arises as a result of a purely rational resolution – and hence (for Kant) it is performed for the sake of the moral law. This will equally have the consequence that the same (moral) conduct will invariably follow under exactly the same empirical circumstances. For if the agent's action arises from reason alone, the principle of action will be expressed in the form of a universal maxim, e.g. to help others whenever they are in a certain degree of distress. Accordingly, if on one occasion the agent's action does result from such a principle, that same action will always result under the same empirical circumstances. The very notion of causation, whether through nature or through reason, requires regularity in its operation: 'For every cause presupposes a rule according to which certain appearances follow as effects. This uniformity is, indeed, that upon which the concept of cause (as a faculty) is based' (A 549/B 577). If an agent in virtue of its purely rational nature – that is, in virtue of its existence as an intelligible being – can ever be held to have acted on the basis of a certain principle of reason, the same action will result whenever that principle is perceived to apply (and all other relevant circumstances remain the same). For no difference of time can affect the choice of an intelligible subject, since that subject is an atemporal entity.

So a rational agent's empirical character should be thought of as an amalgam of dispositions to act. Some of these dispositions express how, under certain circumstances, the agent is disposed to act from sensuous impulses; while others can be regarded, without self-contradiction, as expressing how, under other circumstances, he is disposed to act from purely rational resolutions.[3] Whether an action is produced, on a given occasion, through a sensuous impulse or spontaneously through reason, the same action will constantly occur under the same circumstances (thereby allowing us to ascribe a particular empirical character to the agent). Consequently, whichever ground prevails on a given occasion, sensuous or rational, there will be no break in the natural law of causality, according to which everything that happens in the sensible world must fall under a universal law:

> But I say: the law of nature stands, whether the rational being is the cause, by reason and through freedom, of effects in the world of the senses, or whether it does not determine these effects out of grounds of reason. For, in the first case, the act happens according to maxims the

[3] Kant does *not* hold that when a rational agent acts as a result of sensuous impulse, reason never plays any part in aiding what actions are carried out. Rather, his view (like Hume's) is that reason can, and usually does, play a *supportive* role in such cases: it can determine the best *means* to a desired end. But when reason only shows the means to a desired end, it has no role in activating the agent; that is entirely owing to sensuous impulse. Where Kant differs from Hume is in allowing that we can at least think that there are other cases where reason does not play a merely supportive role, viz. where the agent acts for the sake of the moral law, and hence on reason alone. This difference between the two philosophers will be further discussed when we look at Kant's moral philosophy.

effect of which in appearance will always be in conformity with constant laws; in the second case, the act happening not in accordance with principles of reason, it is subject to empirical laws of sensibility, and in both cases the effects are connected according to constant laws; we demand no more for natural necessity, indeed we know nothing more of it. (*Prol*, Sect. 53; 4: 345–6)

We can now see how Kant's notion of an empirical character, on the one hand, and his distinction between the noumenal and phenomenal worlds, on the other, come together in his defence of transcendental freedom. According to the standpoint of the subject, considered as an intelligible being, there is nothing in the series of appearances which renders inevitable any morally discreditable action that occurs in the temporal series. Rather, each of the agent's acts – creditable or discreditable – can be considered as expressing the free choice of the intelligible subject. From the point of view of the noumenal world, it is the intelligible subject that creates *the whole empirical character*. This subject can be seen as choosing, for each set of empirical circumstances, whether to act through the causality of reason or to allow – by default (see A 555/B 583) – a given sensuous impulse to be *operative*, i.e. to produce an action. (An agent's sensuous impulses are not, therefore, inevitably included in his empirical character: only those sensuous impulses which he not only feels but also *acts upon* are included in the empirical character.)

Of course, on the grounds already explained, a rational agent's actions must exhibit a constancy in their appearance in the temporal series, whether any given action be determined through sensuous impulse or through reason alone. Indeed, it is this very constancy that permits us to ascribe a particular empirical character to the agent in the first place, i.e. from past observation of his actions, thereby enabling us to predict his conduct on future occasions. But the fact that actions can be predicted in this way is consistent with affirming that nothing in the appearances – including, most notably, the agent's empirical character – can have determined the intelligible subject to produce *any* of the actions that appear in the temporal series. So the agent, *qua* intelligible subject, can be thought of as transcendentally free and morally responsible for each one of his actions in the phenomenal world. For every feature, every disposition, of the empirical character merely expresses a transcendentally free choice of the intelligible subject, which we first learn about through observation of the agent's actions under phenomenal conditions. From the point of view of the intelligible subject, the whole of a rational agent's empirical character should be seen as *a consequence of* the intelligible subject's free choice; that empirical character cannot possibly be seen as *determining* the agent, *qua* intelligible subject, to begin any series of events that occur in the phenomenal world. On the contrary, a rational agent, *qua* intelligible subject, can be thought of as responsible for every one of his actions that appears in the phenomenal world – even though we can, in principle, use our knowledge of that agent's empirical character (gleaned from our observation of his past actions) in order to predict future actions.

> [E]very action . . . is to be regarded in the consciousness of his intelligible existence as nothing but the consequence and never as the determining ground of his causality as a *noumenon*. So considered, a rational agent can now rightly say of every unlawful action that he performed that he could have omitted it even though as an appearance it is sufficiently determined in the past and, so far, is inevitably necessary; for this action, with all the past which determines it, belongs to a single phenomenon of his [empirical] character, which he gives to himself and in accordance with which he imputes to himself, as a cause independent of all sensibility, the causality of those appearances. (*CPractR*, 5:97–8; italics original)

Although this last quotation comes from the *Critique of Practical Reason*, I do not see any difference of treatment in that later work of the fundamental issue of whether it is self-contradictory to ascribe transcendental freedom to beings in the spatio-temporal world. The quotation is not only consistent with everything that is said in the *First Critique*, but is one of the best summaries of its main line of argument.

But, it may be said, even if we admit that the intelligible subject is not causally determined by anything in the world of appearances, we have been given no account of *why* it makes the particular choice of actions which appear in the phenomenal world. Given that the intelligible subject creates the empirical character, why does it create one particular type of empirical character instead of some other? Kant replies that it is impossible for us to know, since, from our phenomenal standpoint, we have no access to the noumenal world. Without such access, we should not expect to have an answer. As he puts it: 'we can get so far as the intelligible cause, but not beyond it . . . to explain why in the given circumstances the intelligible character should give just these appearances and this empirical character transcends all the powers of our reason, indeed all our rights of questioning' (A 557/ B 585).

I have tried to rebut the best-known and, so far as I am aware, the most powerful criticism of Kant's defence of transcendental freedom within the world. In my view, he does successfully show that it is *logically possible* to acknowledge both a thoroughgoing determinism in the spatio-temporal world and our transcendental freedom. This is all that he is arguing for in the *First Critique*. At the same time, I have no wish to deny that serious – and, so far as I can see, insurmountable – difficulties remain if he is to prove (as he further thinks that he can prove) the *reality* of our transcendental freedom. We shall take up this issue when we consider the place of transcendental freedom in the *Critique of Practical Reason*.

Fourth Antinomy

We have seen from the discussion of the Thesis and Antithesis of the previous Antinomy that, if transcendental realism is accepted, Kant believes that we are committed to accepting both that there must be a free acting causality to explain the beginning of the series of spatio-temporal events and that everything that begins in that world must itself be caused. In a similar vein, he now argues that, granted transcendental realism, we are committed to accepting both that there must be a being, belonging to the spatio-temporal world, whose existence is unconditionally necessary (and so does not depend for its existence on any preceding conditions) and that there cannot be any unconditionally necessary being, whether within or outside the world.

The dogmatist opens up his argument by pointing out that there must be a series of alterations in the world in order for us to have a consciousness of time. But this series, he urges, requires an unconditionally necessary being. Without such a being to begin the series, no given alteration would be necessary. Moreover, this being must belong to the spatio-temporal world, since the ultimate condition for the beginning of a series of alterations must precede that series.

The empiricist counters that we cannot conceive, within the world, a necessary being who begins a series of alterations. If there exists in the spatio-temporal world a being who is the cause of an alteration or a series of alterations, we must search for a prior condition determining the existence of that being. We could never have experience of a being whose existence is unconditioned; we must always regard the cause of an alteration as itself determined in its existence by a preceding condition. Nor can there be a being outside the world who unconditionally begins a series of alterations. For this being must itself begin to act, and hence, after all, must be in time (its existence cannot, therefore, be regarded as unconditioned).

Kant's attempted resolution of this conflict of reason depends, of course, on distinguishing between viewing the series of alterations from the phenomenal and from the noumenal standpoints. The empiricist is right that, in so far as we consider any such series only from within the spatio-temporal world, we cannot allow any unconditionally necessary being as its cause. Our reason demands that for any cause that exists in the spatio-temporal world, we must always search, and expect to find, a prior condition determining its existence. But the empiricist is wrong to claim that we cannot *additionally* postulate a different cause, outside the world, by which the whole series of appearances may be thought to arise. In rejecting the logical possibility of an unconditionally necessary being outside the world, as the cause of alterations within it, the empiricist is presupposing transcendental realism (in which space and time are things in themselves, or relations between things in themselves). On this presupposition, it does indeed seem correct to say, as the empiricist urges, that in order to conceive of a cause beginning a series of events, that being must itself be regarded as preceded by some condition through which its existence is explained.

However, if the serial events are nothing but mere appearances, it is not self-contradictory to hold *both* that for every appearance that causes a series of alterations in the spatio-temporal world, we must search for, and invariably expect to find, a prior condition (appearance) *and* that the whole series of appearances is itself caused to exist in the subject's consciousness by a noumenal ground (the transcendental object). The whole series of appearances is, for the transcendental idealist, not a series of self-standing entities, existing independently and prior to the subject's acts of synthesis. It is, as the discussion of the first two Antinomies has shown, nothing but an incompleted series of representations in the subject's mind. This whole series, both actual and possible, may without self-contradiction be thought of as grounded in a transcendental object which, since it is outside the temporal series, cannot depend for its existence on any preceding conditions. In this way, it is possible to accept that there can be no unconditionally necessary being within the spatio-temporal world, while also accepting that there may be an unconditionally necessary being outside this world as the ultimate cause of all that happens within it.

Given transcendental idealism, then, the assumption of an intelligible ground of the whole series of representations is not in conflict with the requirement that we must always seek, within the appearances, the conditions on any being in the spatio-temporal world. No unconditionally necessary being can be accepted within the world of appearances – here everything must be regarded as conditioned, and so contingent – but we may yet assume, without self-contradiction, an intelligible ground of this whole series of dependent representations.

Indeed, Kant insists that our reason *requires* us to make such an assumption. Once it is acknowledged that everything that exists in the world of appearances must itself be conditioned, our reason demands that we postulate something different from all possible appearances through which this contingency can be explained. '[T]he existence of appearances, which is never self-grounded but always conditioned requires us to look around for something different from all appearances, that is, for an intelligible object in which this contingency may terminate' (A 566/B 594). Our reason always demands an unconditional ground for what is acknowledged to be conditioned. Accordingly, the assumption that the world of appearances is grounded in a transcendental object does have a foundation in the nature of our reason. Reason would be at odds with itself if it could not admit *both* the unceasing requirement to find, within the world of appearances, the conditions for the existence of an appearance *and* something sensibly unconditioned (an intelligible object) upon which this whole series of sensibly conditioned beings is grounded.

Without the assumption of a sensibly unconditioned ground for all that is conditioned in the world of appearances, our intellectual faculties (understanding and reason) could not consistently prosecute the search for *empirical* knowledge. Reason, instead of invariably requiring the fullest extension of natural explanations within the empirical world, would seek an unconditioned existence in order to explain a given series of alterations. By assuming the existence of a sensibly unconditioned being entirely outside the spatio-temporal realm, the possibility of our acquiring empirical knowledge can proceed unhampered, while yet satisfying the demand of our reason for a noumenal ground wherein all contingency of the sensible world would terminate.

The Ideal of Pure Reason: Three Speculative Arguments for the Existence of God

The three speculative arguments are intended to be the most rigorous attempts to establish the existence of God (or the *ens realissimum*) by means of theoretical reason. If it is asked why Kant supposes that there can be only three speculative arguments, the answer is that he thinks that there are only three possible forms which such an argument can take: first, one that makes no reference to experience at all, being based upon the analysis of a priori concepts; second, one that is based only on the very existence of experience, irrespective of any reference to its actual content; and, third, one that is based on the specific content of experience.

The Ontological Argument

Kant's attack on the Ontological Argument can be divided into two halves. In the first half, the discussion centres on the concept of an absolutely necessary being. Exponents of the Ontological Argument claim that the *ens realissimum* – the being that has all positive qualities to the highest degree – should be identified with an absolutely necessary being. However, before turning, in the second half of his attack, to the *ground* that is offered for this identification, Kant wants first to see whether talk of 'an absolutely necessary being' is comprehensible. Clearly, if it is not – at least in the way in which it is used in the Ontological Argument – then the argument will be a non-starter.

To this end, he asks what can be meant by saying of any attribute or property that it necessarily belongs to an object, and in what way we can reject such an attribution. He takes the case of an analytic judgment and, in particular, the judgment that a triangle necessarily has three angles. It cannot be said without self-contradiction that there exists an object answering to the concept of a triangle but that it does not possess three angles. Once an object has been identified, instantiating the concept of a triangle, it is self-contradictory to deny of that object that it has three angles. Yet one can deny that such an existential judgment obtains: that is, one can deny that there exists any object answering to the concept of a triangle. There is no contradiction involved here, because one is rejecting the existence of both any object answering to the concept of the subject term and any set of properties answering to the concept of the predicate term.

So Kant's position is that when we say that a triangle necessarily has three angles, we are saying that *if* there exists an object answering to the concept of a triangle, it must have three angles. Hence, it is not self-contradictory to say either that there are no triangles or that there are no figures having three angles, even though it is self-contradictory to say that triangles do not have three angles.

In the light of the triangle case, let us now consider the concept of an absolutely necessary being. Kant plausibly contends that the concept of an absolutely necessary being is not an easy one to grasp. It is said to be the equivalent of a concept of a being whose non-existence is impossible or unthinkable. The trouble is: how can any *object* be thought of as necessarily existing? Standardly, the explanation of what can be meant by the concept of necessary being (or a being whose non-existence is unthinkable) is to give examples like 'A triangle necessarily has three angles' or 'A triangle that has more than three angles is inconceivable.' But such examples are of necessary *judgments*, not of concepts of necessary *things* or *objects*. And, as we have seen, Kant has argued that what these judgments assert is that 'If there exists a triangle, then it necessarily has three sides.' Consequently, these examples have not explained what can be meant by the concept of a necessary being.

Kant plainly thinks that these criticisms have by themselves put paid to the Ontological Argument. It is merely a confusion to suppose that the alleged necessity of an object existing can be understood in the same way in which we understand a judgment about the necessity of a triangle existing with three angles. For the way in which the judgment is to be understood precisely does make it possible to deny the existence of triangles or of the three angles (provided that the existence of the object, the triangle, is likewise rejected). Further, the only way in which it has been shown that we can legitimately talk of necessity when referring to an object is *within* a judgment. No sense has been attached to the alleged concept of a necessary being, at least as it is employed in this first speculative proof.

None the less, he admits that, according to the Ontological Argument, there is just *one* case where we cannot deny that the concept of a possible object does legitimately require or necessitate that object's existence. This brings us to the second half of his attack. Exponents of the argument declare that the *ens realissimum* must contain existence as one of its attributes. For, they argue, the concept is a *possible* one, and its object is thought of as possessing all reality – that is, all positive attributes to the highest degree. But a being that did not exist could not possess as much reality as one that did exist. Consequently, since the *ens realissimum* is that which does possess all reality, it follows that it must exist.

Against this position, Kant employs his well-known claim that 'existence' is not a real predicate, or, in other words, that it does not refer to an attribute of a thing. Hence, the *ens realissimum* is not required to exist in order to possess all positive attributes to the highest degree.

In accepting the possibility of the concept of *ens realissimum*, we are admitting the existence of its object in one sense only: we are admitting that the thought of the object is not self-contradictory. Moreover, when I say 'God exists', if I am doing more than asserting that my concept is not self-contradictory, I can only be claiming that my concept is actualized. To suppose that I am characterizing the object of my thought would be to hold that an object 'answering' to my concept of God contains more attributes than those referred to by the concept itself. In which case, my so-called concept of that object would fail to be its concept, because it would fail to capture all of the object's attributes. This point is well brought out in the case in which Kant invites his readers to think of an object possessing all of its attributes save one:

> If we think in a thing every feature except one, the missing reality is not added by my saying that this defective thing exists. On the contrary, it exists with the same defect with which I have thought it, since otherwise what exists would be something different from what I thought. When, therefore, I think a being as the supreme reality, without any defect, the question still remains whether it exists or not. (A 600/B 628)

To say that an object of a concept exists is to say at most that there is an object answering to that concept; it is not to ascribe a further attribute to the object. Consequently, the Ontological Argument fails because the *ens realissimum* cannot contain existence as one of its attributes.

The Cosmological Argument

The Cosmological Argument begins with some experience or other of the world (irrespective of its content) and argues from that experience to the necessity of a being as the first cause. This unconditionally necessary being is then identified with the *ens realissimum*.

Kant maintains that the Cosmological Argument can never achieve its goal of showing that the unconditionally necessary being is the *ens realissimum*. In order to achieve this goal, it has to fall back on the Ontological Argument. In fact, he contends that the motive force behind the Ontological Argument derives from the felt need to determine the nature of a being whose existence is unconditioned. But whereas with the Ontological Argument, we start with the concept of the *ens realissimum* and argue to the necessity of its existence, with the Cosmological Argument, we first reach, or suppose ourselves to have reached, the necessity of a being as the first cause, and then argue that this unconditionally necessary being must be the *ens realissimum*.

The cosmological proof is briefly stated thus:

> If anything exists, an absolutely necessary being must also exist. Now I at least exist. Therefore an absolutely necessary being exists. . . . The necessary being can be determined in one way only; that is, by one out of each possible pair of opposed predicates. It must therefore be *completely* determined through its own concept. Now there is only one possible concept which determines a thing completely a priori; namely, the concept of the *ens realissimum*. The concept of the *ens realissimum* is therefore the only concept through which a necessary being can be thought. (A 605–6/B 633–4; italics original)

Although a number objections are made to the proof, Kant's attack concentrates on this one. Even if it is permissible to move from the existence of some experience to the necessity of a being as the first cause, it is undoubtedly fallacious to conclude that the concept of the *ens realissimum* is the sole concept by which we can think of a necessary being. To suppose that it is would be to fall back on the Ontological Argument, which has already been shown to be invalid. (The nature of the necessary being has to be wholly determined *on the basis of its own concept – and hence through reason alone*, since we have now passed beyond experience.)

The claim that the Cosmological Argument relies on the (invalid) Ontological Argument has been criticized on the ground that Kant fails to show that the Ontological Argument must play any part in the cosmological proof. It is not easy to understand why he thinks that the Ontological Argument is needed, but I suggest the following as his line of thought. He acknowledges that the properties of the *ens realissimum* are eminently *suitable* ones for an absolutely necessary being. But in order to establish that this object is alone capable of fulfilling the conditions essential to an absolutely necessary being, it is required that from the concept of the *ens realissimum* – and from no other concept of a possible object – unconditional necessity of existence can be inferred. Unless it can be, it would be impossible to conclude, solely on the basis of concepts of possible objects, that the *ens realissimum*, and only the *ens realissimum*, contains all of the properties that an absolutely necessary being must possess. For only a being whose existence can be determined as necessary from its own concept can be thought of as absolutely necessary through reason alone. As Kant puts it: 'reason recognises that only as absolutely necessary which follows of necessity from its concept' (A 613/B 641). However, since the Ontological Argument is invalid, the set of properties that an absolutely necessary being must possess cannot be identified with those of the *ens realissimum*. On the contrary, once it is acknowledged that 'existence' is not a real predicate (and hence that unconditional necessity of existence cannot be inferred, and uniquely inferred, from the concept of *the ens realissimum*), the exercise of pure reason has given us no ground for concluding that the *ens realissimum* is alone capable of fulfilling the role of an absolutely necessary being. So far as we can tell a priori, unconditional necessity of existence can belong to a being with a far less exalted set of positive properties than those that must be possessed by the *ens realissimum*. The cosmological proof, therefore, has failed to determine the properties which are essential to such a being. (It might also be objected that the proof has failed to show that there can be only *one* unconditionally necessary being for all that is experienced or may be experienced. Perhaps there are a number of such beings, each grounding different series of appearances. But, given the thoroughgoing interconnectedness of everything that exists in the sensible world this objection may be felt to lapse.)

Kant further criticizes the cosmological proof on the ground that no decisive argument has been given against the possibility of an *infinite* series of causes. To maintain that the cause or ground of the objects of experience must be unconditioned by any condition governing these objects – and so by the Principle of Sufficient Reason – does *not* warrant us inferring that this ground has no cause at all. Admittedly, as the Fourth Antinomy has shown, our reason does require us to assume the existence of a *sensibly* unconditioned cause (the transcendental object). But we are not entitled to hold that what, from the point of view of the world of experience, is unconditionally necessary has no intelligible ground of its existence. Once we pass entirely beyond experience, we are unable theoretically to employ any of the pure concepts, including those of *cause* and *substance*, in order to characterize any object, including the transcendental object. Even the claim that there must be a *cause* of the sensible world cannot be assigned any determinate meaning, since it employs a category outside our possible experience.

Our reason, unaided by any specific empirical evidence, has been found incapable of proving the existence of a supremely perfect and unconditionally necessary being. But what justification can there be for our reason even to form the idea of such a being – and to do so without basing it on any specific content of our experience? Kant's answer is that the idea's defensible employment, with regard to our theoretical knowledge, is its role in a *regulative* principle of our reason. While we must never cease to search for a cause for any given appearance within the spatio-temporal world, the principle that we should treat the whole world of appearances *as if* it originated in a supremely perfect and unconditionally necessary being serves as a spur to our empirical enquiries. This regulative principle leads us to search for natural laws that are maximally simple and unifying, rather than to rest content with complex and disparate sets of specific causal laws. But although the idea of a supremely perfect original being is strictly defensible only as part of a regulative principle, we naturally, but illusorily, take it as referring to an actually existent being. The illusion arises because of reason's demand to find the unconditioned for any condition, despite the fact that, once we pass beyond the world of appearances (in which everything is necessarily conditioned), our theoretical reason is unable to prove anything determinate. Accordingly, within the context of our search for scientific knowledge, the justified use of reason's idea of the perfect original being can only be within a regulative principle: a principle that aids in the discovery of systematic unity in the world of experience.

The degree of harmony and seeming design that our empirical investigations of nature do uncover is the starting-point for the third and final speculative argument for the existence of God.

The Physico-Theological Argument (the Design Argument)

Unlike the Cosmological Argument, which does not rely on any particular content of experience, the Design Argument seeks to prove the existence of God from our experience of overall coherence and (apparent) purposiveness in nature, including its organic parts.

In general, Kant's criticisms of the Design Argument will be familiar to anyone who has read Hume's classic objections.[4] In fact, a number of the latter's most famous critical points are given, at best, a passing general mention: e.g. Hume's claim that, even if we presume systematic order and harmony of the entire experienced universe, it is

---

[4] See David Hume, *An Enquiry concerning Human Understanding*, Sect. XI, and *Dialogues concerning Natural Religion* (London, 1779).

impossible for us to know whether any designer has not 'botch'd and bungl'd' innumerable productions before succeeding in our own experienced case. Of course, a transcendental idealist (and Hume of the *Treatise*, for that matter) will insist that any experienced universe must conform to the pure (transcendental) natural laws. But this could still leave room for a great deal of diversity in the more specific laws, and hence for the possibility of a considerable lack of systematic unity between the different parts of nature.

Kant expresses some reservation about whether the Design Argument can justify us in inferring a supersensible designer of nature. (He does not here specify the source of his reservation: he will do so chiefly in the teleology part of the *Critique of Judgment*; see below, chapter 12.) At the same time, he does affirm that once we allow a cause at all of the apparent purposiveness in nature, we are justified, at least as a necessary *subjective* means of discovering causal explanations for the organic parts of nature, in thinking of this cause as a supersensible one, and of crediting it with understanding and will – thus personifying the supersensible ground. His acceptance, albeit from a subjective or regulative point of view, of the necessity of hypothesizing a supersensible designer is not plausible today. The harmony and apparent purposiveness of the organic parts of nature – which, more than anything else in the sensible world, seem to suggest an overarching cause acting through reason and intention – have been successfully, not to say spectacularly, accounted for by Darwinian evolutionary theory. This *natural* explanation of the behaviour of, and interconnections between, organisms dispenses with the need for a supersensible cause of the phenomena, at any rate in the straightforward way proposed by Kant. Still, following Hume, he does stress one of the strongest objections to the Design Argument: even admitting a cause of the world, this cause can be validly conceived only as its *designer*, and not as the *creator* of its materials. (On analogy with artefacts and their human designers, it is not even clear that we have strong grounds for supposing that the designer of the universe still exists.)

In two ways at least, the Design Argument is seen to fall short of what is required for a proof of the existence of God. First, it cannot establish a creator of the universe. Second, our observations of the workings of the universe are necessarily insufficient to credit its acknowledged designer with *supreme* perfection: they permit us only to credit the designer with a *relative* degree of perfection, i.e. one which is proportional to the experienced order and power of nature (and no further). Yet our idea of God is of a being who is supremely perfect. The nature of this being must transcend any degree of perfection that can be experienced, since, whatever the experienced perfection may be, it is always capable of being exceeded in thought.

The most, then, that the argument can achieve is to give us encouragement to search for grounds that *will* prove the existence of a being that answers to our idea of God. Consequently, so long as we remain within the realm of theoretical reason, we must appeal to one of the speculative arguments previously discussed, viz. the Cosmological and Ontological Arguments (as Kant would have it, the only other speculative arguments available). But we have already found that the Cosmological Argument fails to prove the existence of an absolutely necessary being; and even if it succeeded in doing so, it could provide this being with a nature that is suitable to our idea of God (supreme perfection) only by relying on the Ontological Argument. On the other hand, the Ontological Argument would, if valid, prove by itself the existence of a supremely perfect absolutely necessary being. But that argument too has already been found wanting. None the less, despite being dubbed 'a quite unnatural procedure and a mere innovation of scholastic subtlety' (A 603/B 631), it has emerged that the Ontological Argument is the only serious candidate for a successful speculative proof. Only the Ontological Argument, if it had been valid, would have succeeded in proving the necessary existence of a supremely perfect being (from which all reality must come). It is, accordingly, the only speculative argument which, given our idea of God, could possibly have succeeded in proving his existence.

Conclusion to the Dialectic

The discussion of the speculative proofs for the existence of God effectively brings to a close the attack in the Dialectic on the attempt to employ theoretical reason to establish the central claims of metaphysics.

This attack has shown that once the distinction is made between the world of appearances and things in themselves, theoretical reason is powerless to prove or disprove a judgment affirming the immortality of the soul, the freedom of the will, or the existence of God. Each of these central metaphysical judgments is not only synthetic, it is also a priori – since it cannot be confirmed or disconfirmed by sense experience. Yet, unlike the synthetic a priori judgments of mathematics and natural science, there is no bridge, no 'third something' – viz. the possibility of sense experience – by which a link can be effected between the subject and predicate of any of these metaphysical judgments. For none of them contribute anything to the possibility of our having sense experience (although, taken merely as regulative principles, some of them can be effective in improving our systematic grasp of nature). Since the central claims of metaphysics have no relation to sense experience – being neither confirmable or disconfirmable by sense experience, nor capable of making it possible – it follows that theoretical reason is entirely unable to prove or disprove any of them.

It remains to be seen whether any of the central claims of metaphysics can be established by showing that they make our *moral* experience possible.

Part II

Critique of Practical Reason

6

The Analytic of Pure Practical Reason: Reason, not Sentiment, as the Foundation of Morality, and how Freedom of the Will is Proved

The *Critique of Practical Reason* – known also as the *Second Critique* – is much more than a treatise on moral philosophy narrowly conceived. It is also, and centrally, a work of metaphysics. In the *First Critique*, Kant maintained that there are three major questions of transcendent metaphysics: concerned with the existence of God, the freedom of the will, and the immortality of the soul. With regard to these questions, the *First Critique* merely attempted a *defence*, that is, it attempted to show that it is at least *logically possible* that all three concepts – *God, freedom* and *immortality* – are actually instantiated. It is in the *Critique of Practical Reason* that Kant attempts to prove the *reality* of their objects, and thus to provide positive answers to all three of the great questions of metaphysics.

Freedom of the will, or transcendental freedom, is the pivotal concept in this whole metaphysical endeavour. For it is through, and only through, the knowledge that, Kant claims, we possess of this freedom that he thinks we shall be able to prove the immortality of the soul and the existence of God. Our *knowledge* of transcendental freedom? How so, given what was said in the *First Critique* about the impossibility of using theoretical reason to gain knowledge of anything that transcends the world of the senses? This is where Kant's moral philosophy comes in. By analysing our concept of duty, or moral obligation, he will maintain not only that moral agency presupposes transcendental freedom, but that its existence is *proved* by our moral experience. His proof, whatever else may be said of it, does not conflict with his own strictures on the use of theoretical reason. What it does require, as he well appreciated, is that we view his moral philosophy as an integral part, perhaps the culminating part, of his

Copernican revolution. It seems to me doubtful whether there is much that can be thought of as both original and important in his moral philosophy unless it is placed within that revolution. I hope that this throw-away remark may gain some plausibility in the sequel.

Kant's moral philosophy, like his theory of knowledge, is best approached as a reaction to former positions, and, in particular, to Hume's. For Book I of the *Critique of Practical Reason*, entitled the 'Analytic of Pure Practical Reason' (much the largest part of the whole work), is above all a critique of the claim that only sensuous desires can influence the will. This claim is one of the corner-stones of the empiricist theory of morals – of which Hume's theory is the most distinguished example.

It may be objected that although Kant is opposed to the empiricist theory of morals, he is equally opposed to *traditional* rationalist theories. The most notable of these sought to place the supreme object and foundation of morality either in the will of God or in the realization of our own perfection. Now it is quite true that Kant does see himself as opposing, and as opposing in the Analytic of Pure Practical Reason, traditional rationalist theories. But this is not incompatible with holding that the Analytic is, before anything else, an attack on the claim that only sensuous desires can influence the will. For he makes it abundantly clear throughout, and most conspicuously in the chapter entitled 'On the concept of an object of pure practical reason' (*CPractR*, Bk I, ch. II), that he thinks that *all* ethical theories other than his own must appeal, either explicitly or implicitly, to sensuous desires and feelings. Say, for instance, that the will of God is taken as the supreme object and foundation of morality. How can an agent be motivated to obey God's commands? Only, according to the Kantian view, through the agent's sensuous desire to receive his rewards or to avoid his punishments. Consequently, the theory that it is God's will which is the supreme object and basis of morality has implicitly appealed to one's own pleasure or avoidance of pain in order to ground obligation (since sensuous desires are always the product of the consciousness of one's own pleasure or pain, on the Kantian view). However much traditional rationalist theories may allege that reason is the sole foundation of morality, conceived as a practical discipline, Kant believes that there must always be a surreptitious resort to our sensible, and so to our non-rational, nature. As he sees it, then, any moral theory which attempts to found morality on some supreme object – whether it be a traditional rationalist one, like the will of God, or an empiricist one, like the happiness of others –

inevitably appeals to the agent's sensuous desires in order to motivate his will.

The Humean Theory of Morals

Hume held, in contrast not only to traditional rationalist claims but, as we shall see, to Kant's own highly original rationalist position, two central theses concerning the foundation of morality. He held, first, that reason does not determine what the *content* of our duties is ('Moral distinctions [are] not derived from reason'); and, second, that reason cannot *motivate* the will ('reason alone can never be a motive to any action of the will').

Rather than immediately confronting the first Humean thesis (that reason does not determine the content of our duties), Kant sets out to respond to the second (that reason alone cannot motivate the will). In his response to the second thesis, he produces a moral principle, *the moral law*, which, he maintains, is both the motivating principle of pure reason, i.e. of reason alone, and which does, at the same time, fundamentally determine our duties.

But how does Hume himself account for our practice of morality, if not on the basis of reason alone? In common with earlier empiricist moral philosophers, most conspicuously Francis Hutcheson, he explicitly sets out to explain both our capacity to judge morally and our capacity to act morally primarily, though not exclusively, in terms of our feelings of pleasure and pain. Thus, on the question of distinguishing between virtuous and vicious actions or characters – i.e. on the question of *making* moral distinctions – the Humean theory affirms that it is feelings (or sentiments) of pleasure or pain, aroused in contemplating actions and characters, which enable us to make these distinctions. Of course, not all pleasing or painful sensations, which may be produced by such contemplation, count for Hume as *moral* feelings. But he does hold that moral distinctions are dependent on a subset of these feelings. Moreover, for Hume, feelings of pleasure and pain can alone activate our desires (our 'sensuous' or 'pathological' desires, as Kant calls them); and it is our desires, so produced, that always provide *the motivating force* for action.

On this empiricist theory, therefore, the explanation of how it is that our judgments of virtue or vice can motivate is that, in the very making of these moral distinctions, certain of our sentiments are intrinsically involved; and these particular sentiments, in turn, lead to the production of corresponding desires, and, through these desires (assuming that there are no stronger countervailing desires), to appropriate action.

Has reason, then, no part to play in Hume's moral theory? Certainly it has, and in two ways. First, our reason can show us the likely *consequences* of certain actions or ways of life; and it thereby plays a major part in helping us to determine the content of our long-term ends or objectives, whether in the moral sphere or outside it. Still, whether we denominate any possible objective as *good* or *bad* – and hence as providing us with a motive to action – is never, according to Hume, decided by the exercise of reason. It is our sentiments that enable us to make this decision, after the circumstances have been found out by reason. Second, our reason needs to be employed to show us the best *means* to some end. And in this case, we can even talk, as Hume admits, of certain courses of action being 'rational' or 'irrational'. For instance, a course of action may rightly be described as 'irrational' if it is a causally inappropriate way of going about obtaining an end, e.g. drinking salt water in order to quench thirst. None the less, reason, if properly employed, can only show us how best to obtain an end. That we *value* the end (whether from a moral or a non-moral point of view), and so *desire* the best means for gaining it, is not provided by reason, but by feelings of pleasure or pain.

In brief, on the Humean analysis, reason alone can never be practical; that is, it can never motivate the will. Motivation, even in the moral arena, is fundamentally an affair of our non-rational nature: of our naturally produced feelings and desires (where the latter are always conceived as causally dependent on the former).

Now there are a number of consequences, or apparent consequences, of this moral theory. First, no moral principle can be said necessarily to require all human beings, let alone all (possible) rational creatures, to act on that principle. In Kantian terminology, no moral principle can claim to hold with strict universality and necessity. The most that can be claimed is that, *as a matter of fact*, all human beings have the same set of sentiments (aroused by the same type of circumstances), and that there is, accordingly, *contingent* agreement among them as to what morally ought to be done. But there can be no ground for claiming that a moral principle *necessarily* binds *every* human being without exception, provided only that the being has the capacity to motivate itself by means of the recognition of rules – provided only, in other words, that it has *a will*. A being is said by Kant to possess a will *in so far as that being is capable of acting on the consciousness of rules;*

and, hence, through the employment of reason (CPractR, 5:32). Second, even assuming that all human beings do in fact possess the same set of sentiments, it is noticeable that these sentiments are very variable in their strengths, not only *between* individuals, but even, in many cases, within the *same* individual at different times. The upshot is that there would be a strong element of *luck* about whether a particular individual's moral sentiments happened to be sufficiently strong and unwavering to motivate the will on appropriate occasions.

I think that both of these consequences would have been acknowledged by Hume. But there is a third consequence that Kant sought to draw from the empiricist theory of morality which Hume would not, perhaps, so readily have conceded (and which, undoubtedly, many commentators would oppose attributing to him). This is that all our moral obligations, all our duties, have, as the ground of their motivation, our own pleasure or happiness and are, therefore, self-interested. None the less, despite passages where Hume may seem to suggest otherwise, there is powerful textual evidence that he did accept this third consequence. Thus, in the concluding chapter of his *Enquiry concerning the Principles of Morals* (London, 1751), he asks what ground there could be for interesting ourselves in moral obligation; and he suggests that performing our duties is, all things considered, the best means for giving us – the persons whose duties they are – the greatest personal happiness:

> Having explained the moral *approbation* attending merit or virtue, there remains nothing but briefly to consider our interested *obligation* to it, and to enquire, whether every man, who has any regard to his own happiness and welfare, will not best find his account in the practice of every moral duty. . . . And, indeed, to drop all figurative expression, what hopes can we ever have of engaging mankind to a practice, which we confess full of austerity and rigour? Or what theory of morals can ever serve any useful purpose, unless it can show, by a particular detail, that all the duties, which it recommends, are also the true interest of each individual? The peculiar advantage of the foregoing system seems to be, that it furnishes proper mediums for this purpose. (Sect. IX, Part II; italics original)

It is, incidentally, compatible with claiming that the *ground* of obligation is self-interested also to claim that its *object* may be the welfare of others. If the determining ground of your performing a moral obligation is that it will increase your own happiness, then the motive is, in Kantian terminology, self-interested *even though* the object of that moral obligation is e.g. the helping of others in distress (see *CPractR*, 5:34).

On the basis of these three consequences – as well as another which will be discussed later – Kant rejected the empiricist theory as providing a satisfactory elucidation of our concept of duty or moral obligation. He held that if we examine that concept, we shall find that, contrary to this theory, we do think (1) that moral obligation applies *without possible exception* to all (finite) rational beings in possession of a will; (2) that it is conceived as applying to them *whatever* the strengths of their sensuous impulses may be; and (3) that in so far as any rational being is acting for the sake of duty, that action *cannot* be performed from the motive of personal happiness or self-interest.

Kant's Opposing Strategy (the Analytic of Pure Practical Reason)

In opposition to the empiricist theory, Kant begins by asking what a subjective principle of action – what he also calls 'a maxim' – would be like if it *were* also fit to stand as a practical law; that is, if it *were* capable, at the same time, of applying necessarily to all rational beings in possession of a will.

A subjective principle or rule of action is a practical principle that the subject is personally considering acting upon. Since it is a principle, it specifies a general recipe for action (though only for the subject); and when fully spelled out, it normally contains not merely a description of the action contemplated, but the reason for it as well, e.g. 'I shall give aid to those in distress, in order to relieve their suffering', or 'I shall make lying promises, whenever it will help me out of difficulties.' Now the question is: Under what conditions could a subjective principle of action also stand as a practical law? In the first place, it is clear that the principle, if it is to be adopted as a practical law, could not motivate in virtue of its content stimulating our sentiments, since this would imply that the principle could *not* hold with necessity or strict universality. As we have already noted, it is a *contingent* truth, if it is a truth at all, that all human beings, let alone all rational creatures, share the same sentiments. Accordingly, the principle, when held also as a practical law, could not owe its motivational force to any *material* features referred to in the principle. For the *matter* or *content* of a principle, where it does motivate, motivates by appealing to our sentiments (on this, Hume and Kant are agreed). On the other hand, what is concerned with the mere *form* of any principle of action

– with whether it is, for instance, singular or universal, hypothetical or categorical – can have no direct motivational effect upon our *sensuous* nature. This is, indeed, a point upon which Hume had particularly insisted. For, he maintained, what is concerned with a principle's form can only be determined by *reason*; and the exercise of reason, he insists, never 'takes possession of the heart' – never by itself stimulates our sentiments – and cannot, therefore, generate a desire or an aversion. In two important respects, Kant agrees. He agrees that the form of a principle can be determined only by reason, and he agrees that reason cannot *by itself* produce any feeling. But he does not conclude, as does Hume, that reason alone can never motivate.

Instead, he points out that since a practical law cannot motivate in virtue of its matter or content (if it did, the 'law' could not hold with necessity or strict universality), it can do so only in virtue of its form. But, Kant urges, not all subjective principles of action, not all maxims, have a form that fits them for *universal* application. For instance, a maxim like 'I shall make a lying promise whenever it will extricate me from difficulties' would, he claims, destroy itself if it were accepted as a rule holding for all rational beings in possession of a will: when I attempt to apply my own maxim in concrete cases, I find that the universal rule, which is generated from the maxim, makes it impossible for the maxim to be fulfilled. (We shall see *why* he holds this in a moment.) Only a maxim that can be consistently conceived or willed as holding for *all* rational agents can hold as a (strictly) universal principle of action – that is, as a practical *law*. But, as we noted above, the mere *form* of a principle can have no direct motivational effect upon our sensuous nature. Indeed, as an object of *reason* alone, the universal form of a law cannot be considered as an object of the senses, as an appearance, *at all*. Hence, if a practical law as such – that is, a practical law merely in virtue of its universal form – is the sole initiating ground of the will, it follows that the will cannot then be subject to the law of natural causality. For that law, as the *First Critique* has shown, applies only to what is a possible object of the senses; and the universal form of a practical law is an object *not* of the senses, but of reason.

Accordingly, *if* the will is determined solely by the universal form of a practical law, and hence through reason alone, it must be a free will. For it is here determined in its operation *independently* of anything among the appearances (e.g. a sensuous desire). As such, the will originates an action *spontaneously* precisely because there is nothing in the appearances, which precedes the operation of reason, through which the will is determined. Reason, in such a case, motivates the will *of itself*. In Kant's terminology, where the will does act spontaneously – and thus solely on the basis of the universal form of a practical law – it is said to be *transcendentally free*.

Equally, *if* the will is transcendentally free, it can only have as the law of its operation the universal form of a practical law. A free will cannot be determined to act by means of the matter (or content) of any practical law, since, if it were so determined, it would be dependent on *empirical* conditions, and therefore not transcendentally free: it would, rather, be subject to the law of natural causality. But once the content of a practical law is discounted, nothing remains to determine the will but the mere *universal form* of the law. This alone can be its governing principle. Even a free will must act according to a law: a will that is law*less* is not a free will – not one that can be responsible for anything – but one that cannot be thought of as *producing* anything at all.

From these considerations, Kant concludes that a will that is transcendentally free and a will that is determined by a practical law mutually imply one another (*CPract R*, 5:29). If the will is free, then it must be determined to act by the mere universal form of a practical law; and if the will is determined to act merely through the universal form of a practical law, then it must be a free will.

Yet, despite this mutual implication holding between a will that is free and a will that is determined by the mere form of a practical law, we are not in a position to infer the will's capacity to be so determined from any *prior* knowledge of its transcendental freedom. For no (theoretical) experience, no sensible knowledge of what happens in the spatio-temporal world, can divulge our transcendental freedom to us. It cannot, because everything that is given in experience must, as an appearance or object of the senses, fall under the law of natural causality. Moreover, our conceptual grasp of what is entailed by a transcendentally free will is only negative. It tells us only that such a will cannot be determined to act by anything in nature. We do not learn from this negative concept of transcendental freedom what it is like *positively* to will freely, or whether we actually *possess* such a will.

In sum, we cannot discover that we have the capacity to motivate ourselves by means of the mere form of a practical law (and hence by reason alone) through any antecedent knowledge that we possess transcendental freedom. It is instead, Kant claims, the other way round: it is our consciousness of the necessity of acting only on practical laws as such that first gives rise to the recognition of our freedom. This consciousness comes about when we devise for ourselves a subjective principle of action (a maxim). He thinks that whenever, in formulating a subjective principle, we ask ourselves whether the maxim of our action is one that it is morally right or lawful for us to perform, we always determine our answer by seeing whether the maxim can hold as a universal law. When, by the use of reason, we test our maxim in this way, we become immediately conscious that we *ought* only to act on the maxim if it can stand as a universal, and hence as a practical, law.

The examples that are offered in the *Second Critique* to illustrate how the universalizing test determines our duties are really too perfunctory to be helpful. Fortunately, a rather fuller treatment is provided in the earlier *Groundwork of the Metaphysic of Morals*; and we shall briefly examine two of the examples. Take the maxim that in order to borrow money, when I find myself in financial difficulty, I shall make a lying promise to repay the money borrowed. ('A lying promise' is understood here to mean 'a promise that I intend not to honour'.) What has to be done, in order to see whether my maxim opposes duty or conforms to it, is to ask myself whether I can will it in the form of a universal law, i.e. as a rule that holds not only for myself but for all rational beings. Kant thinks that I cannot: if, in obedience to the universal law, everyone accepts that it is permissible to make a lying promise, my own maxim would be defeated because no such promises could be taken as genuine. The very attempt to conceive of my maxim in the form of a universal law would make it impossible to suppose that my so-called promise would be believed. For each rational being is not only permitted to act on the maxim himself, he would *also* know that it is a maxim that everyone else is permitted to act on – since we are assuming that each of us is complying with the rule that everyone may make a lying promise to repay when in financial difficulty. Hence, provided others realize the circumstances under which my promise to repay is made, viz. that I am in financial difficulty, it is impossible to suppose that they would take my expression of intention to repay as genuine. It is, after all, *permitted* that I make the lying promise, and it is here in my perceived *self-interest* to do so (this latter point is specifically written into the example). It follows, therefore, that other rational beings can be certain that the promise I make is a lying one. For, on the Kantian view of motivation, finite rational beings always act, and are always taken to act, in their perceived self-interest, unless controlled by their sense of duty.

Another type of case is illustrated by the example of a comfortably situated agent who adopts the maxim not to help those whom he can relieve from distress, on the ground that the good or bad fortune of others is none of his business. This maxim, unlike the maxim in the first example, can be consistently *conceived* as a universal law; but it cannot, Kant argues, be consistently *willed* as such. For if the agent is to test the consistency of his maxim, when transformed into a universal law, he has to consider those possible states of affairs where he finds *himself* in distress and where there are others in a position to help him. This point is made clear in the Preface to the *Groundwork*: 'the ground of obligation . . . must not be sought in the nature of the human being or in the circumstances of the world in which he is placed' (4:389). (In order to grasp Kant's line of argument, both here and more generally in his ethical writings, it is vital not to confuse the object with the ground of obligation. The *object* of a duty may refer to the nature of human beings, e.g. to their need for happiness, and/or to their particular circumstances, e.g. to their situation of distress. But the *ground* of moral motivation must depend only upon whether the given maxim can be conceived or willed as a universal law.) Accordingly, when the comfortably situated agent attempts to universalize his maxim, it transpires that he cannot consistently will it as a universal law. As a finite rational being, he necessarily has needs (in particular, the need for happiness and the avoidance of pain); consequently, in a condition of distress, he requires – and so, by means of his reason, he wills – the assistance of others. Yet, by universalizing his original maxim, he has willed that every rational being complies with the rule that no one is to help those in distress, even when in a position to do so. Accordingly, the agent, by his own act of universalizing, has willed that no one comes to his aid, even though he also wills that someone does.

Despite the substantial amount of criticism that these two examples have attracted, it does seem to me that, given his premisses, Kant has argued validly in both cases.

When, in the attempt to universalize a maxim, it is found either that the maxim cannot consistently be conceived as a practical law (as Kant claims of the first example) or cannot consistently be willed as such (as he claims of the second), the action enjoined in the maxim is morally *prohibited*, and the opposite action is a *duty*. So, in the two examples, the universalizing test shows that a promise, made in order to extricate oneself from difficulty, ought only to be given when there is the intention to honour it, and that one ought to offer help to those in distress when in a position to do so. (If no inconsistency results from attempting to universalize both the maxim and its opposite, the action enjoined by the maxim is morally *permitted*.) It must be emphasized, however, that Kant's suggestion is not that whenever we recognize that we morally ought or ought not to act on a given maxim, we are always *aware* of having gone through a process of testing whether our proposed maxim can hold as a universal law. Clearly that would be an implausible claim, as he remarks himself (see *Groundwork*, Sect. I; 4:403–4). His point is, rather, that if we analyse our recognition of duties and moral prohibitions (as well as moral permissions), we shall find that such recognition always arises from our explicitly or implicitly asking ourselves whether our maxim can stand as a universal law.

It is, Kant insists, *a fact of reason* – a datum of which pure reason makes us immediately conscious – that we acknowledge the unconditional necessity of acting only on maxims that can stand as universal laws. We acknowledge, in other words, that whatever our sensuous desires may urge, we ought to act only on maxims that can be willed as practical laws. Consequently, the universal form of a practical law is recognized by us as the *supreme* or *overriding* condition on the will. What Kant calls *the moral law*, or *the fundamental law of pure practical reason*, expresses the rule always to act on maxims in virtue of their capacity to be willed as practical laws. He gives several versions of the moral law, but his formulation in the *Second Critique* runs: 'So act that the maxim of your will could always hold at the same time as a principle in the giving of universal law' (5:30).

There are two related reasons why he calls our consciousness of the overriding requirement to obey the moral law *a fact of reason*: (a) because this consciousness is not *deduced* by us from some other item of knowledge, but is instead an *immediate datum* (once we ask ourselves whether our maxim can be willed as a universal law); and (b) since we acknowledge the binding force of a maxim in virtue of its capacity to be willed universally, our consciousness of its necessity must arise not in virtue of the maxim's *content* but in virtue of its *form*; and hence it must be our *reason* that makes us immediately conscious of the necessity of obeying the moral law.

But why does Kant suppose that it is our consciousness of the necessity of acting for the sake of the moral law that first discloses our transcendental freedom to us? The answer is that in acknowledging, as he is adamant that we do, the overriding requirement of acting on unconditional practical principles, we thereby admit that we have the capacity so to act. We can only be conscious that we *ought* to act for the sake of the moral law provided that we *can* so act. Now since, as he has urged, our consciousness that we ought to obey the moral law arises from reason alone, it follows that reason alone can motivate the will. In short, our recognition of duty shows us that reason alone can be practical, and hence that we can will freely.

> It is therefore the *moral law*, of which we become immediately conscious (as soon as we draw up maxims of the will for ourselves), that *first* offers itself to us and, inasmuch as reason presents it as a determining ground not to be outweighed by any sensible conditions and indeed quite independent of them, leads directly to the concept of freedom. . . . [Each of us] judges, therefore, that he can do something because he is aware that he ought to do it and cognizes freedom within him, which, without the moral law, would have remained unknown to him. (CPractR, 5: 29–30; italics original)

Where reason alone motivates the will, there exists what Kant calls *autonomy* of the will. Here the will is not only motivated to act independently of anything empirical (anything in the appearances); it is also determined by a law of reason's *own* devising, i.e. by the mere universal form of a practical law. So, in the case of autonomy, the will is motivated by the *self-legislation* of reason. This is to be contrasted with *heteronomy* of the will, where the motivation comes from naturally produced feelings and desires, and reason merely devises a rule for obtaining the desired object. Here, the (naturally produced) desires *precede* reason's formulation of a rule of action, and are the determining ground of the will. Only autonomy of the will produces actions that have moral worth, since only in this case is conformity of one's maxims to the moral law the sole motivating ground of the actions. Heteronomy of the will is opposed to the production of morally commendable actions because, even when the acts produced do accord with duty, the will's motivation comes not from the mere conformity of one's maxims to the moral law – and so not through reason alone – but from naturally produced desires.

Review of the Kantian and Humean Moral Systems

In terms of the distinction between autonomy and heteronomy of the will, let us review some of the differences, at least as Kant sees them, between his own, rationalist view of morality and the Humean, empiricist view.

On the Kantian view, all ethical principles, all moral ought judgments, are *categorical* imperatives. They arise immediately from the agent's use of reason (in determining whether his proposed maxims can stand as universal laws), and they state what an agent ought to do *whatever* his naturally produced, sensuous desires may urge. Consequently, our acknowledgement of an action as a duty, as morally binding upon the will, is not conditional upon any naturally produced desire preceding the use of reason and determining the will. On the contrary, our recognition of duty must arise independently of anything empirical; it must arise solely through the exercise of pure reason. All ethical principles, therefore, in so far as they are acted upon for the sake of duty, motivate through *autonomy of the will*.

On the Humean view, all practical principles, all ought judgments – including moral ones – are *hypothetical* imperatives. They arise as the result of naturally produced desires, and they state what an agent ought to do *if*, or *given*, he has these desires. The desires themselves result from the perceived pleasure (or avoidance of pain) that the attainment of certain ends arouses in the agent. Reason is employed only to discover the best means for obtaining these desired ends. Consequently, our acknowledgement of an action as a duty, as morally binding upon the will, is always conditional upon the occurrence of a naturally produced desire; and the role of reason, even with regard to moral motivation, is merely to work out what we ought to do – what is morally obligatory – in order to attain the object of the desire. On the Humean view, therefore, all ethical principles, even if they are acted upon for the sake of duty, motivate through *heteronomy of the will*.

When Hume says that 'reason is, and ought only to be, the slave of the passions, and can never pretend to any other office than to serve and obey them' (*Treatise*, Book II, Part III, Sect. III), he is giving forceful statement to his claim that every practical principle, in so far as an agent accepts it as binding upon his own will, depends for its motivational power upon the stimulation of his passions (felt as desires). Reason alone can never determine the will; its role in the production of action is limited to calculating how best to obtain the objects of our passions.

Now, as Kant realized, Hume maintained that only certain of our passions lie at the basis of our formation of specifically *moral* conceptions. The passions of benevolence and sympathy play key, though not exclusive, roles here. And Hume develops a sophisticated theory of how, on the basis of such 'other-regarding' passions, human beings together come to accept certain courses of action as morally binding upon them. None the less, it remains the case, even at the end of this elaborate theoretical development, that, for each of us, our acknowledgement of any course of action as morally obligatory depends on our belief that the action commanded will achieve certain of our own desired ends. It remains the case, in other words, that moral motivation is heteronomous: certain naturally produced desires must precede the operation of reason and provide the impetus to the will. The role of reason is still confined to determining how best to achieve the objects of (certain of) our naturally produced desires.

A point, however, that is sometimes overlooked, especially by those in the Kantian tradition (though not by Kant himself), is that an empiricist theory of morals is able to affirm that moral obligations apply to all human beings under the same circumstances. Of course, they cannot be held to apply, as they do on Kant's theory, with *strict* universality and necessity to all human beings (still less, to all possible finite rational beings). On the contrary, for an empiricist, the universal application of moral obligations is dependent upon experience, viz. upon the (supposed) contingent truth that human beings share sufficiently similar affective natures. As Hume himself claims, there is enough uniformity in human nature to allow for a *standard of morals* to exist.[1] It is not, as some writers have implied, a peculiar virtue of a *Kantian* moral system that its concept of moral obligation applies to every human being under the same circumstances. Moral judgments for an empiricist can be – and for Hume actually are – *universalizable* with respect to human beings (albeit the universality implied can be only *comparative*, not strict, since it rests on a contingent, rather than an a priori, basis). The really significant difference between the two systems concerns the *motivation* of moral obligations – whether it arises through reason and transcendental freedom (the Kantian system) or through sentiment and natural determination (the Humean system) – and not with the *generality* with which these obligations are conceived as applying to human beings.

Kant's Antipathy to the Humean Moral System

There is no doubt that Hume's ethical theory was seen by Kant as *demeaning* morality – and, *a fortiori*, human beings – even granting that the naturally produced desires (or passions) underpinning our moral obligations are wholly other-regarding with respect to their objects, as

---

[1] See *An Enquiry concerning the Principles of Morals*, Sect. IX, Part I, and 'Of the Standard of Taste', in *Essays Moral, Political and Literary* (London, 1775).

with benevolence and sympathy. There is a passage in the Dialectic of the *Second Critique* which seems to me to illustrate very well his antipathy to the Humean, empiricist system (Kant here employs the term 'inclination' to refer to what Hume usually calls a 'passion'):

> [T]he inclinations change, grow with the indulgence one allows them, and always leave behind a still greater void than one had thought to fill. Hence they are always *burdensome* to a rational being, and though he cannot lay them aside, they wrest from him the wish to be rid of them. Even an inclination to what conforms with duty (e.g., to beneficence) can indeed greatly facilitate the effectiveness of *moral* maxims but cannot produce any. Inclination is blind and servile, whether it is kindly or not; and when morality is in question, reason must not play the part of mere guardian to inclination but, disregarding it altogether, must attend solely to its own interest as pure practical reason. Even this feeling of compassion and tender sympathy, if it precedes consideration of what is duty and becomes the determining ground [of the will], is itself burdensome to right-thinking persons, brings their considered maxims into confusion, and produces the wish to be free from them and subject to lawgiving reason alone. (*CPractR*, 5:118; italics original)

We earlier noted some of the grounds on which Kant took exception to the Humean moral system: (1) that no duty can be held necessarily to bind all human beings, let alone all finite rational beings; (2) that sentiments and inclinations are variable in their strengths, even within the same individual; and (3) that the ground of our pursuance of duty, or moral obligation, is always self-interested. But the chief ground to which Kant took exception is brought out in the passage just quoted. It is that motivation through heteronomy of the will, if it should be the *only* way in which the will could operate, entails that all our actions are necessarily the product of sensuous feelings and desires. Accordingly, far from any of our actions arising or, at any rate, being capable of arising from our own *self*-legislating will (and hence solely through pure reason), it must follow that the will is inevitably determined by states or events which precede any exercise of reason. Hence, freedom of the will, as Kant understands that notion, would not obtain, since the will could not operate *spontaneously*; and no action could arise through autonomy of the will. On the contrary, human beings would merely be highly complicated mechanisms, whose decisions and actions were the result of naturally produced phenomena which pre-exist, and render necessary, the operation of their wills.

This picture of human motivation, and more particularly of moral motivation, Kant saw as the unavoidable consequence of the empiricist theory of morals. Since that theory rules out any capacity for our wills to operate through transcendental freedom, and hence autonomously, he regarded the theory as denying to human beings any intrinsic worth. It is for this reason, above all, that Kant rejected the Humean theory. The point needs to be emphasized, because of the contentiousness of Kant's claim that sensuous motivation, at least in so far as it can be a ground of (hypothetical) obligation, is always *self-interested* (although, as I have indicated, this view seems to have been shared by Hume). Even if it is allowed that there can be *altruistically* grounded hypothetical obligations, these obligations cannot arise from autonomy of the will. Hence the will is still inevitably determined by preceding sensuous impulses (whether self-interested or altruistic), and cannot, therefore, possess transcendental freedom. As mere mechanisms – and so lacking the capacity to exercise self-legislating acts of will – our existence could have no true dignity. Or so, at least, Kant sees it.

Hume, of course, did not deny that human beings must be free in order to be responsible. But he did deny that we possess *transcendental* freedom, arguing that the most that we can understand by 'freedom' is not only entirely *compatible* with the will itself being determined by prior causes (sensuous desires), but positively *requires* it. If Hume is right, if it is impossible for us justifiably to mean more by 'freedom of the will' than can be implied by this type of compatibilist account, then however much it may be admitted that Kant has correctly elucidated our present concept of duty or moral obligation, it must none the less be confessed that this concept is *inapplicable* to us. For, as Kant explicitly maintains, the very possibility of the moral law applying to us requires transcendental freedom: 'without this freedom . . . which alone is practical a priori, no moral law is possible and no imputation in accordance with it' (CPractR, 5:97).

So if it is true that transcendental freedom is impossible (and Kant's analysis of moral obligation is largely correct), it follows that our common conception of duty must be rejected; and Hume's conception of our moral obligations as a system of hypothetical imperatives, based on other-regarding passions like benevolence and sympathy, will be the most that we can salvage from our notion of morality. The idea that we are conscious of the *unconditional* necessity of obeying the moral law – that our moral obligations are recognized as *categorical* imperatives – will have to be given up as a sheer delusion. Kant may, perhaps, have given an accurate analysis of our present concept of duty; but Hume will have provided us with the only acceptable kind of operative concept of morality. (However, there can be little doubt that Kant himself would not regard the Humean position as giving us even an acceptable *reductive* conception of morality. He holds that, in denying to us autonomy of the will, the Humean position effectively rules out our being moral agents: see *Groundwork*, Section II, final paragraph.)

Clearly, the issue of freedom of the will requires further discussion, and we shall be returning to it. But, in order properly to determine the force of Kant's response to the empiricist, and more particularly the Humean, theory of morals, we need first to outline the place of the feeling of respect in Kant's account of moral motivation.

The Feeling of Respect

From what has been said so far, the reader could certainly be forgiven for supposing that, on Kant's rationalist account, feelings can play no part in *moral* motivation. After all, the moral law is a law of pure practical *reason*. No feeling can *precede* the exercise of reason and provide the motivation of the will, in so far as the ensuing action can have moral worth. If a feeling were to precede the consciousness of the moral law, and be the ground for acting on that law, the will could not then have been determined autonomously, but heteronomously. In such an eventuality, the agent would have acted *in accordance with* the moral law, not *for the sake of* it. (Of course, not all cases of heteronomous action are cases of acting *in accordance with* the moral law: that is only one example of heteronomy.)

Nevertheless, Kant does maintain that there is a specifically *moral feeling* which is the invariable incentive for a genuinely dutiful action. By an 'incentive' he means 'the subjective determining ground of the will of a being whose reason does not by its nature necessarily conform to the objective law [the moral law]' (*CPractR*, 5:72). How can it be consistent with his rationalist ethics to claim that there is, for us, a feeling that acts – indeed, always acts – as the incentive to conformity with the moral law? The answer is that the particular feeling in question arises as the result of pure practical reason overcoming, or at least opposing, our sensuous feelings and desires. In our experience of objects, feelings of pleasure or pain are immediately stimulated by the matter (or content) of these objects; and sensuous desires are thereby first generated for these objects, i.e. prior to any determination of our practical reason. To the extent that we act on maxims so motivated, we are, of course, acting from heteronomy of the will. If, however, reason alone – through consciousness of the moral law – opposes this motivation, it *checks* the impulse of these sensuous feelings and desires upon the will. This is said to give rise to a specifically moral feeling: it is experienced, in the first instance, as a feeling of constraint, in that it thwarts, wholly or partially, our self-love (our natural desire for personal happiness, independent of any moral considerations); but, in the second instance, it is experienced as a feeling of respect or reverence for the moral law, in that our consciousness of the binding force of this law directs us to a purely intelligible realm: a realm where we recognize ourselves as transcendentally free beings who can oppose – even overcome – our sensuously determined nature. It is this moral feeling, when experienced in the form of a *feeling of respect* for the moral law, that always acts as our incentive to genuine moral action.

So the feeling of respect does not *precede* our consciousness of the moral law, but is the effect of it on our existence as phenomenal beings. Although Kant calls the feeling of respect 'this singular feeling', its existence wholly depends upon the action of our rational nature on an *already existing* sensuous impulse. Were we incapable of any sensuous impulses – as is God – we could not be aware of any moral feeling. Reason would, in that eventuality, motivate the will without any rationally produced incentive. As phenomenal beings, however, we are invariably subject to sensuous impulses. Consequently, the moral law always first makes itself known to us in the form of a *constraint* (through opposing these impulses); and this explains why, as imperfectly rational wills, we conceive of the moral law as *obliging* or *necessitating* us, and its deliverances as *duties*. For a perfectly rational will – one that is incapable of acting other than for the sake of the moral law – there could be no question of the law *demanding* respect or of its deliverances being expressed in the form of *ought* judgments. A perfectly rational will *would* always act for the sake of the moral law, since, for such a being (God), there could be no opposition to the will's autonomy. However, in our case (and in the case of any other finite rational wills), the action of pure practical reason always manifests itself in the form of unconditional *ought* judgments.

It is a mistake, then, to suppose that, on Kant's ethics, a feeling can never be the incentive, the determining ground of the will, in so far as the ensuing action can have moral worth. Although it must be possible to think of reason alone as providing the *initial* motivating force on the will whenever an ensuing action has moral worth, it determines that action, in phenomenal beings, *through* opposing their sensuous feelings and desires (themselves aroused by the content, the matter, of empirical objects); and this product of practical reason is made known to us through a feeling of respect for the moral law:

> [A]nything empirical that might slip into our maxims as a determining ground of the will *makes itself known* at once by the feeling of gratification or pain that necessarily attaches to it insofar as it arouses desire, whereas pure practical reason directly *opposes* taking this feeling into its principle as a condition. The dissimilarity of determining grounds (empirical and rational) is made known by this resistance of a practical lawgiving reason to every meddling inclination, by a special kind of *feeling*, which, however, does not precede the lawgiving of practical reason but is instead produced only by it and indeed as a constraint, namely through the feeling of respect such as no human being has for inclination of whatever kind but does have for the law. (*CPractR*, 5:92; italics original)

In sum, at the *phenomenal* level, even moral motivation is always experienced as produced by means of a feeling: a 'special kind' of feeling, the feeling of respect or reverence for the moral law. This feeling has arisen, through the exercise of pure practical reason, from what Kant calls the 'higher faculty' of desire (*CPractR*, 5:22). Sensuous desires, on the other hand, are produced by the feeling of gratification or pain. Consequently, on the Kantian moral system, *all* actions can be said to arise in the phenomenal world from desires or inclinations.[2] Those actions that arise from heteronomy of the will are motivated by *sensuous* desires or inclinations, themselves determined by the feeling of gratification or pain. Those actions that arise from autonomy of the will, or the higher faculty of desire, are first made known to us, as phenomenal beings, by means of the feeling of respect. But this feeling is, in truth, nothing other than pure practical reason thwarting the action of sensuous impulses on the will, thereby allowing us to be conscious of the capacity of our non-sensuous, our rational, nature to overcome our empirically conditioned, or sensuous, nature. To the extent that we act from the feeling of respect (and

---

[2] See *The Metaphysic of Morals*, Introduction, Sect. II (6:211–14), where Kant acknowledges the existence of non-sensuous inclinations or *habitual* non-sensuous desires. He stresses that these inclinations are the effect of practical reason, and not its determining ground (unlike sensuous inclinations (Hume's 'passions'), where the situation is reversed).

thereby from a *non-sensuous* desire or inclination), we are motivating ourselves by means of pure practical reason – and so acting for the sake of the moral law.

It is important to Kant's enterprise that he can convince us of the existence of this feeling of respect for the moral law. In the first place, it was widely accepted, at least among empiricists, that nothing could *oppose* our feelings and desires (in the direction of an action) but *other* feelings and desires. As Hume puts it, in his *Treatise*, summing up a point which he considered perfectly evident: ''Tis impossible reason cou'd have the . . . effect of preventing volition [a sensuous impulse or passion], but by giving an impulse in a contrary direction to our passion' (Book II, Part III, Sect. III). Kant accepts this position: 'every sensible impulse is based on feeling, and the negative effect on feeling . . . is itself feeling. Hence we can see a priori that the moral law, as the determining ground of the will, must by thwarting all our inclinations produce a feeling' (CPractR, 5:72–3). Remember that, for Kant, we – as sensible creatures – always experience a sensuous impulse *before* exercising, or attempting to exercise, our practical reason. So if pure reason is ever to be practical, it must be capable of producing a feeling (granting, as Kant does, that the negative effect on feeling is itself experienced as feeling). Accordingly, if he is to present a plausible case in favour of moral rationalism, he needs to show that motivation by means of felt desires and inclinations is compatible with the exercise of pure practical reason. His account of the feeling of respect for the moral law is intended to do just that. In the second place, he clearly recognizes that we normally *are* aware of experiencing a feeling when we take ourselves to be acting for the sake of duty or to be witnessing others doing so. A theory which held that moral feeling plays no genuine, central role in our practical life would be implausible – especially when we consider the actions of many ordinary people, for whose moral probity Kant often expresses the highest respect (see e.g. CPractR, 5:76–7).

No Deduction of the Moral Law: Instead, a Proof of our Transcendental Freedom

Kant's strategy has been to show what a practical principle would be like if it were a practical law. He shows that since, as a law, it has to hold for all rational beings, it must motivate solely on the basis of its universal form. Hence, the will must here be determined to act by reason alone. He maintains, further, that we are conscious that practical laws, unconditional practical principles, impose an overriding requirement upon us. When we formulate for ourselves a maxim, or subjective principle of action, and ask ourselves whether it is right so to act, we always determine the answer by seeing if the maxim can stand as a universal law; and in so doing, we are immediately conscious of the requirement, the necessity, of acting only on a maxim that can stand as a universal law. This consciousness of the binding force of the moral law Kant calls *a fact of reason*. The moral law, or the fundamental law of pure practical reason, simply articulates the rule to act so that the maxim of our action can always at the same time stand as a principle of universal legislation.

But can we explain *how* this fact of reason is possible, i.e. *how* it is possible for us to be conscious of the necessity of always acting for the sake of the moral law? In asking for an *explanation* for our acknowledgement of the moral law's binding force upon us, Kant is asking for an explanation which is, at the same time, a *justification* of that acknowledgement. He thinks that no such explanation can be given. It is a fundamental datum, provided by our reason, that we are conscious of the moral law's binding force upon us. We cannot, for instance, explain our experience of its unconditional necessity from previously acquired knowledge that we possess transcendental freedom. Certainly, if we *assume* that our will is free, we can provide an explanation of our consciousness of the moral law's necessity. Since the moral law is the law of an autonomous will, it would be self-contradictory to think of ourselves as autonomous while yet denying that the moral law applies to us. Moreover, because from the phenomenal side of our nature we are invariably subject to sensuous impulses, it follows that we must always experience the moral law as *obliging* or *necessitating* our will, rather than, as with a perfectly rational will, merely expressing how the will *would* always operate. (This last point was discussed in the previous section.) On the assumption, then, that we are correct to think of ourselves as acting freely, we can give an explanation of our consciousness of the moral law's necessity. However, as Kant has already insisted, we possess no positive knowledge of our freedom *independently* of this very consciousness. We cannot, therefore, furnish a non-circular explanation of our acknowledgement of the binding force of the moral law from the knowledge of ourselves as transcendentally free.

In this regard, there is a significant difference between the moral law and the laws of nature. For example, in the case of the natural law of causality, we *are* in a position to explain our recognition of the law's necessity: viz. by showing that it makes our experience of succession possible. With causality, however, our experience of succession is *already* given: what we need to show is that the experience is possible only in so far as the natural law of causality can be applied to the appearances. In other words, the ability to explain our recognition of the causal law's necessity depends on proving that our admitted experience of succession is possible only *through* the application of the causal law. This proof is found in the Second Analogy of the *First Critique*. But we cannot explain our recognition of the necessity of obeying the moral law by reference to something that is *already* given (freedom of the will). Indeed, it is precisely our prior acknowledgement of the necessity of obeying the moral law that enables us to prove the reality of freedom, as we shall see. So whereas, with theoretical reason, what is first given is the experience of succession (by means of which we can explain our recognition of the natural law of causality), with practical reason, what has first to be given is our recognition of the necessity of obeying the moral law (by means of which we can prove the reality of freedom). In the case of our recognition of the moral law's necessity, there is nothing previously given *through which* that recognition can be explained. That is why Kant concludes that we cannot provide a deduction of the moral law (see *CPractR*, 5:46 and 5:93).

At the same time, he does think that the moral law can fulfil a function that is an adequate *substitute* for its own justification: it can be used to prove the reality of our transcendental freedom. The *First Critique* has shown that, in order to avoid a contradiction into which our theoretical reason would otherwise fall, we must be able to assume that transcendental freedom is at least logically possible. Such an assumption, it was there argued, can indeed be upheld provided we distinguish between the world of experience (the phenomenal world) and the supersensible world (the noumenal world). We considered the argument for the logical possibility of our transcendental freedom in our discussion of the Third Antinomy, and Kant offers substantially the same argument in the *Second Critique* (5:93–100). However, since everything in experience must be thought of as governed by the laws of nature, all that can be disclosed of a free acting cause by means of our theoretical reason (which can properly concern itself only with sensible knowledge and its possibility) is merely *negative*: viz. that a free acting cause must be able to give rise to events without itself requiring any prior cause. Still, once it has been shown that, so far as concerns our *theoretical* reason, there is nothing self-contradictory in our possession of transcendental freedom, Kant believes that we can confidently appeal to our *practical* reason – viz. to our clear consciousness of the unconditional necessity of obeying the moral law – as legitimately allowing us to affirm the reality of our freedom. While our practical reason cannot be employed to gain knowledge in the theoretical realm, our consciousness of the binding force of the moral law must be allowed to prove the reality of our freedom in the practical sphere.

Thus, our consciousness of the moral law, as the supreme practical principle of our reason, both furnishes us with the *positive* concept of freedom – by showing us the law of its operation – and, at the same time, proves to us the *reality*, not merely the logical possibility, of freedom. It therefore converts a required (but unproved) assumption of our theoretical reason – viz. the existence of a free acting cause in the supersensible world – into an objective reality. Furthermore, the human being is also now *positively* defined as a noumenon in respect of its causality. (This additional, positive consequence is crucial for Kant's later endeavour to prove the immortality of the soul and the existence of God.) The capacity of the moral law to prove the objective reality of a required, but merely assumed, concept of theoretical reason (transcendental freedom), and therewith to determine, at least in part, our existence as supersensible beings, is regarded by Kant as a 'credential' for the moral law that can reasonably take the place of its deduction.

How impressive is this substitute for a deduction of the moral law? I think that it is forceful, once it is allowed – as Kant argues, in both the *First* and *Second Critiques*, that it should be allowed – that theoretical reason is able to demonstrate that, with the phenomena/noumena distinction in place, there can be no *conflict* between the determinism of nature and our possessing transcendental freedom. On that presumption, it is reasonable to employ our acknowledgement of the moral law's necessity to prove the objective reality of a required, but unproved, concept of theoretical reason, viz. the existence of transcendental freedom. Such a 'credential' for the moral law does seem a legitimate substitute for a formal proof of its validity, given Kant's emphatic claim that our practice plainly testifies to our consciousness of the law's unconditional necessity.

Can Reason Alone be Practical? Hume versus Kant

Hume maintains that reason alone cannot motivate the will. As we have seen, Kant maintains that it can. In the light of our discussion so far, let us see how Kant's rationalist moral system can deal with Hume's attack.

Hume's denial that reason alone can be practical rests substantially on three grounds. First, our perception of the *content* (or *matter*) of an experience or judgment always appeals to the sentiments, if that content is to motivate at all; reason here plays no initiating role in motivating the will. Kant agrees with this first claim. Second, we do not find that what is the proper object of pure reason (the *form* of a judgment) ever in fact motivates us – or, indeed, ever obliges us to act. Hume is here appealing to our *consciousness*: are we conscious of any motivating force on the will when we consider the form of any judgment? He believes that, as a matter of fact, we are not. Third, if we reflect on the issue at a theoretical level, it really seems inconceivable that our acknowledgement of any duty might be *deduced* from judgments that are based solely on reason. It is this third consideration that is traditionally taken to be the most powerful. Despite its fame, Hume's actual wording is worth quoting in the present context:

> For as this *ought* or *ought not* expresses some new relation or affirmation, 'tis necessary that it shou'd be observ'd and explain'd; and at the same time that a reason should be given, for what seems altogether inconceivable, how this new relation can be a deduction from others, which are entirely different from it. But as authors do not commonly use this precaution, I shall presume to recommend it to the readers; and am persuaded, that this small attention wou'd subvert all the vulgar systems of morality, and let us see, that the distinction of vice and virtue is not founded merely on the relation of objects, nor is perceiv'd by reason. (*Treatise* (London, 1740), Book III, Part I, Sect. I; italics original)

It has not, I think, been sufficiently appreciated, if it has been appreciated at all, that the substance of this passage, in which Hume demands both an explanation of the force – the necessity – affirmed by moral *ought* judgments and, equally, an a priori justification – a deduction – of these judgments, is addressed by Kant in the *Critique of Practical Reason*. Yet, unlike his well-known reply to Hume's causal scepticism, Kant quite explicitly seeks neither to explain the necessity affirmed by our moral *ought* judgments by reference to what is already given (as he *does* seek to explain the necessity affirmed by the natural law of causality by reference to what is already given, viz. our experience of succession) nor to show that we can derive the moral law from other judgments that are already known (which, he thinks, could be achieved *if* we already knew that our will is free). In fact, he agrees with Hume that it is indeed impossible to *explain* the necessity to act affirmed by moral *ought* judgments or to *deduce* the moral law from what we already know. And, as we have noted, Kant believes that we can even see why we should not even *expect* to be able to produce any such explanation or deduction.

But how, in that case, can he be thought of as providing an *answer* to Hume's doubts about deducing an *ought* from an *is*? He shows, or seeks to show, that we *are* conscious of the motivating power of pure reason in just one instance: our acknowledgement of the binding force of the moral law, when it is confronted with sensuously motivated maxims, proves that we *do* recognize that pure reason can motivate the will. Since Hume did not take himself to be sceptical about the existence of morality and duty, it follows that, if Kant is correct in holding that we are genuinely conscious of the overriding force of the moral law (and this law does fundamentally determine duty), Hume should himself accept that, in the moral arena, pure reason can be practical. So the appeal to *consciousness* – Hume's second consideration against pure reason being practical – is answered, in Kant's eyes, by pointing to our manifest acknowledgement of duty: we are conscious that reason alone not only determines what are our duties but unconditionally *obliges* us to act on them.

Certainly, Kant agrees, we can offer neither an *explanation* of the necessity attaching to our consciousness of the moral law nor an a priori *justification* of that law's validity in respect of our will (and so of pure reason's capacity to be practical) from any judgments that are already known. But our clear consciousness of the binding force of the moral law is a sufficient rebuttal of Hume's denial of pure reason's practical role. If it is a fact that pure reason can motivate (and those who acknowledge the binding force of the moral law are, through that very acknowledgement, accepting that it is a fact), then our incapacity to provide any explanation or justification of this power of pure reason clearly cannot be employed as a ground for denying its motivational capacity. From the admitted fact that we are unable to explain *how* pure reason can be practical, we cannot conclude that reason is *not* practical (especially since we have an explanation of why this is inconceivable which is consistent with its possibility). When it is further recognized that we *are* conscious of its capacity to be practical in the all-important area of morality, any residual doubts about pure reason's motivating power, based upon the unanswered demand for a *deduction* of that motivating power, must fall away. 'For, if as pure reason it is really practical, it proves its reality and that of its concepts by what it does, and all subtle reasoning against the possibility of its being practical is futile' (*CPractR*, Preface; 5:3).

The Kantian response to Hume's attack on pure reason's motivational power is undoubtedly tenacious. But it does rest on a premiss that we have not yet examined sufficiently. This is that there is really no clash – as Kant thinks that there is not – between the conception of nature as a determined system and the conception of our transcendental freedom. This issue will be taken up after we have seen how, in the Dialectic of Pure Practical Reason, Kant seeks to further his metaphysical claims.

Summary of the Conclusions of the Analytic of Pure Practical Reason

Kant now takes himself to have established that, in any being who acknowledges the binding force of the moral law, reason alone can really be practical – and hence that transcendental freedom is, for such a being, a reality (not merely a logical possibility). In this way, we can know that the first of the three principal ideas of transcendant metaphysics, viz. *transcendental freedom* is actually instantiated. Once the reality of transcendental freedom is granted, and hence that the category of *causality* has application to the noumenal or supersensible world, we can also license the use of other categories in the noumenal field *in so far as* they can be shown to bear a necessary relation to the moral law. For what has given objective reality to the category of *cause*, in the supersensible realm, is the acknowledgement of the moral law's unconditional application to us: an acknowledgement that is shown in our ordinary moral practice, i.e. quite independently of any theorizing. Consequently, we shall also be warranted in accepting the objective reality of other categories, in the noumenal realm, to the extent that they are connected necessarily with our acceptance of the moral law. These topics will be pursued in the Dialectic in relation to the two other principle topics of transcendent metaphysics: namely, *the immortality of the soul* and *the existence of God*.

7

The Dialectic of Pure Practical Reason: How Morality Establishes the Existence of God and the Immortality of the Soul

There is a natural dialectic, or tendency to make invalid inferences, with regard to ideas of pure practical reason, as there is with regard to the ideas of pure reason. How does it arise in the case of practical reason? As sensuous creatures, we necessarily have needs: the need to be happy and to avoid pain. In fact, considered merely as sensuous creatures, Kant holds that *happiness* is all that counts for us. Consequently, as finite rational beings – beings with a sensuous as well as a rational nature – we require happiness in order to achieve full satisfaction. Now, in so far as we make obedience to the moral law the supreme condition of all our acts of will (as duty demands), we have, from the rational side of our nature, fulfilled the condition necessary for satisfying our need for happiness. Kant puts this by saying that by becoming *virtuous* – that is, by becoming fully disposed to making the moral law the supreme condition of our acts of will – we make ourselves *worthy* of being happy. Although, therefore, obedience to the moral law is the *supreme* condition on our wills, limiting the fulfilment of our desire for happiness (since it must always take precedence over it), it cannot alone constitute our *summum bonum,* our *complete* or *highest good.* As beings with a sensuous as well as a rational nature, our complete or highest good must, rather, consist in virtue and happiness combined in exact proportion. 'For', as Kant puts it, 'to need happiness [in order to achieve full satisfaction], to be also worthy of it [by becoming virtuous], and yet not to participate in it cannot be consistent with the perfect volition of a rational being that would at the same time have all power, even if we think of such a being only for the sake of the experiment' (*CPractR,* Dialectic, Ch. II; 5:110).

But if, for finite rational beings, the highest good must be the object of their wills, how can the synthesis of such heterogeneous concepts as *virtue* and *happiness* be accomplished? Only two ways are conceivable: either the desire for happiness must produce virtuous conduct, or virtuous conduct must produce happiness. Yet, both these avenues seem incompatible with reason's requirement that happiness should be proportionate to virtue. If our desire for happiness were to produce 'virtue', then there could be no genuinely virtuous acts: everything that was produced would result from heteronomy of the will. Accordingly, no act would arise out of obedience to the moral law, which, as we have seen, must always be the supreme condition of everything that is good. On the other hand, if we attempt to make virtuous conduct the condition of happiness (of others as well as ourselves), it seems that it could only be a matter of *chance* that the two should be co-ordinate: for the satisfaction of a finite rational being's needs depends upon the contingencies of the natural world. We could have no assurance that our dutiful acts would lead to happiness, whether for ourselves or for others. Yet the requirement of reason is that happiness *must* accord with virtue. We cannot expect to meet this requirement, because our knowledge of the particular laws of nature, as well as our capacity to use them to our own and others' advantage, are necessarily limited. So reason's demand cannot, apparently, be fulfilled: we cannot expect either of the two ways by which we might try to fulfil it as actually doing so. This is the dialectic of pure practical reason, and it can be put in the form of an antinomy: our reason demands that we achieve the highest good, the *summum bonum*, and yet our reason shows us that we are incapable of meeting the demand. Since this self-contradictory demand arises from the requirement always to make the moral law the supreme condition on our will, it follows that this fundamental imperative of morality must be rejected.

Kant's solution to the antinomy depends, like his solution to the Antinomies in the *First Critique*, on distinguishing between the phenomenal (or sensible) world and the noumenal (or supersensible) world. If the sensible world – in which the harmony of virtue and happiness must occur – existed in itself, there would be no way in which we could see how happiness must come to be in exact proportion to virtue (indeed, no genuine acts of virtue could even occur on such a hypothesis). But, since this world exists in appearance only, it is possible to think that there exists an author of the world who has so arranged the laws and substance of nature that happiness will strictly harmonize with virtue. The antinomy, then, can be resolved: reason shows us that we ought to achieve the *summum bonum*; it must, therefore, be *possible* for us to achieve it; we can only expect to realize this possibility by presupposing an author of the world who has so arranged nature that a virtuous disposition does lead to proportionate happiness. Consequently, it is for us a necessary presupposition of the consistency of reason, in its practical aspect, that we postulate the existence of such an author.

But, as we have seen, in order to make ourselves worthy of happiness, it is necessary that we first make ourselves virtuous: that is, we must first be fully disposed to make the moral law the supreme condition of our acts of will. Yet, as finite rational beings, we are subject to temptation from sensuous impulses, and we can only hope to overcome this temptation completely through an endless progression towards virtue. Admittedly, we may have evidence that we are approaching a wholly virtuous disposition; but there can be no point, in the temporal continuum, where we can be in a position to claim that we have entirely conquered our tendency to transgress the moral law (and have thereby fully acquired the disposition to virtue). Since this virtuous disposition is necessary in order to make ourselves worthy to be happy, we must postulate an endless period of our existence – that is, the immortality of our soul (the noumenal subject) – in order to achieve the *summum bonum*. Note that the immortality of the soul is not postulated to ensure a *balance* of a finite being's happiness with his virtue. It is postulated in order that a finite being should be able fully to achieve *a virtuous disposition*. That we should strive continually to be virtuous – thereby seeking to make ourselves worthy of happiness – is the first and most important requirement laid down by the moral law.

In light of these considerations, Kant thinks that we can specify the type of object that must answer to the concept of the author of nature. The cause of nature must be a rational being with a will, since the harmony of nature with our virtue must depend upon the author's capacity both to judge the moral character of our acts and to fashion nature accordingly. It must, in other words, be capable both of assessing our worthiness to be happy and of possessing a causality that acts on the basis of the conception of the moral law. 'Therefore the supreme cause of nature, insofar as it must be presupposed for the highest good, is a being that is the cause of nature by *understanding* and *will* (hence its author), that is God' (CPractR, Dialectic, Ch. II, Sect. V; 5:125; italics original).

As it stands, it is not evident that this argument – a version of the so-called moral argument for the existence of God – shows that God is the *creator* of the materials of nature; but only that he is the author of their arrangement. Admittedly, Kant does later hold that, *from the practical point of view*, we can determine the attributes of God in still greater detail: 'He must be *omniscient* in order to cognize my conduct even to my inmost disposition in all possible cases and throughout the future, *omnipotent* in order to bestow results appropriate to it, and so too *omnipresent, eternal*, and so forth. Thus the moral law, by means of the concept of the highest good as the object of pure practical reason, determines the concept of the original being as the *supreme* being' (CPractR, Dialectic, Ch. II, Sect. V; 5:140; italics original). Still, even granting this further specification of God's attributes, it might be objected that God need not be the creator of all the materials of nature, although it may perhaps be necessary that he be the creator of some of them. However, it needs to be borne in mind that Kant is not concerned with ascribing attributes to God that go *beyond* his existence as the supreme *moral* author of the world (and so a suitable object of religious worship): the being to whom all finite rational agents owe their allegiance. In this regard, his moral argument for God's existence is logically coherent.

He calls the existence of God and the immortality of the soul *postulates* of pure practical reason. By this he means that they are necessary presuppositions of reason's demand that we achieve the *summum bonum* in the world. It is true that transcendental freedom is also called a postulate of pure practical reason. But there is this distinguishing feature. Whereas freedom is necessary in order to make possible obedience to the moral law even in this life, and on every single occasion, the other two postulates (immortality of the soul and the existence of God) are specifically required only for our realization of the highest good. Our right to assert their reality is entirely dependent on this latter demand of our practical reason. Moreover, although we must assume that a finite being will achieve happiness commensurate with his virtue (in order to make sense of reason's demand that we continuously strive to make ourselves worthy to be happy), Kant remains steadfast in his belief that the motive of all our actions can only be the necessity of obeying the moral law. If we were to act out of a desire for happiness, albeit *in accordance with* virtue, we would be acting heteronomously, and our act could have no moral worth. He allows that in striving always to act for the sake of the moral law (in seeking to be virtuous), we may further *hope* for commensurate happiness not only for others but even for ourselves. None the less, the *motive* for our action must only be the necessity of obeying the moral law. Indeed, the postulates of God and of immortality of the soul arise only *because*, prior to all considerations of the highest good, the categorical imperative requires us, as finite beings, always to act for the sake of the moral law. It is this prior imperative that leads to the rational idea of the highest good, and hence to the postulates of immortality and the existence of God. If we were to allow a *consequence* of these postulates to enter into the motivation of our will, viz. the thought of the harmonizing of our happiness with virtue, the purity of the moral motive would be destroyed – and our progress towards achieving the *summum bonum* would be thereby reduced.

A number of the main points in the argument for the *summum bonum*, and its realization, are summarized in the following passage:

> In the preceding analysis the moral law led to a practical task that is set by pure reason alone and without the aid of any sensible incentives, namely that of the necessary completeness of that of the first and principle part of the highest good, *morality* [viz. the attainment of a virtuous disposition]; and, since this can be fully accomplished only in an eternity, it led to the postulate of *immortality*. The same law must also lead to the possibility of the second element of the highest good, namely *happiness* proportioned to the morality, and must do so as disinterestedly as before, solely from impartial reason; in other words, it must lead to the supposition of the existence of a cause adequate to this effect, that is, it must postulate the *existence of God* as belonging necessarily to the possibility of the highest good (which object is necessarily connected with the moral lawgiving of pure reason). (*CPractR*, Dialectic, Ch. II, Sect. V; 5:124; italics original)

How is any Knowledge of the Transcendent Possible?

But how can we assert the objective reality of the three ideas necessary for the achievement of the highest good (God, freedom and immortality), given that the *First Critique* has declared that it is impossible for us to tell, by the use of theoretical reason, whether these ideas have real objects corresponding to them? Has not Kant gone back on his claim that, without sensible intuition, we cannot acquire any theoretical knowledge of objects – including, of course, any determinate theoretical knowledge of what exists, or may exist, in the supersensible world?

His answer is that our right to assert the objective reality of these three ideas does not amount to any theoretical knowledge *about* them. For this, sensible intuition is indeed required (and none is available). Admittedly, pure practical reason, through its demand that we seek the highest good, *has* extended our theoretical knowledge beyond what can be achieved by theoretical reason. But this knowledge concerns only the *reality* of these objects; nothing is thereby learnt with regard to their attributes *so far as* this may help us to increase our theoretical knowledge. We may, indeed, be enabled to characterize, to determine, some of these objects *for moral purposes* – as we have seen, Kant clearly thinks that this is possible with the concept of God – but we can tell nothing about how these attributes (omniscience, omnipotence, etc.) are to be understood or employed *outside* the moral sphere.

The categories allow us to *think* any (non-contradictory) concepts although, without experience or its possibility, we cannot know whether objects corresponding to these concepts exist. Now the demands of our *moral* experience – more especially, the necessity of our seeking the highest good – require us to presuppose the existence of God and immortality as well as freedom of the will. We are therefore justified in asserting the reality of these objects *just to the extent that* they make possible our attainment of the highest good. But their proven reality does not enable us to gain any *determinate* theoretical knowledge about them, or to extend our theoretical knowledge of the sensible world.

8

The Importance of Kant's Copernican Revolution to his Moral Philosophy

Within the confines of his Copernican revolution, Kant believes that he has successfully brought together our common conception of duty or moral obligation with our metaphysical yearning to prove the reality of transcendental freedom, the immortality of the soul, and the existence of God. He thinks that our *theoretical* reason shows that the determinism of nature and the existence of transcendental freedom within the world can be combined. And he thinks that, given the possibility of this combination, our *practical* reason – in the form of our clear acknowledgement of the unconditional demand made upon us by the moral law – removes the need for a deduction of pure reason's capacity to motivate, while at the same time proving the *reality* of our transcendental freedom. Once we have thus established our freedom, he further thinks that reason's requirement that our happiness be proportionate to our virtue must also establish the existence of God and the immortality of our soul. Equally, Kant believes that, without his Copernican revolution, neither morality nor our transcendent metaphysical hopes can be sustained.

He is undoubtedly right on the second score, granted his conception of transcendental realism. In the absence of the distinction between the phenomenal and noumenal worlds – an integral part of his Copernican revolution – there could be no reconciliation between the determinism of nature and the transcendental freedom of the subject. Moreover, without transcendental freedom, there could be neither morality (as he conceives it) nor, consequently, any practical proofs of the existence of God and of the soul's immortality.

But is he right to suppose that even *within* his Copernican revolution, he has justified our common notion of morality and, at the same time, the reality of our transcendent metaphysical concepts?

That is far from evident. In order for his attempted justification to be successful, he needs to have demonstrated the possibility of transcendental freedom in a way that is more robust than he has actually achieved. What Kant has shown, in his resolution of the Third Antinomy, is that we can conceive of ourselves as transcendentally free while acknowledging the existence of a thoroughgoing natural determinism in the spatio-temporal world. What he has not shown is that we can justifiably regard ourselves as transcendentally free *whatever* causal determinism in fact exists in nature. If he is to establish the reality of our transcendental freedom in the face of the actual causal determinism in nature, he needs to do more than show that our recognition of the moral law justifies us in accepting that the will can be motivated by reason, when reason operates independently of sensuous impulses. He also needs to show that it justifies us in accepting that reason can motivate the will undetermined by any phenomenal factors. It is difficult for us now to accept that the capacity to exercise practical reason is not determined by physical causes. For it looks highly likely that this capacity is dependent for its existence on physical structures and events in the brain, which themselves depend for their existence on earlier phenomenal causes, and so on. This makes it correspondingly hard to be persuaded that Kant's 'fact of reason' – our clear consciousness that we ought to obey the demands of the moral law, whatever our sensuous impulses may direct – can be relied upon as disclosing to us a genuine recognition of our capacity to act for the sake of the moral law. Indeed, given the strong empirical evidence in favour of the dependence of our familiar mental life on physical (brain) structures and events, there is substantial ground for *distrusting* a conviction that we can will an action undetermined by any prior causes. Even though the 'fact of reason' may, perhaps, be allowed to show that we do have the capacity to motivate the will independently of *sensuous impulses*, it does not show that we possess the capacity to motivate the will independently of, and undetermined by, anything existing in the phenomenal realm, including physical states and events.

Still, would it matter to the Kantian enterprise if the capacity to exercise the causality of reason were determined by physical structures in the brain? It seems clear that it would. For it would mean that the agent's ability to exercise practical reason is itself wholly dependent for its existence upon phenomenal factors, viz. upon certain physical states of his brain, which themselves have phenomenal causes, and so on. The whole of an agent's empirical character – all of his dispositions to act – would inevitably depend upon antecedently existing factors. Before we observed any of the agent's actions, we could *already* determine the whole of his empirical character through a knowledge of the physical structure of his brain. (In fact, since this physical structure itself has a prior set of physical causes and so on, it would seem possible in principle to determine an agent's entire empirical character prior to his conception.) On this account, the noumenal subject simply has no power to intervene within the phenomenal series of events, thereby giving rise to *spontaneous* acts of will. Our existence as noumena could not, after all, be determinately known, since it now transpires that we have no good reason for thinking of ourselves as transcendentally free agents.

It is all very well showing – as, I believe, the resolution of the Third Antinomy does show – that, given the phenomena/noumena distinction, it is logically possible to combine our transcendental freedom with the existence of a spatio-temporal world in which all changes of state are subject to natural (causal) law. Kant needs to do more than this if he is to prove that freedom and natural causality are not *actually* in conflict in our world (and hence that the so-called 'fact of reason' can legitimately be employed to demonstrate the reality of our freedom). He needs to prove that our capacity to exercise pure practical reason is not dependent on physical structures in the brain. While it is, quite obviously, not a requirement of the Kantian conception of the thoroughgoing determinism of nature that the capacity to exercise pure practical reason should itself be causally dependent upon antecedently existing phenomenal factors (in fact, upon physical phenomena), the empirical evidence strongly suggests that it is.[1] Yet Kant took it that, provided he could show that an agent's capacity to exercise pure practical reason need not conflict with our explaining his conduct *by reference to his empirical character* (in conjunction with his beliefs about the surrounding circumstances), there could be no logical inconsistency between the transcendental freedom of a human agent and the thoroughgoing causal determinism that exists in our spatio-temporal world. But if it is the case, as the empirical evidence strongly suggests, that our

---

[1] All that the thoroughgoing causal determinism of nature requires is that every change of state can be assigned some cause or other in the phenomenal world. In the present context, this requirement is sufficiently met if, whenever the agent acts, his acts of will (changes of state) can be explained by reference to his empirical character (in conjunction with his beliefs). Within the Kantian system, the dispositions themselves (constituting his empirical character), do not *require* a phenomenal explanation for their existence in order to preserve the thoroughgoing determinism of nature.

very capacity to exercise reason, as well as our actual exercise of it, *is* wholly causally dependent on antecedently existing phenomenal factors (which themselves depend wholly for their existence and operation on earlier phenomenal factors, and so on), then it follows that his attempt to render compatible our acknowledged existence as phenomenal beings with the thought of ourselves as transcendentally free agents must have failed.

So, while it may well be that some kind of a distinction can still be made between acts of will that are heteronomous and those that are 'autonomous' (i.e. those that are not caused by sensuous desires), this distinction will not allow Kant to claim that when an agent acts through the causality of reason, and so 'autonomously', the operation of his will is spontaneous and self-legislative. Hence, acting for the sake of the moral law cannot bestow any *intrinsic* worth on human beings, since motivation even in this case (as in the case of heteronomy of the will) can now be regarded as arising only as part of an unending regressive causal chain in the phenomenal world. Additionally, the revised account of 'autonomy' of the will must render problematic our pursuit of the *summum bonum*, because, from a subjective point of view, we can only make sense of this pursuit given the immortality of our soul and the existence of God. But these two postulates themselves depend for their proof on the reality of transcendental freedom. Without that freedom, it cannot be a legitimate demand of our reason that we make the moral law the supreme condition of our wills (since *ex hypothesi* reason is not, after all, practical of itself). Accordingly, we can have no ground for postulating immortality in order fully to realize that demand, or, in turn, God's existence in order to render happiness coordinate with our attainment of virtue. The Kantian notion of the *summum bonum*, together with the requirement that we continually strive to make it possible, does seem wholly inapplicable under these circumstances.

When Kant affirmed that transcendental freedom, in so far as its existence is proved by the moral law, 'constitutes the *keystone* of the whole structure of a system of pure reason, even of speculative reason' (CPractR, Preface; 5:3–4; italics original), he did, I suggest, accurately locate the centrality of transcendental freedom within his system. But once it is conceded that the determinism of nature does in fact conflict with our transcendental freedom, and hence that the latter's reality cannot be proved by our (supposed) consciousness of the moral law's unconditional necessity, Kant's Copernican revolution with regard to the establishment of our *transcendent metaphysical concepts* must collapse – together with his claim that we are subject to the moral law. Neither God nor freedom nor immortality can be shown to exist by means of our moral experience; and, assuming the Kantian analysis, that experience must itself be declared illusory since, without transcendental freedom, we cannot be subject to categorical imperatives. However, his Copernican revolution with regard to the establishment of our *theoretical concepts and principles* will not, on these grounds, be endangered. Independent arguments are produced in the Transcendental Aesthetic of the *Critique of Pure Reason* for the ideality of space and time; and the force of his claim that the Third Antinomy (so far as concerns the beginning of the world), like the other theoretical Antinomies, can be resolved given transcendental idealism, but not given transcendental realism, is unaffected. For the freedom of *our* will – more generally, of any beings existing *within* the world – is not required for resolving the Third Antinomy with regard to the beginning of the world.

How might Kant attempt to respond to this attack? There is a passage in the Paralogisms which suggests that he might seek to resist it by appeal to his idealism. The claim that thought depends on the activity of matter amounts to the claim that, without the existence and operation of matter, thought would not exist. But, according to the transcendental idealist, the correct position is that since the whole material world is mere appearance, the subject (as noumenon) must exist, *and be able to think,* logically prior to, and hence independently of, the existence of matter. For it is the operation of the subject, *qua* thinking being, on the given representations that makes possible the very existence of the material world. If the thinking subject did not exist and have the capacity to operate independently of matter, there could be no such thing as matter at all:

> [T]he intent of securing our thinking self from the danger of materialism . . . is achieved by the rational concept of our thinking self that we have given. For according to it, so little fear remains that if one took matter away then all thinking and even the existence of thinking beings would be abolished, that it rather shows clearly that if one were to take away the thinking subject, the whole corporeal world would have to disappear, as this is nothing but the appearance in the sensibility of our subject and one mode of its representations. . . . Matter thus signifies not a species of substances quite different and heterogeneous from the object of inner sense (the soul), but rather only the heterogeneity of the appearances of substances (which in themselves are unknown to us), whose representations we call external in comparison with those that

we ascribe to inner sense, even though they belong as much to the thinking subject as other thoughts do. (*CPR*, A 383–5)

On this account, the materialist claim – that thought depends on
matter – is self-contradictory. For the claim entails that matter exists
(since it is accepted that thought exists). But if matter exists, then,
given transcendental idealism, the thinking subject must exist and
engage in an activity of thought logically prior to, and so independent
of, matter. The materialist claim, therefore, both asserts and denies
that thought depends on matter. Since the claim is self-contradictory,
the materialist cannot be justified in holding that thought is dependent on matter, whether that claim is said to be based on empirical or
on theoretical considerations.

But although an argument along these lines does show that, for the
transcendental idealist, *some* features of the subject's mind must exist
and operate independently of matter, it does not show that the existence and exercise of practical reason are free from the determinism
of nature. To hold that the representations given to us through sensibility must first be *thought* by the understanding, in order for spatio-
temporal objects and events to exist, hardly rules out the possibility
that *other* mental capacities and acts, including those of practical
reason, can be assigned physical causes in the brain, i.e. as a result of
empirical investigation. Or, if it does, I remain unclear why this is so,
even though Kant himself does seem confident that, on his system, we
cannot ascribe any empirical conditions to the exercise or capacities
not only of the understanding (in his technical sense) but of reason as
well (see *CPR*, A 547/B 575).

Let us grant that what an agent is thinking about when he is conscious of the necessity of obeying the moral law is not an object of the
senses, not an appearance, but rather the mere *form* of a universal law.
Even so, it is not evident that one can go on to argue, as Kant does,
that in such a case the agent's will cannot be subject to the natural law
of causality. For what such an argument overlooks is that the agent's
consciousness of the necessity of obeying the moral law may *itself* be
determined by physical states and events in the brain. And, in fact, I
do not think that there is any less ground for maintaining that our consciousness of duty is subject to such physical determination than there
is for any other familiar act of consciousness.

In certain of his writings, there is a suggestion that Kant seeks to
defuse this type of objection by claiming that, in so far as we regard
our reason as genuinely capable of *assessing* data (as we do), we cannot

possibly regard its exercise, whether in the theoretical or the practical arena, as initiated by determining causes that lie outside the rational faculty. Yet even *if* this reply is acknowledged to have some force, it can hardly be said, by itself, to deal adequately with the strong, accumulating evidence for the dependence of the mental on the physical. If transcendental freedom is to be defended, more will need to be done to meet the objection, especially as Kant himself asserts that if the determinism of nature cannot be shown to cohere with freedom of the will, it is the latter, freedom of the will, that must be sacrificed (see *Groundwork*, Sect. III; 4:456).

I conclude that Kant's moral philosophy, which itself incorporates his transcendent metaphysical aspirations, has not been shown to offer a genuine alternative to a subtle version of the empiricist's moral system. Admittedly, if transcendental freedom is a non-negotiable condition of moral agency (as Kant himself was convinced), this implies not that the empiricist theory has correctly identified the foundations of morality, but that, for us, there can be no such thing as morality at all. Rather than jumping to this unedifying conclusion, it would seem worth asking whether, in the spirit of Kant's own approach in the second edition of the *First Critique*, we should not rather begin with the certainty that morality *does* apply to us, and then ask ourselves not *whether* it is possible, but *how* it is possible.

— Part III —

Critique of Judgment

9

The Analytic of Aesthetic Judgment: Defending a Third Way between an Empiricist and a Traditional Rationalist Theory of Taste and Beauty

The *Critique of Judgment* (or *Third Critique*) has as its overall aim to show that the two realms that were discussed in the *First* and *Second Critiques* – namely, those of nature and of freedom (or morality) – can be bridged by means of the faculty of judgment. Following a general Introduction, the *Third Critique* is divided into two parts: the Critique of Aesthetic Judgment and the Critique of Teleological Judgment (the latter dealing with teleological or purposive explanations in nature). Of these two, it is mainly in the first part that Kant seeks to link the realms of nature and freedom via the faculty of judgment. This is because he believes that it is only the judgment of taste – and, more specifically, when it is applied to the beauties of nature – that can effect the bridging role.

It is surprising that analysis and justification of the judgment of taste, together with an examination of artistic creation and apprecia-tion, should take up so very much of the Critique of Aesthetic Judgment, given the importance that Kant attaches to bridging the realms of nature and freedom by means of our perception of natural beauty. None the less, this bridging role does gradually emerge, with the fullest treatment to be found in the Dialectic of Aesthetic Judgment. Having said that, there is some extremely interesting addi-tional material to be found in the Introduction to the *Third Critique* (and in the earlier so-called First Introduction, which Kant replaced with the published Introduction, apparently largely because of the former's considerable length). But it will be best to approach this additional material in relation to some of Kant's views on teleology, which will be considered in chapter 12.

*

As regards the judgment of taste – characteristically expressed by 'This is (or is not) beautiful' – Kant contrasts his own position with those of an empiricist and a rationalist. There are, of course, various forms of the empiricist position; but the views that Kant seems most obviously to have in mind are those of Hume ('inevitably', one feels like saying) and of Francis Hutcheson. In the case of rationalism, he specifically mentions the views of the Leibnizians, although he may also have had in mind the views of Thomas Reid. From now on, when I refer to the empiricist or to the rationalist position, I shall be referring to the views of these philosophers. This point needs especially to be borne in mind with respect to the rationalist position, because, near the end of the Dialectic of the Aesthetic Judgment (CJ, 5:347), Kant identifies his *own* view as a version of rationalism, although it is to be distinguished from the version that, up until that time, he has identified by that rubric. His own view he considers to be a rationalist one, because it entails that the judgment of taste must be based on an a priori rule (although a very different one from the Leibnizians'). Such a rule could never form the basis of an empiricist's analysis of the judgment of taste.

According to the empiricist position, the judgment of taste is determined by a feeling of disinterested pleasure or displeasure. Certainly, there will be features in the object which are responsible for the spectator's feeling. But the ground for making the judgment depends ultimately on the existence of a disinterested or contemplative pleasure. Any standards of taste, by which certain features of objects are denominated an appropriate target of aesthetic judgment, will be *empirical* generalizations based on how spectators, or certain spectators, feel when viewing the aesthetic object.

According to the rationalist position, the ground of a judgment of taste depends upon the *perfection* of the perceived object – more particularly, upon whether its parts are well adapted for the object's conceived end or purpose. Admittedly, as the rationalist acknowledges, a judgment that an object actually is beautiful will be attended with a feeling of pleasure; and it may well be that the spectator is *only* consciously aware of the object's beauty (= perfection) by means of this feeling. However, the determining ground of the judgment is dependent not strictly on the feeling of pleasure, but on whether the particular object perceived is perfect of its kind. Consequently, on this account, the object's beauty is determined by a definite concept, viz. by the determinate rule governing how the parts of the perceived object should be arranged to be well adapted for the end or purpose of an object of that type. Since the aesthetic judgment is based on a definite concept, the judgment, if correctly made, *must* hold for *anyone* who judges the beauty of the same object. In short, on the rationalist analysis, an aesthetic judgment can rightly claim necessary and strictly universal validity – and it will be possible to prove the adequacy of any proffered aesthetic judgment by recourse to a definite rule or concept. More will be said about both the empiricist and the rationalist positions in the sequel.

Kant's own position goes between those of the empiricist and the rationalist. He agrees with the empiricist that a pure judgment of taste is determined by a disinterested feeling of pleasure or displeasure. Accordingly, he accepts that the judgment is not determined by the application to the object of any definite rule. But he also agrees with the rationalist that the judgment claims universal necessary validity. On the face of it, this is paradoxical. If the judgment of taste were based on a definite *concept* of the object (e.g. that of perfection), then it could indeed claim necessity and strict universality. But if, as Kant thinks, the determining ground of the judgment is a *feeling* (of pleasure or displeasure), then how can it be possible to make such a claim? Surely, it may be said, the most that could be claimed is *comparative* universality, based on an empirical generalization concerning how a particular group of people *happen* to feel about certain features of objects.

Kant's attempt to bring together these apparently conflicting positions – and the way in which he connects this task with his Copernican revolution – may reasonably be seen as constituting his major contribution to aesthetics.

The Judgment of Taste: Analysis and Justification

In the opening chapter (Book I) of the *Third Critique*, entitled 'Analytic of the Beautiful', the analysis of the judgment of taste is divided into four parts, or moments. Together these four moments are intended to identify the necessary, and jointly sufficient, conditions for making such a judgment. In the following chapter (Book II), entitled 'Analytic of the Sublime', Kant officially turns to the question of the justification of the judgment of taste or, as he entitles it, the 'Deduction' of judgments of taste (*CJ*, Sect. 38; 5:289–91). Although this is his official strategy, I share the common belief that much of his attempted justification is already to be found in the four moments. The Deduction, properly so-called, seems to do little more than repeat arguments that have already been given in these moments.

——— **185** ———

In examining Kant's analysis and justification of the judgment of taste, I shall not methodically go through each of the four moments in turn, and then pass on to the Deduction. Except in the case of the First Moment – which does set the agenda for much of his subsequent argument and deserves its own separate discussion – I shall try to bring out the main points of Kant's analysis in a continuous thread. In the case of the justification, I shall pick out what I see as his key considerations, whether they are presented in one of the four moments or in the Deduction itself.

It is in the First Moment that Kant shows that, on the all-important issue of our ground for asserting that an object is beautiful, he is in fundamental agreement with the empiricist position. For he there signals that the judgment of taste is always determined, and determined immediately, by *a disinterested feeling of pleasure or displeasure*. As he understands it, the feeling of delight or unease attending the consciousness of an object, if it is to be a disinterested or merely contemplative one, must neither arouse a desire for the actual existence of this, or similar objects, nor be based on any such desire. He also expresses this by saying that in a judgment of taste, the real existence of the object must not interest us.

The disinterested nature of the judgment of taste leads him to make the further, and initially surprising, claim that the delight in an object's beauty can never be dependent on the *matter* or *content* of the object. Pleasure accompanying the consciousness of the content of an object – its specific colours, sound tones, smells, gustatory tastes and so on (in short, any of the secondary qualities) – is, he thinks, always an *interested* one; that is, it always either arouses or gratifies a desire for the object's actual existence. Clearly this view is related to Kant's claim in his practical philosophy: namely, that in so far as any sensuous desire is aroused, this is the result, and only the result, of the pleasure we take in some aspect of the content of a representation. But here he seems to go further than this, now maintaining that the content (rather than the form) of any given representation, in so far as it leads to a feeling of pleasure at all, *always* leads to an interested pleasure.

In fact, he believes that our terminology shows that we acknowledge a distinction between the disinterested pleasure that is immediately aroused by the form of certain objects and the interested pleasure that is the immediate effect of their content. Where the pleasure arises immediately from content, we say that the object is *agreeable to*, or *gratifies*, the senses; where the pleasure arises immediately from reflection on the object's form, we say that the object is beautiful. A judgment that is based wholly on the pleasure arising immediately from an object's content, from any of its agreeable features, Kant calls a 'judgment of sense'. To repeat, such judgments, as opposed to judgments of the beautiful, are held by him always to be accompanied by an interest in the real existence of the object.

This view can strike one as especially unappealing with regard to colours and sound tones. On the face of it, it is bizarre to claim that the sensed colours in the stained-glass windows of Chartres Cathedral are not an intrinsic part of their beauty. Yet, in so far as sensations of colour contribute to an object's beauty (or deformity), they do so, for Kant, only through their capacity to show up more conspicuously the *form* of the object. Similarly, in music, whether a Bach unaccompanied cello suite is played on that instrument or on the piano is, Kant holds, irrelevant to its beauty, provided the form of the piece can be fully grasped either way. Colours and sound tones can have, he admits, their *charms* – they can please in themselves, like other agreeable features – and this may add an additional aesthetic attraction to an object; but since they are always coupled with interest, they cannot strictly contribute to an estimate of the object's beauty.

While it is not wholly implausible to hold that sensations of smell and tastes of the palate are, in so far as they please at all, always associated with an *interested* pleasure, it seems most implausible to hold that this is always true of colour and tonal sound sensations. The colours, and their variations, in Notre-Dame de la Belle Verrière (a window in Chartres Cathedral) are certainly visually arresting; yet they would appear to be no more calculated to arouse an *interest* in the actual existence of the object than the window's unusual design. But although Kant's claim that colours and tonal sounds are invariably coupled with interest is not convincing, a case can perhaps be made for his rejection of these empirical sensations as contributing to an object's beauty. Given (as he maintains in the Second Moment) that the judgment of taste claims to hold universally, and given (as he also maintains) that there can be no assurance that the intrinsic nature of our empirical sensations is shared by others, it is arguable that we should reject colours and tonal sounds as capable of entering into a genuine judgment of taste. In other words, the rejection would be motivated not because these sensations always arouse an interest (as Kant contentiously alleges), but because he thinks that a judgment that is grounded upon them cannot claim to hold with universal validity – which a genuine judgment of taste always does.

Despite the official difference between the delight aroused by an object denominated beautiful (a disinterested pleasure) and one denominated agreeable (an interested pleasure), Kant holds that both are alike in this respect: the pleasure felt is always *immediate*. Indeed, it is for this very reason that he affirms that both types of judgment are correctly thought of as *aesthetic* judgments. As he understands it, an aesthetic judgment is one that is determined immediately by subjective sensation, viz. by the feeling of pleasure or displeasure. In this respect, both types of judgment are to be contrasted with the pleasure attending a judgment that an object is good, whether it be thought of as good as a *means* to some desired end or whether it be thought good *in itself* (morally good). With a judgment of the good, the pleasure is dependent upon our first applying a specifiable rule to the object. Kant expresses this point by saying that the pleasure accompanying the judgment that the object is good is always dependent upon the prior application of some determinate concept. Since the pleasure is mediate – dependent on the prior application of a specific rule – it follows that the pleasure accompanying a judgment of the good is never immediate, as with that of the agreeable and the beautiful.

For instance, I may take pleasure at the sight of a restaurant because I am hungry and I realize that the object before me will satisfy my desire. The pleasure felt is not immediate, because it depends upon my belief that, since the object in front of me falls under the concept of a restaurant, a visit to it would be a good *means* to satisfy my desired end. Equally, to take delight in something because it is good *in itself* requires that I have a rule by which I can determine whether it answers to our concept of the morally good. Here too the pleasure is not immediate but dependent upon the prior application of a determinate concept.

Kant additionally holds that the pleasure that accompanies a judgment of the good is always an *interested* one. With objects that delight us because they are seen to be a good means to a desired end, it is obvious why he should maintain that we are interested in the actual existence of the means in question. In fact, it is also clear in the case of what is denominated morally good. For although, unlike the case of what is good as a means, the feeling does not depend upon any *antecedent* desire, it does call one forth. In the case of our consciousness of the morally good, the feeling produced – the feeling of respect – results from our practical reason determining the will in respect of a given object; and so this feeling is immediately coupled with an interest in, or a non-sensuous desire for, the actual existence of the object.

On the question of the immediacy of the pleasure determining judgments of sense, it has been objected that we should reject Kant's view that our consciousness of the so-called agreeable features – colours, tastes of the palate, and so on – can please although unmediated by any concept. We should reject it because *all* perceptual consciousness, even of the secondary qualities, requires the application of a suitable concept. For instance, we can only be aware of a spatial expanse as red through first recognizing that it falls under the concept *red*. Consequently, the Kantian distinction between judgments of the agreeable and those of the good breaks down because of the unfounded claim that only the latter are dependent on the prior application of a concept.

This objection seems to me of no substantial force. We need only draw the distinction between the application of our concepts of a particular colour, smell, taste, etc., where each concept is applicable in virtue of, and only in virtue of, the existence of the single feature in question; and those where the application of the concept is governed by rules applicable to a manifold of features. To judge that an object is e.g. red, each of us no doubt needs to compare the content of our present colour sensation with our colour sensations of paradigm cases of red objects (both under optimum conditions); but there are no rules applicable to the content of the colour sensation itself. However, in the case of judging that an object's surface is e.g. circular, there are formal rules for determining whether the relationship between the apprehended parts of a given manifold constitutes a circle; and these must be satisfied in the case of the present apprehension *before* the surface can be justifiably termed a good or perfect example of a circle. The essential difference, therefore, between judgments of sense and those of the good remains: the first are not reliant on the application of any rules to a number of features in order to take delight in them, while the latter are. Indeed, as I understand it, Kant's chief ground for holding that we can never have the right to claim that the intrinsic nature of our empirical sensations is shared rests on there being no rules applying to the manifold by which we can prove or disprove the correctness of any claim. (From now on, I shall revert to Kant's own usage of the term 'concept', according to which a concept always denotes a rule for unifying a number of features.)

The upshot of the First Moment is that the judgment of taste is determined immediately by a disinterested feeling of pleasure or displeasure. In this, it is to be distinguished both from the judgment of sense (or of the agreeable) and from any judgment of the good. The judgment of sense, like the judgment of taste, is determined immediately by the feeling of pleasure or displeasure, but it is always interested (concerned with the real existence of the object). Judgments of the good are neither immediately determined by pleasure or displeasure (since they are determined by the prior application of a definite concept) nor disinterested.

The identification of an immediate disinterested feeling as the determining ground of the judgment of taste is, in many ways, the crucial one for shaping Kant's overall position. He points out himself that the main conclusion to emerge from the Second Moment, viz. that the judgment of taste claims the agreement of everyone, is a natural extension of his argument in the First Moment. Since we do not consider that the feeling determining the judgment of taste is based on any factor that is private to ourselves, it is natural that each of us should insist that anyone else who judges an object's beauty should be in agreement with our own judgment. After all, the feeling is, in this case, not dependent on consciousness of the matter or content of the object (any of its secondary qualities); nor, since it is independent of the application of any determinate rules, can it result from fulfilling any private interest or end. In asking whether the object before me is beautiful, I need to detach myself from all such individual factors, and, without employing any determinate concept whatever, decide whether the object's mere *form* gives me a disinterested feeling of pleasure. In taking up this aesthetic attitude, I am conscious of making a judgment that is, so far as possible, free *both* from factors that may be peculiar to myself *and* from the rule-bound constraints arising from the employment of any determinate concept.

Moreover, Kant believes that if we investigate *directly* whether the judgment of taste makes a claim to universality, we shall find that it does. When we judge that an object is beautiful (as opposed to agreeable), we do not think that our judgment holds merely for ourselves personally: we claim, rather, to speak with a universal voice, insisting that anyone else who makes a judgment of taste on the same object ought to find it beautiful. (He notes that to hold that an object is merely 'beautiful *for me*' is an improper use of the concept *beautiful*.) Yet the universality claimed in our judgment is not one that we base on experience: that is, on the contingently discovered general agreement in our judgments of taste. We *demand* the agreement of others, holding that those who judge differently from us are in error, just as though our judgment *were* based on some specifiable concept of the object. On Kant's analysis, the judgment of taste claims universal *nec-*

essary validity: in holding that an object is beautiful, one is claiming that everyone's judgment *ought* to be in agreement with one's own.

But how can a judgment of taste make such a demand without being based on any determinate concept? Here we have to consider material from both the Second and the Third Moments. The demand requires that the feeling, which determines the judgment of taste, must arise from those cognitive faculties of the mind, viz. imagination and understanding, that are jointly needed in order to have any perceptual knowledge of objects. For in making judgments about the beauty of objects, each of us is evidently presupposing that our perceptual knowledge of the world is shared with anyone else who makes such judgments. The issue with regard to judgments of the beautiful is how they can be anything more than expressions of personal taste, even *granting* that we do all possess the same perceptual knowledge of the objects about which we are exercising our taste. Consequently, in asking how a judgment of taste can legitimately claim universal necessary validity, we are justified in assuming that the cognitive faculties must themselves be universally shared. Further, only perceptual judgments about formal qualities of an object (not secondary qualities), and those judgments that solely employ the two faculties – imagination and understanding – enabling us to make such determinate objective judgments, can possibly be said to hold necessarily for everyone. For no other perceptual judgments, or judgments immediately related to perception, *must* hold for all of us, rather than merely doing so *as a matter of fact*. Hence, the feeling determining the judgment of taste must arise from the joint employment of the faculties of understanding and imagination, if the judgment is to make a legitimate claim to hold with necessity and universality.

However, since the feeling for an object's beauty has to arise *independently* of the application of any definite concept of the object, the question remains as to how the cognitive faculties can co-operate in a judgment of taste. At this point, we need to recall Kant's explanation of how our everyday perceptual judgments of objects are made possible. In the case of a normal judgment of experience – let us take the perception of a manifold of representations as constituting a house – it is first required that the imagination, in its productive capacity, connects the representations of the given manifold so that they can be apprehended, in accordance with categories of the understanding, as existing together in *one* spatial intuition. Certainly, the perception of the spatial unity as constituting a particular sensible object (a house) relies on the application of a definite concept; and this requires the use of both imagination and understanding in their *empirical* capacities (the former to associate the contents of the representations by means of the law of reproduction, and the latter to supply the appropriate empirical concept). But this process is made possible only because of the non-empirical role of the productive imagination in connecting the representations of the manifold together so that they can form a single, spatial or temporal, intuition.[1] In this latter, non-empirical role, the imagination is subject only to the most general unifying constraints of the understanding.

Now, in the case of a pure judgment of taste, the imagination is *merely* productive: that is, it arranges the manifold so that it can be grasped together as a spatial or temporal unity; but the imagination is left free from the law of reproduction (whereby the contents of the diverse representations are associated together in accordance with some specific empirical concept of an object). So the spectator needs to *suspend* his normal attitude of attempting to identify the particular type of empirical object that a manifold of representations is presenting to him. Instead, he needs to estimate the degree of harmony that exists between the productive imagination and the understanding, as the former connects the given manifold together (to form a single spatial or temporal intuition) subject only to categories of the understanding. And, as Kant later points out, those manifolds of representation which are the *most* adapted for putting the two cognitive faculties into harmonious free play are the ones that possess sufficient formal *variety* to allow the imagination as fully as possible to exercise its productive powers while, at the same time, sufficient *unity* to allow the understanding to grasp with ease how they fall under one or more of its a priori concepts. For, if the pleasure in the beautiful is to arise from the free play of the imagination, it is those manifolds that allow it maximum free play consistent with the facility of the understanding to conceive the manifold as a whole that will be most adapted to their harmonious interplay. The suitability (or lack of it) of any particular manifold for allowing the productive imagination and the understanding to work together as harmoniously as possible deter-

---

[1] See e.g. *CPR*, B 162–3, where Kant argues that a definite cognition of an object in space or in time requires as its basis that we apprehend the manifold of representations in one spatial or temporal intuition; and, as he argues at B 151–2, it is the *productive* imagination which, in conformity with the categories, makes possible this basic sensible apprehension (without which no experience of an object can occur). The same fundamental apprehension is required whether we are actually perceiving an object or only imagining ourselves doing so.

mines the intensity of the feeling of pleasure (or displeasure). Briefly, the estimate of an object's beauty, since it is determined immediately by feeling, yet claims universal necessary validity, must be dependent upon the degree of harmonious free play that the manifold, by means of which the object is given, permits to the cognitive faculties (imagination and understanding).

This estimate bears *some* resemblance to the estimate that is made when judging the perfection of an object. In the latter case, the question is whether the parts of the presented object are well suited to satisfying our concept of the end or purpose of the object; and the pleasure or displeasure felt is a *consequence* of making this estimate of suitability. In the case of estimating an object's beauty, the judgment depends not upon whether the parts of the manifold are well suited to satisfying any definite concept of an object, but upon whether the manifold is well suited, well adapted, for putting the cognitive faculties into harmonious free play. Admittedly, in both cases, the decision is consciously based upon the feeling of pleasure or displeasure. But it is only in the case of the judgment of taste that the estimate depends on the degree to which the manifold puts the cognitive faculties into harmonious *free* play. Here, the estimate hinges on the suitability or purposiveness of the manifold to produce pleasure *without* the intervention of any definite concept of the given object's end or purpose. Kant puts this by saying that, with a judgment of the beautiful, it is a question of estimating the manifold's purposiveness without the thought of some end or purpose served by the object. Whereas, with a judgment of perfection, the estimate hinges precisely on whether the parts are well formed to satisfy our concept of the object's end or purpose; and the feeling produced does here depend on the success of the presented object's form in answering to that empirical concept.

Kant accuses the rationalist of failing to distinguish the judgment of beauty from the judgment of perfection. The judgment of beauty is not, as the rationalist asserts, merely a *confused* judgment of perfection: in other words, a judgment that is, in reality, based upon the suitability of a manifold to answer to our concept of an object's end or purpose, yet is *unconsciously* so based (while consciously this conceptual judgment is experienced as a resultant feeling of pleasure or displeasure). A pure aesthetic judgment is never dependent on the application, conscious *or* unconscious, of such a concept. It is determined by the feeling of pleasure or displeasure unmediated by *any* definite concept. And, in the case of a pure judgment of taste (as opposed to one of sense), the feeling must be consequent upon the free employment of the cognitive powers. In no other way can the judgment demand universal agreement without the intervention of a definite concept.

Why, though, should it be supposed that the free play of the cognitive powers is attended with any feeling at all? I do not believe that Kant produces an argument that can be taken as a free-standing proof for this supposition. It is true that he observes, in the Introduction to the *Third Critique* (5:187), that the successful completion of any intellectual task is attended with pleasure. But this observation appears to be an empirical generalization, not one that carries a priori validity with it. And in any case, the generalization is based on instances where we already have a determinate concept grounding the success of the judgment (as with judgments of perfection) or where we successfully fabricate a new determinate concept to fit the discovered evidence (as in scientific theory construction). It is doubtful whether these instances can provide sufficient ground for confidently extending the generalization to the judgment of taste, since in this latter case there is *no* determinate concept to mark our successful completion of the act of judging. At the same time, I do not doubt that Kant thought that these instances do provide collateral evidence for claiming that the harmonious free play of the cognitive faculties is attended with pleasure.

In fact, given his strategy in the Four Moments, it is arguable that he is not especially concerned to provide an *independent* proof that the harmonious free play of the imagination and understanding is attended with pleasure. Rather, that strategy begins by affirming that a disinterested feeling *is* the determining ground of the pure judgment of taste, and then sets out to show that when we make such a judgment, we always and only attempt to reflect freely on the mere form of an object. Hence, the feeling that alone determines any pure judgment of taste must be employing the cognitive faculties in their free play. The challenge is then to show that a feeling which does arise from this free play can give us the right to claim – as we do – universal necessary agreement for our pure judgments of taste. So far, Kant has established not only that it must be the free play of the cognitive powers that enables us to make a pure judgment of taste, but that we are justified in assuming that all of us have the same cognitive faculties (in order for us to share objective judgments).

But, it may be objected, even if the feeling which grounds the judgment of taste must itself be dependent upon estimating the harmonious free play of the cognitive faculties, what reason is there for supposing that it is the *same* relation between the understanding and imagination that produces, in all who make a judgment of taste, the pleasure in the beautiful? It is one thing to hold that since the feeling determining the judgment of taste demands the agreement of everyone, it must be consequent upon estimating the free and harmonious relationship between the cognitive faculties; it is a further thing to hold that such a method of estimating must actually produce *agreement*. Why should it be that the relation between these cognitive faculties, *when in free play*, is the same for all of us with respect to any given manifold? Perhaps another spectator's pleasure arises from a *different* interplay between the two cognitive faculties (here felt as harmonious) than in one's own case. And if that is so, there can be no reason to claim that the objects whose mere form gives one personally a disinterested feeling of pleasure ought also to please that other spectator. On the contrary, beauty would be dependent on the different ways in which our respective cognitive powers are put into harmonious free play.

In short, while the objector concedes that we determine the beauty of an object on the basis of a disinterested pleasure, and that this determination must result from estimating the degree to which the object's mere form is suited to putting the cognitive faculties into harmonious free play (faculties that must be shared by all of us), he does not accept that, even with these concessions, one can *justifiably* claim the agreement of everyone else's judgment with one's own. As we noted earlier, Kant holds that this claim to universality is not a mere empirical generalization: it does not predict that, as a matter of fact, we shall all be in agreement in our pure judgments of taste. It claims the *necessary* agreement of everyone, just as if the judgment were based on a definite concept of the object. In this respect, the rationalist's analysis looks much more attractive than the empiricist's. For the former analysis, unlike the latter, since it is grounded on a definite (empirical) concept, is in a position to explain how a claim to universal necessary agreement can be justified. The difficulty for Kant's analysis is that although he wishes to affirm that, provided we *have* succeeded in making a pure judgment of taste (and not confused the matter with the form, or the perfection with the beauty), we can claim the necessary agreement of everyone, it is not obvious how he is going to justify this demand.

Here we move on to Kant's discussion in the Fourth Moment and in the Deduction. Nominally, the Fourth Moment is concerned only with elucidating the point, made above, that the judgment of taste claims universal *necessary* validity. But it is, in reality, equally devoted to explaining how we could be *justified* in making the claim to necessity. Recall that, on the objection we are now considering, it is not enough to show that the feeling of disinterested pleasure must arise from the harmonious free play of the cognitive powers. What additionally needs to be shown is that, when we experience a disinterested feeling, it must be the *same* relation for all of us between the cognitive faculties, in their freedom, that feels harmonious; and hence that the same formal arrangements will necessarily be determined as beautiful by all of us. Is there any reason to suppose that we do possess a shared sensitivity to beauty?

Francis Hutcheson had, indeed, maintained that a shared sense of beauty does exist in human beings.[2] He based his theory upon factual observations. These led him to conclude that when spectators judge objects to be beautiful, they not only do so on the basis of a feeling of disinterested pleasure, but that, once certain disturbing features are discounted, this feeling is almost always aroused by the 'uniformity amidst variety' to be found in the forms of those objects. So far as concerns these conclusions, Kant is in close agreement with Hutcheson. When he comes to give his own unspecific description of the formal basis on which we judge the beautiful objects of nature, he says: 'Forms of this kind are those which by their combination of unity and heterogeneity serve as it were to strengthen and entertain the mental powers that enter into [free] play in the exercise of the faculty of judgment' (*CJ*, 5:359).

But while Kant is evidently not unhappy that experience should testify to a degree of unanimity in our sensitivity to beauty, he does think that resting the case for a common sense of beauty on *empirical* evidence is misguided, if the claim to the necessary universality of the judgment of taste is to be defended. Factual evidence for a common sense of beauty could, at best, support a claim to the *comparative* universality of a judgment of taste (which is all Hutcheson, as an empiricist, holds out for), not one of *strict* universality and necessity.

Accordingly, since on the Kantian analysis, the judgment of taste makes a claim to necessity and strict universality, it comes as no surprise that his own argument for the existence of a common sense of beauty is based on conceptual, and not on factual, considerations. As we have noted, it depends on linking the conditions for our making

---

[2] See *An Inquiry Concerning Beauty, Order, Harmony, Design*, esp. Sects I–III and VI–VII (Treatise I of *An Inquiry into the Original of Our Ideas of Beauty and Virtue*, 4th edn (London, 1738)).

taste judgments with those for our making valid perceptual judgments. In order for us to share perceptual knowledge of objects, the cognitive faculties of imagination and understanding must work together, and the way in which they work together must be the same for all of us. Unless both these requirements are fulfilled, we should be unable universally to agree in any of our empirical claims about the objective world (and hence share perceptual knowledge). The reason why agreement in our empirical judgments requires that both requirements be fulfilled is that no empirical knowledge of objects can occur unless the productive imagination and the understanding are able jointly to unify a given manifold into the form of a single spatial or temporal intuition. But if the relation between these two faculties differed among us, there could be no certainty that we should all apprehend any given manifold of representations as together forming the *same* spatial or temporal intuition. Hence, we should be unable to presuppose that our claimed empirical judgments about objects must be universally shared – since this at least requires that we must all apprehend the manifold in a common spatial or temporal form.

Returning to our judgments of taste, we can now see that provided our feeling of pleasure is based purely on the degree of harmony that a given manifold allows to the productive imagination and the understanding, when these faculties are engaged in their non-empirical role of connecting the manifold together in the form of a single intuition, our taste judgments must be in universal agreement. The agreement must be universal, because the way in which understanding and imagination are here related to one another has to be the same for all of us (for any shared perceptual knowledge of objects to be possible); and it is *only* this non-empirical role of the two faculties that is utilized in a pure judgment of taste. Certainly, with normal perceptual judgments, the two faculties are further engaged in making possible the consciousness of a specific empirical object (here imagination, in its reproductive capacity, is in the service of an empirical concept provided by the understanding). Whereas, with pure judgments of taste, the two faculties merely connect the manifold together into the form of a single spatial or temporal intuition, and the spectator estimates, by means of feeling, the suitability of that manifold for harmoniously engaging the cognitive faculties in this task (here the imagination is in free play relative to any empirical concept, and subject only to the a priori concepts of the understanding). Yet since, in both cases, the *relation* between understanding and imagination, in their non-empirical roles, must be the same for all of us, while the *degree* of harmony between them – in bringing the manifold together in a single intuition – is entirely dependent on the structure of the given manifold and so, for that manifold, must also be the same for all of us, it follows that we are justified in assuming that all pure judgments of taste about the same manifold must agree with one another. For the intensity of the feeling of disinterested pleasure – which determines the judgment of taste – arises from the degree of harmony between understanding and productive imagination, and this, as we have just seen, must be the same for all of us in respect of any given manifold. The supposition of a common sense of beauty is therefore well founded, independently of any empirical investigation. It is established a priori by showing that if the relationship between the faculties of imagination and understanding were different – thereby giving rise to discordant pure judgments of taste with respect to the same manifold – this would have the consequence that we could not share perceptual knowledge of objects.

In seeking to explain how our pure judgments of taste are possible, Kant has been primarily concerned with the following question: Given that an immediate feeling of disinterested pleasure or displeasure is the determining ground of our pure judgments of taste (our judgments of beauty), how can we be warranted in claiming that, with respect to the same object, anyone who makes such a judgment ought to be in agreement with our own? He has answered this question by arguing that our demand is warranted because we are justified in believing that there must be a common sense of beauty: an immediate and identically orientated sensitivity to formal arrangements in all who judge by taste alone. This is not, of course, to assert that we will all be in agreement in our taste assessments. Whether in the case of others *or in the case of ourselves*, there can be no certainty that we have ever made a *pure* judgment of taste (and not mistaken, or partly so, the object's perfection for its beauty, or its matter for its form). But the question at issue is not whether we can *tell* whether a pure judgment of taste has ever been made; it is whether, when one is made (which is in principle possible), it can rightfully claim universal necessary validity.

We have now traced the argument by which Kant seeks to effect a *via media* between the empiricist and rationalist views of the judgment of taste. While agreeing with the empiricist that the determining ground of the judgment is a disinterested feeling, he has shown how to combine this with the rationalist view that the judgment claims universal necessary validity. The resolution is made possible by showing that the disinterested feeling must depend upon the extent of harmonious free play between the cognitive faculties; and that these faculties must be both universally shared and universally employed in the same way whenever we make a pure judgment of taste.

The Finality of Nature as the Bridge between the Realms of Nature and of Freedom

But why do we attach such significance – as Kant is convinced that we do – to judgments of taste or, at least, to those that refer to nature? This issue is raised soon after the 'Deduction of judgments of taste' (Section 38), and taken up seriously in Section 42, entitled 'The intellectual interest in the beautiful'. It brings us for the first time, in the main body of the text, to the issue of the *bridging* role of judgments of taste, linking judgments in the realm of nature with those in the realm of freedom.

The role of design or adaptedness in the objects of our taste is a matter of supreme importance in Kant's aesthetics. Although we should never judge a given object's beauty in terms of the degree to which its parts are adapted to fulfilling our concept of the object's end, we do judge nature's beauties *as if* they have been designed to put our cognitive powers into free play. Moreover, we find instances of natural beauty in surprising abundance. This suitability of many of nature's forms for our sense of beauty – their 'finality', as he terms it, for the free use of our cognitive faculties – calls for an explanation.

> With regard to the beautiful in nature, therefore, we may start a number of questions touching the cause of this finality of their forms: e.g. How we are to explain why nature has scattered beauty abroad with so lavish a hand, even in the depth of the ocean when it can but seldom be reached by the eye of man – for which alone it is final. (CJ, Sect. 30; 5:279)

Going along with the abundance of beauties to be found in nature, Kant claims that those who *take an interest* in these beauties testify to their possession of 'a good soul' – that is, to their strong commitment to realizing the highest good. What he means by 'taking an interest' in nature's beauties is taking delight in the *existence* of the beautiful forms of nature. *This* delight is not purely one of taste (which must itself be free of *any* interest). It is, rather, a delight that first arises from noticing that there exist beautiful natural forms, indeed a profusion of them. As Kant sees it, this profusion of beautiful forms, by suggesting that the natural world is favourably arranged for the free and harmonious use of our cognitive powers, gives us some ground to hope that it is also favourably arranged to allow us to achieve our final (moral) end, viz. the highest good.

Although the connection between our interest in nature's beauties and our interest in the highest good is acknowledged in the section in which our intellectual interest in the beautiful is explicitly discussed (Section 42), it is in the Critique of Teleological Judgment that we find Kant's most explicit statement of the relationship between the two interests. It is, he says, 'in all probability . . . this moral interest that first aroused attentiveness to beauty and the ends of nature', and that 'it is only in relation to the final [moral] end that the very study of the ends of nature acquires that immediate interest displayed to so great an extent in the admiration bestowed upon nature without regard to any accruing advantage' (CJ, Sect. 88; 5:459).

But, more precisely, what is it about our study of the beauties of nature that awakens this aesthetic interest that is allied to the moral? It is a certain similarity of form in our moral and taste judgments. Just as the moral judgment is not based on any interest, yet, by means of the suitability of a maxim to stand as a practical law, produces a feeling of respect which we think of as holding with necessity and universality, so the judgment of taste is not based on any interest, yet, by means of the suitability of a natural object's form for the free use of our cognitive powers, produces a feeling of delight which we think of as holding with necessity and universality. In the case of the moral, the feeling is, of course, produced by a *determinate* rule, the moral law, and an interest in the actual existence of those actions falling under that law is immediately aroused. But Kant thinks that the similarities between the two forms of judgment are sufficiently striking – at least to those who already have, or who are especially susceptible to having, a keen interest in the highest good – to engender a parallel interest in the existence of the beauties of nature. In other words, the similarity in form between the two kinds of judgment leads those who are already possessed of a good soul to take a delight in the actual existence of natural beauties, particularly since they are found in such abundance. For the existence of these beauties suggests that just as nature, or its ultimate cause, may have produced natural forms merely for the free delight of our cognitive faculties, so nature, or its ultimate cause, may be favourably disposed to our achieving, by the free use of our practical faculty (the will), the highest good.

That is why Kant affirms that those who can be seen as taking an interest in the beauties of nature – what he also describes as display-ing a *feeling* for beautiful nature (CJ, Sect. 42; 5:303) – are thereby attesting to their possession of a good soul. Contrariwise, he contends that those who show little or no feeling for nature's beauties, devot-ing themselves to what *gratifies* their senses (the agreeable), are unworthy of their higher calling, i.e. to be active, self-directed beings rather than, like the so-called lower animals, merely passive recipients of whatever nature presents to them. Their habits of mind he describes as 'coarse and low', and he evidently thinks that we are jus-tified in condemning them in moral, or quasi-moral, terms. He even goes so far as to claim that inherent in our judgments of taste on nature is a requirement – a requirement *amounting to a duty* – to develop a feeling for its beauties.[3] He thinks that, by developing this feeling, we are provided with the ideal means of overcoming our inter-est in those properties that primarily stimulate our sensuous pleasures and, at the same time, of replacing it with an interest in those that arouse our moral feeling. For, just as a feeling for the beauties of nature requires one to concentrate on form, not content, and to exercise a *free* activity of the cognitive powers, so the moral feeling requires one to concentrate not on the content, but on the form, of any proposed course of action, and to exercise freedom of the will. Moreover, once a feeling for beautiful nature has been properly cultivated (and with it a recognition of the *lavishness* with which such beauties are to be found), he believes that our resolve to achieve the highest good will be strengthened. It will be strengthened because the natural world – or its ultimate ground – will no longer be seen as hostile or indiffer-ent to our attempts to realize our final (moral) end.

There has been a long-standing debate as to whether the moral or quasi-moral requirement that we take an interest in natural beauty is needed to justify the *necessity* that (on the Kantian analysis) is implied by the judgment of taste. The answer, as it seems to me, is that in so far as Kant is seeking to show that the pure judgment of taste can

---

[3] This requirement does not extend to works of art. Although Kant accepts that fine art may, as a matter of fact, have some beneficial social consequences (as well as some less attractive ones), he denies that these can carry the *moral* significance which we attach to an interest in nature's beauties. It is only a feeling for *natural* beauty which we demand with the force of that necessity that is a defining characteristic of our concept of duty or moral obligation.

justifiably claim the necessary *agreement* of all who judge by taste, there neither need be nor can be any reference to our moral nature (though, as we shall see from the Dialectic, there *does* need to be a general reference to our noumenal or supersensible nature). What is wanted is a proof that the faculties which alone can produce the disinterested feeling of pleasure or displeasure must be shared by, and identically related in, all of us. This proof (which we have already considered) is undertaken in the Deduction properly so called (Section 38), as well as in certain parts of the Four Moments. It applies equally to judgments of taste on natural and on artistic beauty. But in so far as he is seeking to justify the requirement that we *employ and develop* our capacity to feel an immediate delight in natural beauty – and he undoubtedly does believe that we make such a demand with the force of a moral injunction – then the reference to our moral nature is essential. Without this reference and, more especially, the overriding requirement on us to seek to achieve the highest good, he thinks that we would have no convincing explanation for the strict demand that we make, both on ourselves and on others, to cultivate our taste for natural beauty. But this demand is not a constitutive, but a *regulative*, one: reason urges it on us because a feeling for the beauties of nature enhances our capacity to achieve our final (moral) end. In Kant's eyes, it is this connection to morality which, above all else, can justify the *importance* that we undoubtedly attach to developing and displaying taste.

The Sublime

Between the Four Moments and the Deduction of pure aesthetic judgments, Kant sandwiches a discussion of the sublime (CJ, 5:244–78). He thinks that judgments of the sublime, like those of the beautiful, claim universal necessary validity even though they are determined by a feeling, and not by any definite concept of the object. Since they are grounded immediately on feeling, judgments of the sublime constitute the third category of aesthetic judgment, the other two being judgments of taste and judgments of sense. In fact, he does not believe that, strictly, objects of nature (still less of art) can be sublime at all. Rather, it is our *attitude of mind*, sparked by certain experiences, that should strictly be conceived as sublime.

Briefly, our ascriptions of the sublime originate from the formlessness or even chaos that certain natural sights display – e.g. the ocean agitated by a storm or the eruption of a volcano – provided that they also give us the impression of great magnitude or power. These sights stimulate our imagination to try to summon up sensuous presentations of the immensity and the boundless might of the physical universe. Now although our imagination is not up to this task, thereby making us conscious of our own insignificance and helplessness as sensuous beings in the face of nature's limitlessness, we are none the less capable of feeling a real superiority over these impressions. This sense of superiority arises when we recognize in ourselves, as supersensible creatures (noumena), a faculty of far greater worth than anything belonging to the natural world, and which none of its forces need overcome or can destroy. This is the faculty of reason, pre-eminently in its moral capacity to resist and overcome all natural influences. The natural world, then, is not itself sublime; but certain natural occurrences have the capacity to show us that we possess something that is truly sublime, our rational moral capacity: 'sublimity . . . does not reside in any of the things of nature, but only in our mind, insofar as we may become conscious of our superiority over nature within, and thus also over nature without us (as exerting influence over us)' (CJ, Sect. 28; 5:264). This consciousness of our superiority, as rational beings, over nature and its immense forces is manifested as a feeling of delight. Kant seems to think of this feeling as an instance of the moral feeling (the feeling of respect), because it results from our recognition of reason's capacity to disregard or overcome all sensible influences. Accordingly, everyone who possesses the capacity to experience the moral feeling must equally be susceptible to the feeling of the sublime in the face of nature's unbounded magnitude and power.

Since it is not the object, but our attitude of mind, that can strictly be sublime, Kant rightly holds that there is no call for a justification or deduction of judgments of the sublime beyond the explanation of how the feeling which determines these judgments comes about. (This feeling, after all, has been traced to the moral feeling which we both presuppose and require in everyone.) The great difference between judgments of the sublime and those of taste is that we *do* maintain that certain natural objects are beautiful. So the question arises, in the latter case, of how it is possible for us to think of the form of these objects as justifying a judgment which carries universal necessary validity, although it is not determined by any definite objective concept. Moreover, since we in fact find an abundance of natural objects that strike us as beautiful, there is the further question of what attitude we should adopt to a nature that displays such a wealth of beautiful forms. As we have seen, the first issue is taken up in various parts of the Four Moments and in the Deduction, and the second issue is discussed in 'The intellectual interest in the beautiful' (Section 42). Both will be raised again in the Dialectic. But, for the reasons just given, neither of these issues can arise in the case of judgments of the sublime in nature; and that is why Kant does not consider them to have the philosophical importance attaching to judgments of beauty.

Fine Art

Works of art occupy an intriguing position in Kant's aesthetics, because they are intentionally constructed objects. This means that, in order to exist at all, they need to be composed in accordance with determinate rules within a particular art form. For instance, a poem will be written as a sonnet or a villanelle etc.; a painting will be composed as a portrait or a landscape etc. (and many paintings and poems will be devoted to a particular theme, e.g. love or death). This means that works of art cannot be subject to a *pure* judgment of taste, since they must, in addition, be judged on the basis of their perfection. In this way, they differ from natural objects.

> If, however, the object is presented as an object of art, and as such to be declared beautiful, then, seeing that art always presupposes an end in the cause (and its causality), a concept of what that thing is intended to be must first of all be laid at its basis. And, since the agreement of the manifold in a thing with an inner character belonging to it as its end constitutes the perfection of the thing, it follows that in estimating the beauty of art the perfection of the thing must also be taken into account – a matter which in estimating the beauty of nature, as beautiful, is quite irrelevant. (CJ, Sect. 48; 5:311)

How can we explain an artist's creation of a beautiful object? Works of art are intentionally produced, yet what is so produced is a work of beauty. Does this mean that artists have produced their beautiful objects merely by applying, whether consciously or unconsciously, determinate rules of composition? Patently, this cannot be an explanation that Kant would allow, because it would fly in the face of his claim that there are no specifiable rules for assessing the beauty of objects (whether natural or man-made). If putative works of art could be produced by the application of determinate rules, then we, the spectators, could in principle learn to assess their artistic merit by judging the extent to which they accord with these rules of beauty.

If Kant is to allow, as he does, that works of beauty can be created by human beings, he will need to hold that their creation as beautiful objects cannot be reduced to any determinate rules. This is, indeed, his position, and he expresses it by saying that a work of art must display *originality*. But it is vital to note that in making this claim he does not suppose that a work of art can be created without any rule governing it *in respect of which it is beautiful*. There must be such a rule, even though it is not one that can be determinately stated by us; for, otherwise, we could not think of the object as intentionally formed as a work of beauty, and hence as art. In so far as the work is beautiful, its production must arise from the nature of its creator by means of an act of originality. That is why Kant holds that all artists must be geniuses: they must create their art, in respect of its beauty, not by following any determinate rules – even unconsciously – but must themselves *give the rule to art*. Yet this rule cannot then be summed up in any *specifiable* concept (by which we can determine in advance which objects are beautiful); it can only be *shown* or *displayed* in the artwork. Even the artists themselves cannot specify in any algorithmic manner how they achieve their results.

At the same time, the genius is not exempt from having to learn the academic rules of his art form. Without academic skill, genuine originality will be unable to flourish. As we have noted, art, unlike nature, is always the intentional production of some artefact. There are determinate academic rules of composition that need to be mastered within a given art form; and unless the artist has mastered the rules of his medium, there cannot be the proper framework within which originality can operate. The ability to master the academic rules is ascribed to the understanding, while the talent for originality is ascribed to the free play of the imagination.

Kant points out that, connected with originality, as a condition for genius, the works produced by an original mind must be *exemplary*. His idea is that one can produce original work that is nonsense or rubbish; and such work is manifestly not sufficient to warrant us supposing that a contribution has been made to fine art. Accordingly, what is produced by a genius must be exemplary. It must be exemplary in the sense of serving as a model or standard of *judgment* for estimating other work in the same style (as well as for facilitating the development of a spectator's own taste) and, at the same time, as a *stimulus* to another genius to set his own original powers into their creative swing. A work of true genius must be capable of stimulating the imagination to free itself from the constraints of definite rules, while yet allowing it to engage in a train of unbounded ideas that are consonant with the understanding's most general demand for unity.

With these conditions for the production of fine art in mind, we can see why Kant contrasts the production of fine art not only, and unsurprisingly, with what he calls 'mechanical art', i.e. craft, but with the work of even the very greatest scientists (including mathematicians). In all of these contrasted cases, there are, he thinks, methodical procedures that consciously or unconsciously are always being followed to obtain results. No genius is required to give the rules in the first place.

It might appear an obvious objection that from the fact that Euclid's axioms and Newton's principles may be employed by others to obtain further, more specific, results (by the application of scientific methods), it does not follow that no Kantian-style originality is required for the initial formulation of the first principles of these sciences, i.e. by Euclid and Newton. Surely, the mere fact that the rules of a system can be codified does not mean that those who originally put forward these rules do not thereby display genius. But this objection does not tell against Kant because, as he makes clear in the *First Critique* and elsewhere, the *fundamental* rules from which the first Euclidean and Newtonian principles stem are already in us (a priori). In particular, the first principles of Newtonian physics are derivable from the principles of pure natural science (when applied to what in fact moves in space, viz. matter); and these latter principles are themselves held to be derivable from the categories of the understanding (when schematized in accordance with our temporal form of intuition). Consequently, no acts of the free play of the cognitive powers are required in order to produce the Newtonian first principles of physics. (A similar story goes for geometry.) The greatness of men like Newton lies, for Kant, in their capacity to make explicit and to integrate the basic principles of their sciences (from which so many important discoveries can flow). On the Kantian account of creativity, it is only in the production of works of art that the imagination is freed, at least to some extent, from the constraints of definite concepts; and hence only in the production of fine art that genuine originality can be found.

Later developments in physical theory and in mathematics may well lead one to doubt the adequacy of Kant's contrast between the creation of works of art, on the one hand, and the formation of physical and mathematical theories, on the other. For my part, I think that the crucial difficulty for his position lies not so much in his views about the genesis of theories in natural science and mathematics as in his requirement for originality in *art*. I shall return to the issue of artistic originality in the closing section on Kant's aesthetics.

In Section 49, Kant considers how understanding and imagination combine in the production of a work of genius. In order for a work to succeed as fine art, it needs to be more than tasteful (by not offending against any of the academic rules): it must exhibit what Kant calls 'soul'. It is this latter feature which the genius alone can put into a work. This he does by his capacity for presenting 'aesthetic ideas'. These are products of the imagination for which no determinate concept or rule, no definite unifying thought, can be adequate.

There is the familiar, everyday use of the productive imagination which allows us to imagine creatures, occurrences and so on which, though not found in nature, are fabricated from items that we have experienced. The capacity to form aesthetic ideas goes beyond this familiar use of the productive imagination. After all, these fabricated products of the imagination *could* be unified under a determinate concept, e.g. the concept of a griffin. Rather, it is, in the first instance, the capacity to form a wealth of imaginative ideas that illustrate a given determinate concept (love or death, for instance), yet in such a way that *no* further definite concept can sum up the succession of sensuous ideas or images by which the original, determinate concept is being illustrated. And, in the second instance – and what, according to Kant, most separates the true artist from the rest of us – it is the capacity to find the *expression* (in words or other artistic forms) that triggers this train of unbounded sensuous ideas.

It is important to appreciate that an aesthetic idea is one that cannot be clearly expressed or captured in any definite concept. There can be *partial* expressions, associated with the apparently endless variety of sensuous ideas or images comprising the aesthetic idea; but no determinate concept encompassing this whole series of thoughts and images. This is precisely why the ideas are called aesthetic or sensuous ones. Such ideas are to be contrasted with *rational ideas*. These are ideas of reason, e.g. our idea of God, to which no intuition – that is, no sensuous representation – is adequate. Certainly, an aesthetic idea can be used to illustrate a facet of a rational idea (often this is the case in religious art), but it can never succeed in capturing it entirely. This is because the proper medium for the expression of a rational idea is reason or the intellect, and not a sensuous medium.

The genius, then, has the capacity, by means of the expression of an aesthetic idea, to furnish the productive imagination of the spectator with an unbounded set of connected or half-connected sensuous ideas which, while they are consonant with the determinate concept or theme of the art object, are yet such that no definite concept is adequate to unify all these ideas. When this occurs, the mind feels the enlivening power of the free play of the imagination.

Would Kant allow for the possibility of *degrees* of originality? On the face of it, he appears to divide the producers of fine art into those very rare human beings who are geniuses, and those 'clever minds' who, however much they may possess fine taste and be well practised in academic rules, lack originality. The latter form themselves into schools of 'artists' who follow the work of a particular genius, producing tasteful work in the style of the master but without soul (and hence not works of art in the true sense).

Yet, clearly we do possess the idea of degrees of originality. We talk of a 'supreme or towering genius', contrasting such a one with a person who is 'touched with genius'. We also, I suggest, have the distinction between someone whose genius displays itself more in the originating of a *new* style (someone like Picasso or T. S. Eliot) and someone whose genius is more evidently displayed by a highly complex *synthesis* of already existing styles (like Bach).

On the question of degrees of originality, Kant does speak at one stage of 'full-blown' geniuses; and this suggests that he might well allow as a contrast those who possess only a small degree of originality. Since originality consists in the capacity to put the cognitive capacities into free play, someone who is only touched with genius would only very occasionally pull off this feat. Although I think that this account is consonant with a good deal of what Kant says, the fact remains that he does speak of the genius as an extremely rare creature indeed. He even suggests, at one stage, that the limit has very probably 'been long since attained' for the production of genuinely original work (CJ, Sect. 47; 5:309).[4] These claims do not sit well with the idea of the comparatively large number of artists whom we would think of as possessing at least some degree of genius.

Moreover, although Kant is obviously right to say that a genius can be the impetus to a school of 'clever minds' or imitators, there are cases where we think of a school of artists without thinking that only

---

[4] Although he *also* holds that Christoph Wieland (1733–1813) and possibly the 'great king', Frederick the Great (1712–86), have produced poetic work of true originality. Both men are almost exact contemporaries of Kant (1724–1804).

one of them – even if he is thought of as 'the originator' of the school – is a true genius. Thus we talk of the Impressionist School of Painters (e.g. Manet, Monet, Pissarro, Sisley, Renoir) or of the Romantic School of English Poets (e.g. Wordsworth, Coleridge, Byron, Shelley, Keats). These schools are not normally thought to be composed of only one genius plus a lot of clever minds: we would, rather, tend to credit all, or most, of the above-named members of each school as having some genuine originality. Here, the two distinctions of degrees of original-ity, on the one hand, and originality which is primarily displayed through innovation or which is primarily displayed through synthesis, on the other hand, seem to come into play with us. But whether these are distinctions that Kant himself would allow – in particular, whether he would credit those who are considered to be great synthesizers as possessing genius – seems to me less certain.

Kant's conception of the artist as genius raises a question about whether his account of the production of works of art can be consist-tent with his claim, in the *First* and *Second Critiques*, that all the actions of human beings are in principle predictable from a knowledge of their empirical characters (and the circumstances in which they are placed). For – it may be objected – if there are no determinate rules governing artistic creation, it must follow that we cannot predict how, in all circumstances, an artist will act, viz. when he is constructing his work. On the other hand, if the actions of an artist can be predicted with certainty, it must follow that there *are* rules for the creation of beautiful objects.

Now, in fact, I think that the objection does raise a deep issue in Kant's aesthetics which will be taken up in the Dialectic. On the face of it, however, the objection can be swiftly answered. Given his views in the first two *Critiques*, it must indeed be possible to predict an artist's actions, even with respect to his production of an artefact that is a genuine work of art. But it does not follow that the rules by which the artist's actions are predictable can be seen as rules *for the creation of beauty*. Let us suppose that the work produced is a beautiful statue. Kant is committed to accepting that causal laws must exist such that they could predict how, from a knowledge of initial circumstances, the artist would put together the various constituents of that statue. (Compare the creation of a beautiful snowflake. Physical laws, together with a knowledge of initial conditions, could be used to predict how this snowflake will come to be formed.) However, the laws that predict the actions which produced the particular (beautiful) statue do not give us any rules for determining which *further*, qualitatively different statues, even by the same artist, will be beautiful. (Analogously, with snowflakes.) The only way for us to determine whether *any* statue is beautiful must depend on the disinterested feeling that its overall design arouses; and that, according to Kant, cannot depend on any determinate rules – since it depends precisely on the feeling of the *free* play of the cognitive powers. Even if (as with snowflakes) we possessed very full and precise laws for the production of objects of a given type, as well as a knowledge of all the initial conditions from which they are naturally produced, we could not tell from this information *which* of the token objects of that type (e.g. which particular snowflakes) would be beautiful. While the construction of any particular composite object must be fully causally determined, the question of whether the *end result* is beautiful cannot be determined merely from a knowledge of the rules for *building* the object. An object's beauty, whether it be a product of nature or a product of human art, is determined by the degree to which its overall design puts our cognitive faculties into harmonious free play.

Provisionally, then, we can say that Kant's conception of genius is compatible with his conception of the thoroughgoing determinism in the spatio-temporal world.

10

The Dialectic of Aesthetic Judgment: Why the Judgment of Taste and our Attitude to Natural Beauty Require a Copernican Revolution in Aesthetics

> [Those] judgments – called *aesthetic* (having merely subjective princi-
> ples) since they are distinct from all those called 'logical' (whether they
> are theoretical or practical) which have objective principles – are of a
> special kind which connect sensuous intuitions to an idea of nature in
> which its conformity to law cannot be understood apart from a relation
> to a suprasensuous substrate. The proof of this will be produced in the
> course of the discussion.
>
> (First Introduction to the *Critique of Judgment*, Sect. II; 20:246–7;
> italics original)

Just as Kant believes that there are antinomies in our employment of
theoretical and practical reason, so he believes that an antinomy lies
in the background of our judgments of taste. It is normally referred to
as the Antinomy of Taste. This antinomy, and its resolution, constitutes
the main topic of the Dialectic of Aesthetic Judgment.

It has seemed to many commentators that the Antinomy of Taste –
the proposed solution of which is what primarily leads Kant to invoke
transcendental idealism with regard to aesthetics – is a most unconvincing affair. Indeed, the appeal to transcendental idealism in the
Dialectic, as well as the antinomy itself, is often treated as an irrelevance to Kant's aesthetics, which it is best to pass over as rapidly as
possible. This attitude strikes me as seriously mistaken, on at least
three counts. I shall argue that (1) Kant is right to suppose that, on his
analysis of the judgment of taste, there *is* an antinomy in the claims
that we make in our taste judgments; (2) he is correct to hold that the
antinomy can be resolved only by invoking his distinction between
phenomena and noumena (and hence by invoking transcendental
idealism); (3) the relationships that he wishes to bring out in the

Dialectic between beauty and morality depend on accepting transcendental idealism.

The Antinomy of Taste seeks to demonstrate that our ideas about the aesthetic judgment are self-contradictory:

Thesis: The judgment of taste is not founded on concepts, since it is impossible to decide the validity of any judgment by means of a proof; each judgment, rather, is determined immediately by a disinterested feeling of pleasure or displeasure.

Antithesis: The judgment of taste is founded on concepts, since its claim to universal necessary agreement is possible only if there is a rule determining the judgment.

This Antinomy has frequently seemed unconvincing because, it is said, Kant had already explained, before embarking on the Dialectic, how it is possible for the judgment of taste to claim universal necessary validity *without* the ability to justify the judgment by reference to any concept or rule. In the Analytic of the Beautiful, he has argued that, in a properly made judgment, the pleasure must arise from the free play of the cognitive faculties, viz. imagination and understanding. Consequently, it is clearly impossible to provide any determinate rule for the application of the judgment of taste (otherwise the imagination could *not* be in free play relative to empirical concepts provided by the understanding). None the less, since, as he has also argued, we must all have the same cognitive faculties, and they must be attuned identically for all of us, it follows that, assuming that I have not confused the beautiful with the agreeable or with perfection, my judgment of an object's beauty can rightly claim the necessary agreement of everyone else who makes a pure judgment of taste on the same object.

But this expression of doubt, with regard to the existence of an Antinomy of Taste, overlooks a key point. The free play alluded to refers to the freedom of the imagination – the productive imagination – from *determinate* concepts. The imagination, accordingly, is not here under the control of any empirical concept (and hence is not subject to the law of reproduction). But, as Kant had insisted in discussing freedom of the will in the *Critique of Practical Reason*, a will that is free is not a will that is law*less*.[1] If it were, no maxim of any action that is allegedly performed 'freely' could hold with necessity for the will

---

[1] See *CPractR*, Book I, Ch. I, Sects 5–6; 5: 28–30.

of everyone; on the contrary, a will that is lawless is a will that operates randomly. A free will must be subject to a rule (in fact, the rule expressed by the moral law). Similarly, a spectator's pure judgment of taste cannot possibly lay claim to universal necessary validity unless the imagination, in its freedom from any empirical concept, does operate in accordance with a rule (that is, the *same* rule holding for everyone). If the imagination, in reflecting 'freely' upon the manifold by which an object is given, behaved *chaotically*, or if it behaved regularly for each of us but could *vary* among us, it is obvious that no judgment of taste could lay claim to universal necessary validity. There must therefore be – what is for us – an *indeterminate* rule governing the imagination's free play in such cases.

Indeed, if there were no such rule, it would be impossible for us to share our *cognitive* judgments about the empirical world. For it is the spontaneous action of the productive imagination, in initially synthesizing the manifold so that it can be apprehended together in the form of a single spatial or temporal intuition, that also makes possible the application of empirical concepts to the contents of a manifold. Clearly, in the cognitive case, the productive imagination has to be operating in accordance with a strictly universal rule; otherwise we would be incapable of *sharing* ordinary empirical knowledge. This rule must equally apply with regard to pure judgments of taste, since, in their case too, the imagination in its spontaneity has to bring, or attempt to bring, a given manifold together into the form of a single sensible intuition – but here our ordinary activity of connecting that manifold by *empirical* concepts is laid aside.

So the Antinomy of Taste is not unconvincing, despite Kant's earlier claim that a common sense of beauty is well founded. By accepting the existence of such a sense, we are not released from acknowledging that the free play of the imagination must operate according to a rule, albeit – for us – an indeterminate rule. Far from it: what makes it possible to affirm that there exists a *common* sense of beauty is precisely that the imagination, when it reflects spontaneously on a manifold by which an object is given, must be governed by an indeterminate rule. Without the existence of a rule – a *strictly* universal rule – governing the free play of the imagination, it would be impossible justifiably to claim that certain forms are beautiful, i.e. such that they must please anyone who makes a pure judgment of taste upon them. Admittedly, Kant does believe that we can say unspecifically how the parts of a beautiful object must be formally related: they must collectively have both sufficient variety and sufficient unity to put our cognitive faculties into harmonious free play. But this description is so unspecific that it does not enable us to delineate any *definite* law by which the productive imagination must here be operating.

But now the question arises as to how we can *both* think of everything in nature as subject to determinate causal laws *and* think of the form of some of its products (natural beauties) as capable of putting our cognitive powers into harmonious free play. It would be impossible to combine these thoughts if the spatio-temporal world were conceived as existing *in itself*. This would be equivalent to accepting transcendental realism; and, on this theory, everything in nature exists, and only exists, as a noumenon *while yet being subject to the conditions of time*. Consequently, all the operations of our own minds, including those of the understanding and imagination, would be subject to natural law. Of course, the laws governing the operation of our minds would be psychological laws, but they would be natural (determinate) laws for all that. Hence it would be impossible for a feeling of pleasure to be generated by the interplay of the understanding and imagination when these are *not* acting according to any determinate law. Assuming, therefore, that the spatio-temporal world exists in itself, none of nature's forms could put our cognitive faculties into *free* play, nor could there be any judgments of taste (any judgments which, while justifiably claiming universal necessary validity, are determined immediately by a feeling of pleasure or displeasure). The question as to whether a natural form is beautiful could be calculated from a knowledge of its overall pattern and the natural laws governing the mind's operations. Beauty would then be founded on definite concepts, and not upon a feeling which is unmediated by any determinate rule.

If, however, we accept the distinction between phenomena and noumena, it is possible to allow that the judgment of taste can claim universal necessary validity and, at the same time, to allow that everything which happens in the spatio-temporal world (now considered as a mere phenomenon) is subject to determinate natural laws. While the determinate laws of nature must be thought of as responsible for the production of any composite phenomenal object, the end result, the object's overall formal arrangement (upon which the judgment of taste is directed), can yet be regarded as governed by an indeterminate rule and, as such, be capable of putting our cognitive faculties into free play. For, given the phenomena/noumena distinction, these faculties must belong to us as non-temporal (noumenal) subjects, and hence they must be capable of operating free from determinate rules. More particularly, the imagination, when taken in its productive capacity (the capacity in which it operates in aesthetic reflection), cannot be governed by any natural laws. It cannot, because the spontaneous action of the productive imagination is required in order for the phenomenal world – nature (together with its laws) – to exist in the first place.

The same general points go for artistic creativity and appreciation. If the spatio-temporal world is taken as existing in itself, the artist's aesthetic ideas cannot depend on the free play of his cognitive powers (since no free play can exist). Kant's notion of the artist as genius would have to be abandoned, since the so-called originality of his work must be governed by definite concepts. On the other hand, if we distinguish between the phenomenal and noumenal worlds, we can allow for the Kantian notion of artistic creativity. Although the artist's actions in putting together the various parts of his work into a single composite whole must be subject to natural law (like all other actions in the phenomenal world), it is none the less possible to regard the beautiful overall design that the artist thereby creates as the product of the harmonious free play of his cognitive faculties (and so as governed by an indeterminate rule). These faculties, after all, are now conceived as part of his non-temporal, noumenal self. Equally, we, the spectators, can judge the overall design to be beautiful only because this indeterminate rule puts our faculties into harmonious free play. Whether we consider the artist who creates the design or the spectators who appreciate it, that design can only be conceived as beautiful provided that we *distinguish* between our existence as phenomena and as noumena.

The upshot is that we could not think of either the creation of art or the appreciation of beauty (whether in art or nature) as dependent upon the free play of our cognitive powers without distinguishing between the phenomenal and noumenal worlds. Transcendental idealism, far from being an unnecessary excursion into Kant's metaphysics, is a vital ingredient in his justification of the judgment of taste.

Another way of presenting Kant's solution to the Antinomy of Taste is to see it, like his solutions to the Antinomies in the *First* and *Second Critiques*, as a means of demonstrating the truth of transcendental idealism and the falsity of transcendental realism (the only alternative theory, as he conceives it). We have noted that, if the latter theory is correct, our power of judgment must be at odds with itself: we should be making the mutually inconsistent claims that the judgment of taste is not founded on any determinate concepts and that the judgment of taste holds with universal necessary validity. Whereas, if transcendental idealism is correct, there is no contradiction. On that theory, we can accept that the forms of those objects which put our cognitive faculties into harmonious free play must be governed by a rule, but – for us – an indeterminate one. Consequently, although we must judge the objects to be beautiful on the basis of an immediate feeling of pleasure, there is a rule which governs their formal arrangements (and so the harmony of our faculties in contemplating them); but, being an indeterminate rule, it is not one that we can employ to support our judgment. None the less, the rule's existence is what enables each of us to claim the necessary agreement of everyone else's judgment with our own. Hence, the Antinomy of Taste reveals a yet further reason to reject transcendental realism and accept transcendental idealism – since, on the former theory, there really is a contradiction in our judgments of taste, while, on the latter, there is none.

Finally, I turn to the connections that are made in the Dialectic between beauty and morality. Here, again, transcendental idealism plays an indispensable role.

As Kant sees it, there is a striking parallel between our judgments of beauty and those of morality. This is a parallel that he had earlier alluded to in the Analytic, when discussing our intellectual interest in the beautiful, but he returns to it at the end of the Dialectic in the light of his distinction, now made, between the phenomenal and noumenal worlds. In judging the beautiful, we are conscious of a wholly free delight (arising from our non-sensible cognitive faculties) which is held to be valid for everyone; and, in judging the morally good, we are conscious of a feeling of respect (arising from our non-sensible faculty of the will) which is held to be valid for everyone. Just as we find that the feeling of respect in the presence of the morally good gives us a consciousness of ourselves as capable both of rising above the urges of sensuous desires and of determining our own actions, so we find that the feeling of delight, which stems not from the charms of the senses but from reflecting on an object's formal features, gives us a consciousness of ourselves as capable of both rising above sensuous pleasures and of determining the beauties of nature. In each case, we become conscious of that noumenal ground within us: a ground from which, as the Antinomy of Taste has shown, the judgment of taste can alone derive, and from which, as the Antinomy of Freedom had earlier shown (in the *Critique of Pure Reason*), our acknowledgement of moral obligation is alone possible.

Mainly on account of these parallels between the two types of judgment, Kant speaks of beauty as the symbol of morality. And he emphasizes how the cultivation of taste encourages our interest in morality as against the charms of the senses. This it does by teaching us, without undue difficulty, to take a delight in natural objects on the basis, not of their content or matter (a merely *passive* delight), but of the free, yet mutually supporting, employment of our cognitive faculties in estimating their form (a *spontaneous* delight arising from our own intellectual activity).

Quite apart from these analogies of structure between moral and taste judgments, Kant contends that the discovery of an *abundance* of natural objects which accord with the harmonious free play of our cognitive powers provides a significant moral dimension to our aesthetic appreciation of nature. He thinks that the profusion of beautiful natural forms suggests the existence of a cause or ground of nature that is favourably disposed to us (in so arranging nature that we can discover, within it, a profusion of beautiful forms). The existence of such a ground is, he holds, of profound moral interest, because it provides us with reason for hoping that our attempts to realize our final *practical* goal – namely, the union of virtue and happiness – will not prove unavailing. However, Kant's attempt to link natural beauty with morality, via a cause or ground of the abundance of beautiful natural forms, can be admitted only by accepting transcendental idealism.

In order to see why this is so, consider the following objection. 'Kant's reference to a ground of nature as an explanation for the profusion of natural beauties is not compatible with his often repeated claim, both before the Dialectic and within it, that it is *we* who determine the beauties of nature (by an immediate feeling of disinterested pleasure). If this abundance of beautiful forms is really the intentional product of nature's ground, then we must not consult *our* disinterested feeling in order to determine nature's beauties; rather, we must consult the special, purposive, laws *in nature* that determine which forms are beautiful.' But this objection is misguided. Agreed, it would be impossible to render consistent Kant's claim that the beauties of nature are determined by an immediate feeling of pleasure with the claim that, *in addition to* the physical (and psychological) laws of nature, there are purposive laws specifically governing the production of beautiful natural forms. If such purposive aesthetic laws existed, we would need to discover them before being in a position to judge the beauties of nature. For the question of which natural forms are beautiful would not, on this hypothesis, be dependent upon a feeling of disinterested pleasure in us, but upon which natural forms are in fact governed by these purposive aesthetic laws. However, Kant's claim that the beauties of nature are determined by our feeling of disinterested pleasure *is* consistent with his holding, not only that there is a noumenal ground for the whole phenomenal world, but that this ground can be conceived as having fashioned nature and its physical laws so that there will arise an abundance of natural forms which, solely as *by-products* of the physical laws, are capable of putting our cognitive powers into harmonious free play. Accordingly, so far as we are concerned with explaining what happens in the spatio-temporal world, including the production of those objects which we also judge to be beautiful, nothing beyond physical laws need in principle be appealed to. At the same time, by taking the noumenal ground as ultimately responsible for the design of the whole spatio-temporal world, including its physical laws, we can give a purposive explanation for the extraordinarily large number of diverse natural forms which put our cognitive faculties into harmonious free play and which are, consequently, found to be beautiful.[2] But of course, this capacity *both* to explain the existence of beautiful natural forms as arising in the temporal series merely from physical laws *and* to account for the profusion of such forms as perhaps ultimately due to a genuine purposive cause of the whole of nature is possible only in so far as the spatio-temporal world is a mere phenomenon with any purposive cause as its noumenal ground.

We can now see why, given transcendental idealism, Kant maintains that the abundance of natural beauties provides us with a further and vital link between beauty and morality. Although, from the phenomenal point of view, we must always seek to explain the many beautiful forms in nature as arising as mere by-products of physical laws (and we ourselves as alone determining the beauty of these forms), we can, entirely consistently with this position, understand their profusion by reference to a noumenal ground of nature. The abundance of beautiful forms, distributed throughout nature, can suggest to us that this noumenal ground has designed the physical laws of nature so that, in

---

[2] Moreover, this position can explain Kant's observation, earlier noted, of beauties 'even in the depth of the ocean where it can but seldom be reached by the eye of man – for which alone it is final' (*CJ*, Sect. 30; 5:279). If the physical laws do by themselves produce the abundance of forms that are determined by us to be beautiful, it is to be expected that these laws, being universally applicable throughout the natural world, will throw up beautiful forms even in remote places. But if there were additional laws *specifically* for the purpose of designing beautiful forms, it is difficult to understand why such forms should exist in places that are remote from our gaze (given Kant's premiss that it is *only* for us that these forms can produce a free delight).

our empirical investigations into the causes and effects of physical phenomena, there will be ample opportunity for us to experience the free and disinterested delight associated with the contemplation of beautiful forms. And once we have developed this idea that, underlying the whole of nature, there may be a noumenal ground that is well disposed to the spontaneous use of our *cognitive powers*, we are provided with reason for hoping that nature will not prove hostile to our realizing, by means of the free exercise of our *will*, the ultimate end of all our endeavours: the union of virtue and happiness (the highest good).

I conclude that the appeal in the Dialectic to transcendental idealism is far from being an irrelevance to Kant's aesthetics. Without recourse to transcendental idealism, we could neither justify making a judgment of taste (since it would entail mutually inconsistent claims) nor give to our appreciation of natural beauty the role of providing a link between the realms of nature (mechanism) and of morality (freedom). Kant's Copernican revolution does, indeed, run right through his 'entire critical undertaking' (CJ, Preface; 5:170).

11

A Kantian or an Empiricist Theory of Taste?

Kant's aesthetics, as I remarked earlier, is an attempt to take a middle way between empiricism and rationalism. But does he establish that this middle way is more defensible than the alternatives? That is doubtful. In particular, it is not clear that his position is to be preferred to the type of sophisticated empiricist position adopted by Hume in his famous essay 'Of the Standard of Taste'. In this chapter, I shall compare some parts of Kant's theory of our judgment of taste with Hume's theory, as developed in that essay.

Central to Kant's own analysis and justification of the judgment of taste is his contention that, despite being determined by a feeling of pleasure or displeasure, the judgment claims strict universality and necessity, just as if it were an objective judgment. It is primarily from this basis that he goes on to argue that the judgment of taste must be governed by an indeterminate rule. Yet his grounds for holding that strict, rather than comparative, universality and necessity are claimed by our judgments of taste are not, I suggest, compelling. We can see why this is so if we first understand how the Humean, empiricist position differs from the Kantian one.

According to Hume, it is a merely *contingent* truth that there exists sufficient uniformity among the aesthetic tastes of human beings that we are enabled to set up a standard of taste. This standard requires of those who happen to be governed by its empirically based rules that they *ought* to make certain aesthetic discriminations. However, this standard, since it is based only on a contingent agreement among most human beings, cannot claim *strict* universality and necessity. In Kant's own terminology, the Humean standard of taste claims only *comparative* universality and necessity, since it applies only to all those who, *as a matter of fact*, are governed by the same rules of art. (Even if the standard applies to all, and not merely to most, human beings, this will only be a contingent truth.)

But if, for the great majority of humans, their disinterested feelings of pleasure or displeasure are governed by the same rules of taste, it is surely the case that their judgments of taste – since they are determined by these sentiments – must all be *in accord with* these rules. How, therefore, can anyone in the majority group possibly be mistaken, let alone be *shown* to be mistaken, in any judgment? One way is by convincing such a spectator that he lacks the full *delicacy of taste* necessary to appreciate all the aesthetically relevant features in a specific object. These features themselves have been identified through the investigation of what Hume calls 'established models'. The established models are works of art that have survived 'all the changes of climate, government, religion, and language': the works of Homer and Virgil, among others, are mentioned as falling into the group of works that have survived this test of time. The preservation of these classical models strongly suggests to Hume that there are rules of composition that govern the sentiments of all, or the vast majority, of human beings. How could one more reasonably account for their preservation than by the hypothesis of such general rules? These rules lay down ways of composing which, when put into effect, produce relationships between features that, at least in simple instances, will please most human beings.

Now if a spectator fails to feel the (full) effect of any of these rules in a certain work, this will arise from disturbing conditions. One of these is a lack of delicacy of taste. Hume's idea is that although there is good empirical evidence to suggest that we are nearly all governed by the same rules of taste, it is not true that every spectator in this group is equally capable of feeling the full effect of any of these rules in *particular* cases, where e.g. several rules may be operating at the same time and/or some of the rules may apply only to a comparatively small part of the whole composition. No doubt, a spectator himself needs to acknowledge that the rules of taste which govern his own sentiments *are* operating in the work in question, if he is to be convinced that he has made a mistaken judgment (through his failure to spot or react to relationships between features instantiating one of these rules). But that seems to be conceivable, at least in many cases, e.g. by showing the spectator that there are less complex instances of the operation of the given rule, where he *is* moved by the features instantiating that rule. As Hume explains:

> But when we show [the spectator] an avowed principle of art; when we illustrate this principle by examples, whose operation, from his own particular taste, he acknowledges to be conformable to the principle; when we prove that the same principle may be applied to the present case, where he did not perceive or feel its influence: He must conclude, upon

the whole, that the fault lies in himself, and that he wants the delicacy, which is requisite to make him sensible of every beauty and every blemish, in any composition or discourse. ('Of the Standard of Taste')

So a sophisticated empiricist can allow that discussion and proof are possible, given that (contingently holding) rules of taste have been uncovered, and given our agreement that capacities like delicacy of taste are a significant factor in making an accurate judgment. In brief, it is possible to show those human beings (the vast majority) who are governed by the rules of taste that a certain judgment of taste ought to be made in a particular case, i.e. by reference to what a spectator who is subject to these rules and who has full delicacy of taste etc. would feel in that case. (Those comparatively rare individuals – as Hume thinks – whose aesthetic appreciation is not, as a matter of fact, governed by these rules of taste cannot, of course, be shown to have made an appropriate *or* an inappropriate judgment by appeal to them.)

Let us now look at some features of Kant's conception of the judgment of taste which differentiates it from Hume's. Importantly, Kant denies that we can be proved mistaken in any of our judgments of taste by the presentation of (alleged) rules of beauty. In this regard, he mentions the rules of artistic beauty that have been offered by Lessing and Batteux. To the extent that their rules are considered to be *a priori* rules of beauty, Hume would concur. Both he and Kant agree that there are no discoverable a priori rules of beauty, and so no specific rules of beauty that we can recognize as holding with strict universality and necessity. Hence, I can indeed refuse to be budged from my own judgment by means of the presentation of any such purported rule. But it does not follow that, because I cannot be swayed by the presentation of allegedly a priori rules of taste, I can rationally refuse to accept that I ought to withdraw any of my judgments by the presentation of a posteriori rules of taste. For I can be shown that, in a particular case, I failed to feel the operation of an a posteriori rule – a contingently established general rule of taste – that I myself acknowledge to govern my own sentiments. As we have seen, this failure may have arisen because, among other possibilities, I lack full delicacy of taste (and I can be rationally persuaded of this).

It appears that Kant accepts too readily that I cannot be compelled to relinquish any of my judgments of taste by the presentation of (alleged) rules of taste.

> If any one reads me his poem . . . which, all said and done, fails to commend itself to my taste, then let him adduce *Batteux* or *Lessing*, or still older and more famous critics of taste, with all the host of rules laid down by them, as a proof of the beauty of his poem. . . . I stop my ears: I do not want to hear any reasons or any arguing about the matter. I would prefer to suppose that all those rules of the critics are at fault, or at least have no application, than to allow my judgment to be determined by a priori proofs. (*CJ*, Sect. 33; 5:284–5; italics original).

As he sees it, I need to confront the object (the poem) myself and simply rely on my own sentiments in this reflective confrontation. He assumes that, granted there are no determinate a priori rules, the only alternative to relying *solely* on my own sentiments – i.e. without appeal to any a posteriori rules of taste – would be to accept the verdict of the majority in the particular case in hand (*CJ*, 5:284). Clearly, yielding to a majority verdict, merely in virtue of its being the majority, would be unacceptable: it would be unacceptable because the judgment of taste – as Kant and Hume agree – makes a claim to how we ought to feel. This *is* an instance where I can 'stop my ears', on the ground that an appeal to what the majority *happens* to think or feel in a particular case is no proof of what I *ought* then to think or feel. But, in default of an independent argument which establishes that our judgments of taste do claim *strict* universality and necessity, Kant is in no position to hold that these judgments are governed by an indeterminate, and not a determinate, rule of taste (and hence that we have no alternative but to rely solely on our own sentiment in each particular case). For his aim must be to *show* us that a claim to strict universality and necessity is implied by the judgment of taste, even though it is not capable of being proved or disproved by appeal to any determinate a priori rules of taste (as are judgments of perfection). He cannot, therefore, *presuppose* that the appeal to a posteriori rules is out of order on the ground that the judgment of taste claims strict universality and necessity. On the contrary, he needs first to establish that presenting a spectator with a posteriori rules of art cannot be a legitimate ground for convincing the spectator that his judgment is appropriate or inappropriate. This he does not do. Consequently, he has failed to show that the judgment of taste implies strict, rather than merely comparative, universality and necessity.

We can now sum up one significant difference between Hume's and Kant's aesthetic views. While both acknowledge that the judgment carries universality and necessity, only the Kantian position insists that these hold with the same force as in an objective judgment. On the Humean theory, although judgments of taste demand universal agreement, *this* demand is sufficiently accounted for on the basis of an empirical generalization. It is sufficiently accounted for because, in making a judgment of taste, the most that he believes we are concerned to claim is *comparative* universality and necessity. He denies – what the Kantian asserts – that the judgment of taste (though determined immediately by feeling) claims *strict* universality and necessity: that stronger claim would, the empiricist agrees, require the backing of an indeterminate a priori rule. For, assuming that the judgment of taste is immediately determined by the feeling of pleasure or displeasure (as both parties agree) *and* claims strict universality and necessity (as the Kantian asserts), there must be a rule governing the judgment which holds for everyone without possible exception. Yet that rule cannot be a *determinate* one, otherwise the judgment of taste would in reality be based on a concept, not a feeling – just as the rationalist alleges. But, the Humean complains, Kant never produces the evidence to justify his stronger claim (the claim to strict universality). In fact, he fails to recognize that an appeal to an a posteriori rule of taste can be employed to disprove a given judgment. This appeal, however, does not depend upon what the majority of us feel in that case (indeed, the majority may also lack e.g. full delicacy of taste). It depends, rather, on the demonstration that an a posteriori rule of taste, which we acknowledge as governing our own taste, is operating in the case in hand, although owing to a lack of discrimination on our part, we failed either to perceive or to feel its full influence. Such a disproof could never occur if, as Kant supposes, judgments of taste really do imply strict universality and necessity, since no *empirical* generalization could then govern any genuine judgment of taste. The sophisticated empiricist concludes that, at the very least, Kant has not shown that the judgment of taste claims more than comparative universality and necessity.

But there is one important area where Kant's views may seem to be considerably more plausible than Hume's. This is the area of fine art and, more especially, its creation. It may well be felt that our concepts of genius and originality do support Kant's claim that the judgment of taste, at least in the realm of fine art, must be conceived as governed by an indeterminate rule. This point may be developed as follows. Given that exemplary *originality* is the prime condition of the genius, we cannot possibly allow that there are any a posteriori general rules that govern the beauty of genuine works of art: surely (it is objected) that would negate the very idea that these works are original. Hence, Hume's belief that there are discoverable general rules of art, as testified by the survival of established or classical models, cannot be rendered consistent with our conception of the creation of fine art. This is not to dispute the existence or value of classical models – Kant specifically acknowledges their importance – but it is to question that they can be governed by any set of determinate rules of taste.

On the Kantian view, established models are original productions, because they each give a *new* rule to art: one, moreover, that has to be perceived in the individual work itself, and cannot be encapsulated by us in a determinate formula. Accordingly, these works are models, not because they supremely exemplify some rule or rules of taste which can be seen to apply to many *other* works of art; rather, they are models because they are, in respect of artistic merit, *unconstrained* by past masterpieces. They precisely do not utilize the same rules as earlier works (other than academic rules). And it is because of this that they *are* models or illustrations which can be employed to stimulate another genius.

Despite the ingenuity with which Kant develops his views on originality and genius, I think it should be questioned whether our concept of originality in art really does, or indeed can, require that there should be no determinate rules of art. Arguably, it is enough for artists to be considered creative or original if they are able successfully to apply a determinate general rule or rules of taste, perhaps unconsciously, to new situations, just as moral reformers may realize that changed circumstances may call for a novel application of general moral rules. Changes in cultural or metaphysical outlook (as in the differences that characterize the outlook of the Gothic age and the Renaissance), as well as a host of possibly related factors (notably, advances in technology e.g. in the fields of architecture, musical instruments and so on), can have a pronounced effect on the final appearance of works of art, *even though* they may all be governed by a limited set of determinate overarching artistic rules.

What are the results of this all too brief comparison between the Kantian and Humean conceptions of aesthetic taste? So far as I can see, none of the grounds that Kant brings forward in support of his contention that the judgment of taste claims strict universality and necessity are decisive. Plainly, this does not prove that the alternative position of the sophisticated empiricist is correct. It is one thing to point to the persistence of established models as indicative of the fact that the great majority of human beings are subject to the same a posteriori rules of taste: it is another actually to produce these rules.

Although a huge number of theorists have had a crack at formulating rules of taste, few if any of their suggestions have so far commanded even a fair measure of agreement (here there is a noticeable contrast with morality). None the less, in so far as we are inclined to accept some reference to universality in the judgment of taste – possibly requiring us to relativize the judgment to certain groups of human beings or historical periods – the Humean claim to comparative, rather than strict, universality does look attractive. For the alternative position, at any rate as developed by Kant himself, requires us to accept the existence of an indeterminate a priori rule of taste (in order to underwrite the claim to strict universality and necessity, while yet basing the judgment of taste on the immediate feeling of pleasure or displeasure). Not only does the acceptance of such an indeterminate rule require us to embrace transcendental idealism, as Kant himself urges; it also raises the question of whether, even if we do embrace it (possibly for independent reasons), we can now accept that aesthetic appreciation brings into play faculties of the mind that, in this activity, must be conceived as operating free from the causality of nature. This is part of a general problem with Kant's attempt to defend the reality of freedom, which we have already encountered in discussing his moral philosophy. With regard to the appreciation of beauty, whether in art or in nature, his thought is that our cognitive faculties must be subject to an indeterminate rule if a genuine judgment of taste is to be possible. The difficulty is to believe that whatever mental powers we bring into play in the appreciation of beauty, they are not then subject to determinate laws of nature. (An analogous point must cast doubt on the very possibility of the Kantian notion of artistic originality.) Yet, unless our appreciation of natural beauty is subject to an indeterminate and not a determinate rule, the bridge that the judgment of taste is claimed to build between the realms of nature and morality cannot exist.

12

Teleology and the Principle of the Finality of Nature

It may initially appear that the second part of the *Third Critique*, the Critique of Teleological Judgment, has little that is new to offer a reader who is trying to understand Kant's overall critical system. The main body of the text is concerned chiefly with showing that purposive or teleological explanations of certain objects in nature do not endanger the consistency of his system. Although I would agree that Kant's central concern here is with this defence, his discussion can also be connected to some general and highly significant comments which he makes in both the published Introduction and the First Introduction to the *Third Critique*. By considering the discussion of teleological explanations in harness with these comments from the two Introductions, we shall find that some further light is thrown on the structural unity of Kant's critical system – on its 'architectonic', as he calls it – including his claim that the *Third Critique* provides a bridge between the *First* and *Second Critiques*.

As the two Introductions remind us, the *First Critique* has argued that, in order for experience to be possible at all, the manifold of representations, given in sensible intuition, must conform to the pure or transcendental laws of nature (themselves derived from the categories in our understanding). But, Kant now explicitly maintains, such agreement with the categories is not sufficient to ensure the possibility of our having a single experience in which all the objects of our sensible intuition can be thought of as subject to *empirical* laws. It is also required that the (apparently) diverse empirical laws governing these objects should be reducible by us to a system. Since – and here we return to a theme of the *First Critique* – unless we can conceive the given manifold in *thoroughgoing* interconnection according to laws, we can have no single consciousness of the objects of experience. Nature, as the *sum* of these objects, must be governed by a system of laws in order to be conceived by us at all. For it is constituted by appearances, and these can have their objective reality *only* in a possible unified experience, while a unified experience itself requires that the given appearances can be brought under a system of laws. Unless the appearances can be brought to systematic unity, there can be no consciousness of them as collectively possessing objective reality (and so as together forming the objects of nature). But, if the appearances are governed by – what are for us – *irreducibly* diverse empirical laws, we could not conceive of them in thoroughgoing interconnection under empirical laws; and hence we could have no single experience in which they could all be grasped as subject to such laws. Consequently, in order for the appearances collectively to form the objects of our experience under empirical laws, it is necessary that we should be able to unify them into a *system* of empirical laws.

Yet our understanding, by means of the categories, determines only the transcendental laws of nature (laws like 'Every event must have a cause'). Accordingly, there can be no a priori guarantee that we shall be able to reduce the different empirical laws, which we discover, to a comprehensible system. While the categories determine the structure or form of nature in general – that is, without considering any specific differences that our perceptions may disclose among the appearances – our understanding does not possess any a priori concepts for determining in detail the particular (empirical) laws. We must rely on our perceptions to discover how given appearances are governed in their empirical laws. We can therefore have no a priori guarantee that diverse appearances must conform to *our* capacity to grasp the empirical laws and integrate them into a system. Rather, it must be a subjective presupposition of our having a unified experience of these appearances under empirical laws that the empirical laws are reducible by us to a system. As Kant puts it:

> For *unity of nature in space and time* and unity of our possible experience are one and the same, because the former is a sum of mere appearances (modes of representation) which can possess its objective reality only in experience, which itself must be possible as a system under empirical laws if (as one must) one thinks it as a system. Therefore it is a subjectively necessary, transcendental *presupposition* that this dismaying, unlimited diversity of empirical laws and this heterogeneity of natural forms does not belong to nature, that, instead, nature is fitted for experience as an empirical system through the affinity of particular laws under more general ones. (First Introduction, Sect. IV; 20:209; italics original)

The transcendental presupposition that nature (as the sum of appearances) is fitted for being grasped by us as an empirical system is not being advocated by Kant merely as a presupposition for our gaining a complete *scientific* knowledge of nature. His central point is more philosophically radical. He is maintaining that it is an a priori condition of the possibility of our having a unified experience of nature as subject to empirical laws that we think of the various empirical laws as if these laws have been organized by an understanding so that, relative to our cognitive faculties, we can reduce them to a system. He calls the presupposition that we can reduce the empirical laws to a system 'the transcendental principle of the finality of nature'. It is so named because, in order for a unified experience of nature in accordance with empirical laws to be possible for us, we must presuppose that the empirical laws governing the appearances will be *adapted* or *fitted for* our capacity to unite them into a system. (In this system, all the lower-level empirical laws will be derivable from a smaller group of higher-level laws, and so on, until we reach the highest level containing a compact and, as far as possible, homogeneous set of very general empirical laws. Everything that happens in the purely material world can be explained by reference to this empirical system.)

But why does Kant hold that this presupposition is a *subjective*, and not an objective, one? The answer is implicit in what has already been said. We cannot determine a priori any of the empirical laws governing appearances – we must rely on our perceptions to discover them – and we cannot even be assured a priori that, given the powers of our understanding, we shall ever be able to integrate all of the appearances under a system of empirical laws. Accordingly, it is a subjective presupposition of our having a unified experience of nature under empirical laws that we can reduce the multiplicity of the empirical laws to a system. For, whereas the transcendental laws of nature, without which there could be no objects of experience (appearances) at all, are contributed by us, the empirical laws are dependent on the content of the given appearances, not on us, and it is therefore a presupposition of *our* unified experience of the appearances according to empirical laws that these laws should form a system that is comprehensible to us.

In the Critique of Teleological Judgment itself, Kant is concerned with a particular group of material objects, viz. *organisms*, or what he calls 'physical ends'. The activity of these cannot, he holds, be exclusively explained by us in terms of mechanical laws – that is, in terms of mere laws of motion applied either to the organisms, considered as wholes, or to their parts, whether taken individually or in sum. He thinks that physical ends – plants and animal bodies – display self-regulating, reproductive and repairing capacities which we are unable to reduce fully to mechanical laws. They require that we explain their activity primarily in terms of purposes or final causes, as when we say that a tree is shedding its leaves *in order to* conserve liquid. He compares the production and behaviour of an organism with that of a humanly con-structed machine, like a watch. In this latter case, although it is true that a watch's individual parts are adapted to its other parts, and all the parts together exist for and to serve the object's end (to tell the time), there is no suggestion that this object has the power to produce, regulate or repair itself – *still less* that these ends can be achieved by taking in and forming materials that are not already specifically fash-ioned for such purposes. Quite the reverse: the construction, regula-tion and restoration of a watch depend upon an intelligence having conceived the end, and having fabricated raw materials into parts that can, when suitably arranged, serve the final end. If recourse to inten-tional causality (a designing intelligence) is necessary in the case of a watch, how much more so in the case of an organism. It is, Kant holds, inconceivable that we should be able to understand how an organism can achieve its results by thinking of it as governed solely by mechan-ical laws. Its formative powers of generation, self-regulation and repair must be accounted for in terms of a purposive or intentional style of causality, quite different from that of mechanical causality.

In appealing to intentional causality, Kant plainly does not suppose that we have adequately explained thereby *how* organisms achieve their purposes. That we must regard organisms as possessing a forma-tive impulse, and not mere mechanical causality, is clear; but how, pre-cisely, this operates is not clear to us. What we can say is that we have to think of their formative capacities as *designed*, as resulting from the conception of an end, and hence as due to *an intelligence*. From our point of view, the only alternative is to suppose that the material parts have simply come together by 'blind chance', so as to produce the characteristic capacities of the organism in question. This is an alter-native which he rejects as manifestly implausible.

Despite the necessity (as he believes) of our having to account for organisms primarily in terms of purposive explanations, Kant is not denying that mechanical explanations may be found, perhaps in all cases, for the *means* by which an end is produced. So, in the case where a tree sheds its leaves in order to preserve water, he acknowledges that it may well be that we shall discover mechanical explanations of how some leaves fall off branches in the event of a water shortage. What we shall not thereby have explained is how the tree has come to be so organized that the appropriate mechanical processes should be in place to enable this adaptiveness, this purposive behaviour, to occur; nor (he alleges) could we ever expect to find a purely mechanical explanation for this purposiveness. Instead, we must suppose an intelligence that has conceived this end and so designed the materials – either of this type of tree or of some more primitive forbear – so that by mechanical means the adaptive processes will result.

Of course, it may now be reasonably disputed that Kant was right to urge that the generation and behaviour of organisms cannot be fully explained by us in terms of (what he would identify as) mechanical causation. Darwin's theory of evolution, together with more recent advances in Darwinian theory, has made less than satisfactory Kant's claim that, on the basis of our understanding, it is 'contrary to reason' to suppose that even primitive organisms could mechanically arise from 'crude matter', or his claim that it is absurd to hope that another Newton may arise 'to make intelligible to us even the genesis of but a blade of grass from natural laws that no design has ordered'.[1] Admittedly, there is not yet a thorough picture of all the main steps from relatively simple chemical compounds to what Kant himself would have regarded as organisms. But enough is now understood of this process strongly to suggest that an entirely mechanical explanation will be available to us (and, in accordance with which, the myriad different organisms will also be accounted for). None the less, there does still remain the interesting question of how Kant himself is going to deal with the situation, as he sees it.

On the one hand, a great deal of material nature can be fully explained by reference to familiar mechanical laws. Kant holds that there is no reason in principle why these empirical laws should not be reduced to a mechanical system that is discoverable by us. On the

---

[1] This last quotation could be interpreted as merely asserting that, at *some* level, e.g. at the level of the basic laws of physics, an intelligence must be invoked in order to explain the benign conditions of our universe for the (mechanical) emergence of life. From the context, this is clearly not Kant's intention; but it is an interpretation that, in default of criticism, would support a purposive ground of the universe. However, as an argument for the existence of God, it would, even as it stands, be open to at least one of Kant's general objections to Design Arguments, viz. that they are insufficient to establish the existence of a being who is supremely perfect and suitable to form the basis of religion.

other hand, we have found that, in respect of certain objects in material nature – namely, organisms – he supposes that we must invoke, not a form of mechanical causality, but a purposive or teleological causality. There is, he contends, no possibility of our reducing these laws to mechanical ones.

Given this situation, it may now look as though we are confronted with an antinomy. On the one hand, we must seek to explain the purely material objects of nature solely by mechanical laws. On the other, it is necessary for us to explain certain material objects, viz. organisms, by reference to purposive causality. Hence, given the impossibility of our reducing purposive to mechanical explanations, it follows that we cannot explain everything in material nature exclusively in terms of mechanical laws. In fact, as Kant points out, there is no genuine conflict here, because the requirement for us to seek mechanical explanations is only a *subjective* one. It is not a requirement on the very existence of material nature that *we* should be able to reduce its objects to a system governed by mechanical laws. Admittedly, we are enjoined to search for mechanical explanations wherever possible. But where this fails, as it must in the case of organisms, we may have recourse to purposive explanations if this helps us to bring the phenomena under rules. For in employing purposive explanations, we are still employing *a law of causality* (and hence applying a category) to unify the manifold; and to that extent we are *understanding* what is happening – where otherwise we would be unable to see any ground whatsoever (other than pure chance) for the existence of the object. Moreover, once we have conceived the overall behaviour of an organism by reference to final ends, this may well aid us in grasping the operation of many of its internal physical processes, viz. by investigating how, and to what extent, these ends are achieved by means of *mechanical* causality.

So the appeal to an intentional causality, in cases where recourse to a purely mechanical account must fail us, is in accordance with the principle of the finality of nature. We are enjoined by that principle to think that nature is operating as if an understanding has fashioned the empirical laws for our cognitive faculties. When a purely mechanical account cannot be applied by us to the phenomena (owing to the limitation of our faculties), we may employ another form of causal explanation, viz. an intentional or purposive one, if that helps us to reduce the phenomena to rules. The complete system of laws will not be as simple as one that is wholly mechanistic; but since, from our point of view, mechanical explanations are not capable of standing alone, we may still be able to reduce the empirical laws to as unified a system as is compatible with our faculties (see *CJ*, 5:414).

Still, the issue cannot be left there. Even if no antinomy is created by our seeking, so far as possible, mechanical explanations while leaving room for purposive explanations in certain cases, we are confronted with a serious problem. If it is necessary for *any* understanding to employ an intentional explanation in order to account for the production and behaviour of organisms, this must mean that it is an *objective*, and not a merely subjective, condition of the experience of material nature that the existence of at least some of its products be ascribed to an intelligence, and an intelligence that lies *outside* nature (since organisms are not designed by us, and nature itself is not an intelligent being). Yet, if that is so, we cannot, properly speaking, be conceiving organisms as *natural products*. In order to consider anything as a product of nature, it must be possible to think of it as arising wholly from causes which lie *within* the spatio-temporal realm. But, by referring to an external intelligence as an objective condition for the production and behaviour of organisms, we are necessarily ascribing at least some of the things in nature (organisms), and perhaps, by extension, nature as a whole, to a designer who lies *beyond* the sensible realm. Now whereas Kant is unconcerned that it should be a *subjective* condition of our unified experience of nature that we think of some of its products as due to an intelligent supersensible cause – since this is merely a regulative principle for facilitating our grasp of nature, where appeal to mechanism alone must fail us – he would quite certainly be disturbed if the appeal to a supersensible intelligence were an *objective* requirement for the experience of some of the things in nature (and maybe even for the experience of nature as a whole). He would be disturbed, because this would mean that it is a constitutive principle for the very possibility of at least some of the things in nature that there should be an intelligent causality, a designer, in the noumenal world. This would put in jeopardy his whole critical undertaking, according to which (a) the production and behaviour of objects of experience (appearances) do not require recourse to a cause that lies beyond experience; and (b) nothing positive can be known about the noumenal world by means of theoretical reason.

In order to avoid having to admit a supersensible designer as an objective condition for (at least) some things in material nature, Kant distinguishes between *our* understanding and an understanding that can grasp objects in an intellectual intuition. There is no contradiction in supposing that although, for us, the activity of an organism can be understood only by reference to final causes, it is none the less the case that, for a being with an intellectual intuition, this can also be grasped as an instance of mechanism. A being with an intellectual intuition would not seek to understand an organism's overall behaviour from a knowledge of its individual parts and any mechanical laws governing them. Accordingly, there need be no unexplained gap between the mechanical workings of the parts of an organism and its overall behaviour (where that gap requires to be filled by appeal to final or teleological explanation). Rather, such a being would, from an awareness of the activity of the whole organism, fully determine the rule or law governing that activity. In apprehending the whole, an intellectual intuition is able *immediately* to grasp the rule that fully explains the behaviour of that whole, i.e. without thinking, or trying to think, of this rule as arising out of any possible mechanical laws governing its individual parts. At the same time, Kant argues that the application of this explanatory rule to organisms does count as an instance of *mechanical* generation, because it explains the activity of these material objects in terms of their structure, without any recourse to *purposes* or *intentions*, and therefore without any reference to a designing intelligence (see *CJ*, Sect. 77; 5:406 and 408; see also *CPractR*, Bk I, Ch. III; 5:96).

How an intellectual intuition can grasp the rule governing the operation of an organism in this immediate way is not something that we can really comprehend. All we can say is that an intuition of this type has no need to divide an organism into its parts, and that it grasps the organism as *a holistic system*, governed by a rule suited to seeing it in this way. With a holistic system, the behaviour of a whole is greater than that of the sum of its parts, at least so far as we can understand the operation of the parts. Once the appeal to an intellectual intuition has been introduced, to explain how it is possible for us to *think* of whole organisms as governed by mechanical law (even though we cannot *understand* how this mechanistic rule works), Kant points out that it is now possible to think of everything in material nature as governed by a *system* of mere mechanical laws. On the one hand, we can already think of the set of empirical laws governing the objects of nature, other than organisms, as reducible to a mechanistic system. On the other hand, we have now shown how we can think of *organisms* as governed by mechanical law. It therefore becomes possible to think that the whole of material nature is reducible to a system of exclusively mechanical laws, with a single overarching principle determining all the more particular empirical laws. Admittedly, such a system

—— **234** ——

could only be grasped by a being with an intuitive understanding, since the holistic law governing the activity of organisms, and therefore the overarching principle governing the whole of material nature, would require an intellectual intuition.

It needs to be emphasized, as Kant does, that it is not necessary that we should be able to prove that a being with an intuitive understanding exists; it is sufficient that we can think such a being without contradiction. This is enough to establish that the unity of nature, under mechanical laws, could still be grasped by *some* understanding, despite our inability to do so; and hence that no recourse to a designing intelligence is necessary to account for the possibility of organisms, let alone to account for the possibility of nature as a whole. Moreover, the idea of an intuitive understanding enables us to see how an empirical law (and indeed, our whole system of empirical laws, so far as we can ascertain it), which we can establish only by means of experience – and hence as holding only *contingently* – could be recognized as holding necessarily. While we can show only that any empirical law holds contingently (or follows from a higher law which itself is established through experience, and thus can be shown only to hold contingently), it must in reality hold necessarily, if it is a genuine law of nature (CJ, Introduction, Sect. IV; 5:180 and 183–4). For the unity of nature requires that all the objects of experience are connected together by a system of *laws* – that is, by judgments holding with necessity and universality. Now any empirical law would be recognized, by an intuitive understanding, as deriving from the overarching principle. Hence, such an understanding would see that the particular empirical law *must* invariably obtain (under the given phenomenal circumstances). Further, because the overarching principle can be grasped only in an intellectual intuition, it cannot itself be contingent (since it is not established through sensible intuition, i.e. by experience). On the contrary, it would be determined *a priori* by an intuitive understanding, and the whole system of our empirical laws – seemingly contingent but, in reality, necessary – would flow from it.

Despite the lack of clarity surrounding the idea of an intellectual intuition, Kant does seem to me to display considerable resourcefulness in his use of this idea in accounting for the necessity which must be carried by the empirical laws of nature. Indeed, his appeal to an intellectual intuition can be employed in tackling the issue of the necessity of these laws, *without* bringing in any suggestion that organisms must be treated differently from the other things in material nature (as we would now hold). After all, the question of how our empirically discovered laws of nature could form a system carrying *necessity* with it needs, in any case, to be answered. Kant's appeal to an overarching principle that is determined in an intellectual understanding enables him to give an account of how the empirical laws of nature could, one and all, be necessary, despite appearing to us as merely contingent. For even if we were to gather all of our empirically discovered laws into a system, we could still know only that this system held contingently. But, for an intuitive understanding, the whole system would itself rest on what is for us an indeterminate rule: this rule would be grasped immediately and a priori in an intellectual intuition (not as a contingent higher-level generalization incorporating more particular ones), and our whole system of empirical laws – even the most general – would be dependent upon it.

It is striking that, in both the Dialectic of Teleological Judgment and the Dialectic of Aesthetic Judgment, reference is made to what is *for us* an indeterminate rule or principle. In the latter, such a principle is employed in order to justify our claiming universal necessary validity for our judgments of taste, and in the former it is employed to justify the existence of a system of genuinely empirical *laws* (as well as the activity of organisms). If beautiful nature and art are to exist, it must be possible for the formal arrangements of their objects to fall under an indeterminate rule of beauty (a rule which *our* understanding is unable to grasp, but one which could be grasped by a being in the supersensible world). The rule is manifested to us by means of the feeling of pleasure, i.e. when our imagination and understanding are in maximum free play. Equally, if a unified experience of nature under empirical laws is to exist, it must be possible for the individual empirical laws to form a system. This system cannot be cognized by us as necessary (as it must, in reality, be for a unified experience), but it could be grasped by a supersensible being with an intuitive understanding. Although we are unable to grasp the empirical system's necessity, any discoveries that we do make towards the systematic unity of the empirical laws are attended with a feeling of pleasure, i.e. when our judgment finds a general empirical law from which a number of more particular established laws can be seen to follow. But only an intellectual intuition would be able to grasp the a priori principle from which all the empirical laws, in their systematic unity, are determinable. It transpires, then, that just as the categories in our understanding make possible the *transcendental* system of the laws of nature, so the overarching a priori principle in an intuitive understanding can alone make possible the *empirical* system of the laws of nature.

We noted earlier that the principle of the finality of nature – the principle that nature has been organized so that, relative to our cognitive faculties, a system of empirical laws is discoverable by us – can have only subjective, and not objective, validity. None the less, this principle is one that we *must* presuppose for the possibility of our unified experience according to empirical laws. And it is this principle too which, as Kant sees it, is operating in our perception of the beauties of nature. For, given the presupposition, it is, of course, to be *expected* that nature will be suited to our faculties of cognition in their empirical role (of unifying the diverse empirical laws into a system); and it is therefore not at all surprising that certain natural objects, in their individual structures, will *also* be found to display a finality (a unity amidst variety) for these same faculties in their free play, i.e. prior to engaging in any empirical activity (see CJ, Sect. 61; 5:359). Accordingly, although we can know nothing about how any indeterminate rule could operate so as to make the finality of nature possible, it is this finality which is made manifest in the abundance of natural beauty. For judgments of taste, as we have seen, require that there should be an indeterminate rule applying to the structure of all those natural objects that we can judge to be beautiful; and the discovery – as Kant claims – of the lavishness with which nature's forms display beauty strongly suggests that the principle of the finality of nature is actually *operating* in our experience.

So, by distinguishing between the world of appearance and the world as it is in itself, Kant believes that the very principle that we must presuppose for a unified experience of nature under empirical laws – and hence for the existence of nature as a *mechanism* – is, at the same time, the principle that underpins the existence of the beauties of nature. And it is our discovery of the plenitude of beautiful natural forms, together with the collateral recognition that the employment of our supersensible faculties even in their *freedom* can be fully in harmony with the ground of nature's mechanism, that gives us reason for hoping that our final end (the union of virtue with happiness) may really be achievable in nature. That is chiefly why Kant calls the principle of the finality of nature the 'mediating concept' between the concepts of nature and freedom: 'For through that concept we cognize the possibility of the final end that can only be actualized in nature and in harmony with its laws' (CJ, 5:196).

Within his Copernican revolution, Kant has successfully argued that *a* thoroughgoing mechanism of nature, the existence of free natural beauties, and our accomplishing the highest good can all be realized, and realized *together*. The journey through to the critiques has ended in a remarkable synthesis of their three principal claims.

Bibliography

I. Texts in English Translation

I have used the translations marked with an asterisk when quoting from Kant's texts (except for minor changes); but all the listed translations may profitably be consulted.

Critique of Judgment, trans. J. C. Meredith (Oxford, 1952)*, Werner Pluhar (Indianapolis, 1987), and Paul Guyer and Eric Matthews, under the title *Critique of the Power of Judgment* (Cambridge, 2000).

Critique of Practical Reason, trans. T. K. Abbott, 6th edn (London, 1909), L. W. Beck (Chicago, 1949), and Mary Gregor (Cambridge, 1997)*.

Critique of Pure Reason, trans. Werner Pluhar (Indianapolis, 1996), Paul Guyer and Allen W. Wood (Cambridge, 1997), and N. K. Smith (Basingstoke, revised 2nd edn, 2003)*. All these translations give the variant readings from the 1st and 2nd edns, referred to as the A and B edns respectively.

First Introduction to the Critique of Judgment, trans. James Hadden (Indianapolis, 1965)*. Both the Werner Pluhar and the Paul Guyer and Eric Matthews translations of the *Critique of [the power of] Judgment* include translations of the *First Introduction*.

Groundwork of [or for] the Metaphysics of Morals, trans H. J. Paton, under the title *The Moral Law* (London, 1948), L. W. Beck, under the title *Foundations of the Metaphysics of Morals* (Indianapolis, 1959), Mary Gregor (Cambridge, 1997), and Arnulf Zweig (Oxford, 2002).

Metaphysics of Morals, trans Mary Gregor (Cambridge, 1996).

Practical Philosophy, trans Mary Gregor (Cambridge, 1996). Contains in one volume Mary Gregor's translations of the *Critique of Practical Reason*, *Groundwork*, and *Metaphysics of Morals*, together with others of Kant's ethical writings.

Prolegomena to Any Future Metaphysics, trans. Peter G. Lucas (Manchester, 1953)*, J. Ellington (Indianapolis, 1977), and Gary Hatfield (Cambridge, revised edn, 2004).

Religion within the Limits of Reason Alone, trans. T. M. Greene and H. H. Hudson (New York, 1960)*, and Allen Wood and George Di Giovanni, under the title *Religion within the Boundaries of Mere Reason* (Cambridge, 1998).

II. A Selection of Secondary Literature

The secondary literature on Kant's *Critiques* is, of course, vast. What follows is only a personal shortlist of some of the very best work.

General

Ameriks, Karl, *Interpreting Kant's Critiques* (Oxford, 2003).
Warnock, G. J., 'Kant' in D. J. O'Connor (ed.), *A Critical History of Western Philosophy* (London, 1964).
Wood, Allen, W., *Kant: An Introduction* (Oxford, 2005).

Critique of Pure Reason

Allison, Henry, *Transcendental Idealism: An Interpretation and Defense* (New Haven, 1983).
Bird, Graham, *Kant's Theory of Knowledge* (London, 1962).
Gardner, Sebastian, *Kant: The First Critique* (London, 1999).
Lovejoy, Arthur, 'Kant's Classification of the Forms of Judgment' (1907) and 'On Kant's Reply to Hume' (1906), both reprinted in M. Gram (ed.), *Kant: Disputed Questions* (Chicago, 1967).
Strawson, P. F., *The Bounds of Sense* (London, 1966).
Van Cleve, J., *Problems from Kant* (New York, 1999).

Critique of Practical Reason

Acton, H. B., *Kant's Moral Philosophy* (London, 1970).
Herman, Barbara, *The Practice of Moral Judgment* (Cambridge, Mass., 1993).
Hill, Thomas E., Jr, *Dignity and Practical Reason in Kant's Moral Theory* (Ithaca, NY, 1992).
Paton, H. J., *The Categorical Imperative* (London, 1947).
Rawls, John, 'Themes in Kant's Moral Philosophy', in E. Forster (ed.), *Kant's Transcendental Deductions* (Stanford, Calif., 1989).
Rawls, John, 'Kant', in *Lectures on the History of Moral Philosophy* (Cambridge, Mass., 2000).
Schneewind, J. B., 'Autonomy, Obligation, and Virtue: An Overview of Kant's Moral Philosophy', in Paul Guyer (ed.), *The Cambridge Companion to Kant* (Cambridge, 1992).
Wood, Allen W., *Kant's Ethical Thought* (Cambridge, 1999).

Critique of Judgment

Allison, Henry, 'Kant's Antinomy of Teleological Judgment', *Southern Journal of Philosophy*, 30, suppl. (1991).
Allison, Henry, *Kant's Theory of Taste* (New York, 2001).

Guyer, Paul, *Kant and the Claims of Taste*, 2nd edn (New York, 1997).

Guyer, Paul, *Kant's System of Nature and Freedom*, Parts I and III (Oxford, 2005).

McLaughlin, P., *Kant's Critique of Teleology in Biological Explanation: Antinomy and Teleology* (Lewiston, NY, 1990).

Index